Insured Beyond The Grave:
Published Essays, Interviews & Dispatches

Volume One

James Calemine

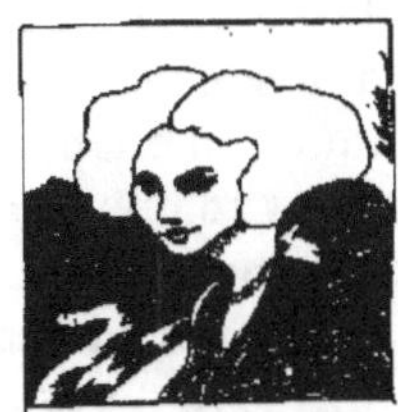

Snake~Nation~Press
Valdosta, Georgia 2017

Snake Nation Press wishes to thank:

Barbara Passmore & The Price-Campbell Foundation
The Porter-Fleming Foundation
The Georgia Council for the Arts
Gloria & Wilby Coleman
Dr. Manual Tovar
Lowndes/Valdosta Arts Commission
Cynthia Schumacher in memory of L. H. St. John
James Najarian in Memoriam: Robin Najarian
Don Hoffman & Sue Hellstern
Dean Poling & *The Valdosta Daily Times*
Morris Smith and the Smith Family
Robin Pennington and Autumn Pennington
    in memory of their Mother, Vicki Pennington
June Purvis
    in memory of Dr. Jerry Purvis
Gloria Mullins
Robert Earl Price
Our Subscribers

Subscriptions:
Individuals $30
Institutions $40
Foreign $40
Sample Copy $10 (includes shipping)

Snake Nation Press, the only independent literary press in south Georgia, publishes *Snake Nation Review*, a book of poetry by a single author each year, and a book of fiction by a single author each year. Unsolicited submissions of fiction, essays, art, and poetry are welcome throughout the year but will not be returned unless a stamped, self-addressed envelope is included. We encourage simultaneous submissions.

Published by Snake Nation Press
110 West Force Street
Valdosta, Georgia 31601
Printed and bound in the United States of America.
Copyright © James Calemine 2017
Photography by James Calemine
All Rights Reserved
ISBN: 978-0-9979353-7-0

Table Of Contents

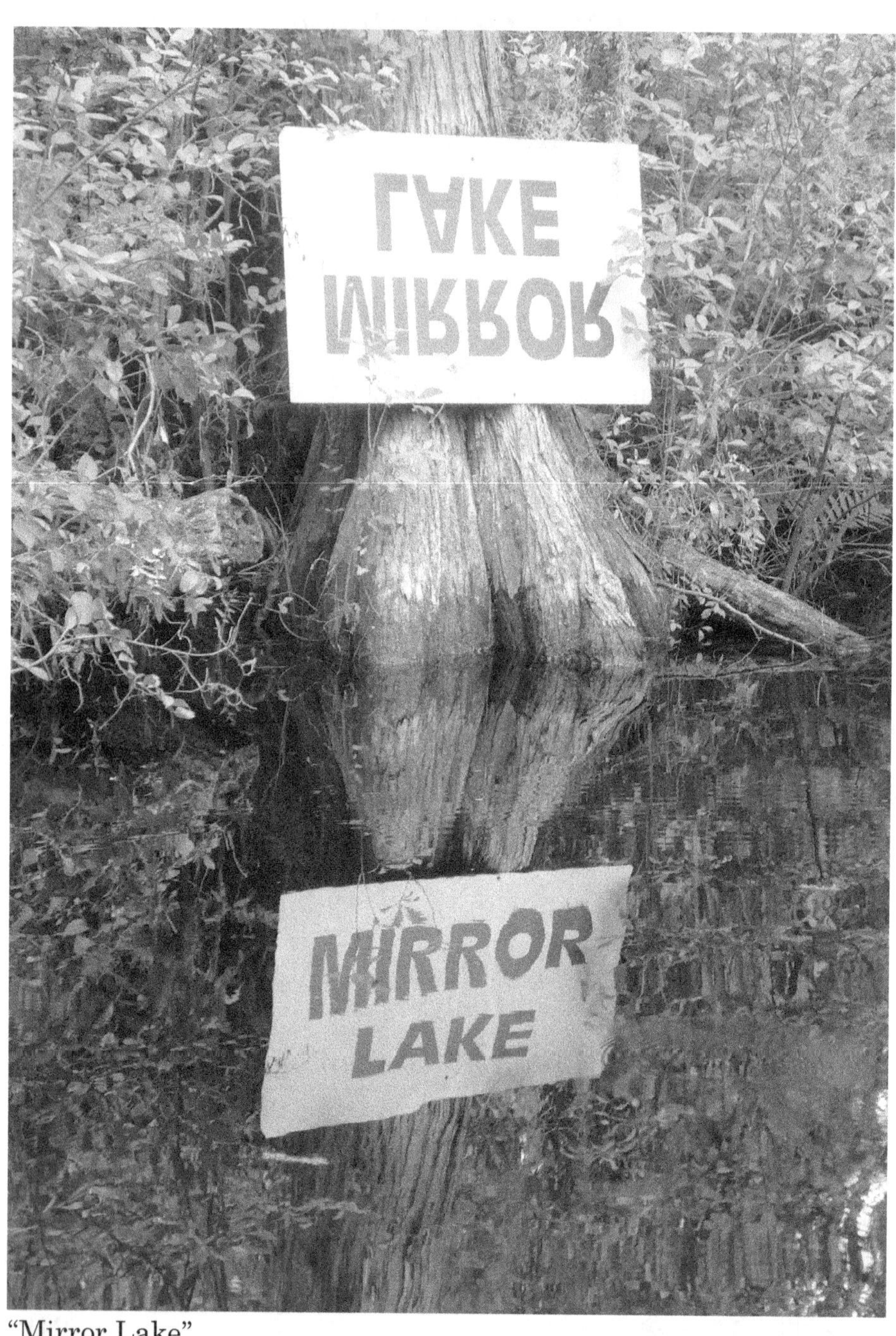

"Mirror Lake"
Deep in the Okefenokee Swamp

•••••••

Introduction

By accident I just sliced my index finger with a Swiss army knife while opening this box I brought along containing a new copy of *The Illustrated Dictionary of Place Names*. Blood spilled on the notebook page to this Introduction. Ah, the irony. Or not?

The soothing May breeze blows outside my sliding glass door here in room 264 at the King & Prince Hotel on St. Simons Island, GA. I grew up on the island. I moved away in 1986, and returned in 2009. I wanted to rent a room on the beach to write this Introduction. I needed solitude. Compiling these stories—and excluding four times times as many—proved a journey through the past. Reading through it all emerges as time travel of the highest order.

Insured Beyond The Grave Volume 1 stands as a collection of my published work from 1995-2016. When I wrote about a subject I wanted to render it untouchable by any other writer. That fueled my intent. I shined a light on and sought out real cultural purveyors. Some remain better known than others. I also wanted the reader to feel a close-to-the-bone perspective regarding the price an artist must pay for the sake of their art.

Several of my closest friends were talented artists, and from first hand experience I learned that talent does not necessarily constitute a lot of expendable income. I refused to compromise, and I paid the price. If the art is good—it lasts. F. Scott Fitzgerald died at 40 thinking he was a failure because *The Great Gatsby* was out of print.

In this day and age, I'm unwilling to wait on anyone to decide my work or fate. So, I've taken matters into my own hands. Again. It's the end of an Era. I bandaged my finger and typed this up. I gaze out at the Atlantic Ocean. The cotton-colored clouds hover above the dark waves. Several stories in this collection will provide clear insight into the significance of St. Simons Island. Folklorist Alan Lomax once said, "The Georgia Sea Islands are the home of the American Song."

These articles appeared in various periodicals, magazines and online publications. This collection leaves footprints in the sand...snapshots in time regarding some of America's finest artists. Everyone in this book is, indeed, insured beyond the grave.

••••••

No matter the cost, I intended to operate where soul, excellence and timelessness existed as my only standards. And I accepted full responsibility....

My photographs hold no direct connection to the articles. However, the images—like the stories—retain an earthy, soulful and rare aesthetic. No glitz.

I'm walking down to the beach to clear my head and think about my next project. Time is always short. When I return to room 264 I'll press 'send' to get this one off. Onward...

James Calemine
May 2017

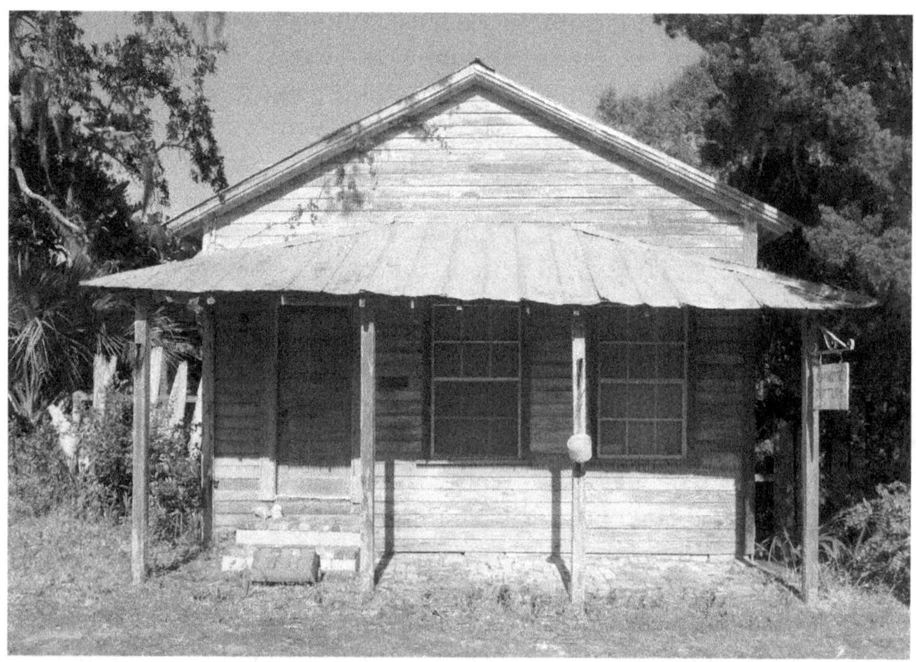

"Cedar Key, Florida"

Can I Get A Witness: The True Adventures of Stanley Booth

I met Stanley Booth in early 1987. Booth exists as one of my great frames of reference. He taught me valuable lessons regarding writing, music, friendship as well as the difference between originality and being a hack scoring a paycheck. Booth's influence runs through this book. Meeting him at 17 proved an adult dose of literary reality. I wrote this article for Hittin' The Note magazine in 2000. It captured the nature of our friendship—then and now. Stanley moved back to Memphis a couple of years ago. In 2017, he visited St. Simons and it was good to see my old friend who knew the Rolling Stones, Elvis, B.B. King, Ray Charles, Al Green and a long list of others.

"Jack Kerouac was a writer. That is, he wrote. Many people who call themselves writers and have their names on books aren't writers and can't write—the difference being a bullfighter who fights a bull is different than a bullshitter who makes passes with no bull there. The writer has been there or he can't write about it. And going there he risks being gored. To write they must go there and submit to conditions they may not have bargained for. The only real thing about a writer is what he has written, and not his so-called life."

—William Burroughs

"The only answer to this is that people without hope do not write novels. Writing a novel is a terrible experience, during which the hair often falls out and the teeth decay. I'm always highly irritated by people who imply that writing fiction is an escape from reality. It is a plunge into reality and it's very shocking to the system. If the novelist is not sustained by a hope of money, then he must be sustained by a hope of salvation, or he simply won't survive the ordeal. People without hope not only do not write novels, but what is more to the point, they don't read them. They don't take long looks at anything because they lack the courage. The way to despair is to refuse to have any kind of experience, and the novel, of course, is a way to have an experience."

—Flannery O'Connor

•••• ••

The silver hair calls to mind an aged wisdom. Without knowing him, you'd never realize this southern gentleman—dressed in khaki pants and tweed jacket, sitting in the passenger seat of your truck, riding up Highway 99 towards Darien, Georgia, to eat alligator tail—is living testimony to the severe price that one must pay for the sake of his art. You wouldn't know that this man, Stanley Booth, epitomizes the survivor. In pursuit of his craft, Booth traveled with the Rolling Stones, overdosed at Graceland, suffered epileptic seizures while withdrawing from drugs, broke his back, went to jail, was crushed by a lumber truck on the Memphis-Arkansas bridge, assaulted by Hell's Angels at Altamonte, and written legendary music books.

No writer documented the progression of American music and its musicians with first hand accounts like Booth. His stories travel in music history from the slave days into 20s jazz through the blues decades into present day music affairs, and he paints the historic and cultural backdrop during each musician's era. There is no substitute for Booth's storytelling.

In May of 2000, Booth's classic, *The True Adventures of the Rolling Stones*, was republished, with a new Afterword written by the author. Also, in October of 2000, Booth's second book *Rythm Oil,* an indelible collection of music essays, was reprinted.

Despite obscurity in the mainstream literary/music/pop culture—where hack journalists write tell-all books and make large sums of money from rehashing old articles and interviews. Booth knew almost all the people he's written about, including Elvis Presley, B.B. King, the Rolling Stones, Furry Lewis, Gram Parsons, Al Green, Dan Penn, Spooner Oldham, Aaron Neville, Hank Crawford, Ernest Withers, Lash Larue, Bobby Rush, James Brown, Dewey Phillips, William Bell, Sam Phillips, Rufus Thomas, Sam the Sham, Mose Allison, Frank Sinatra, Ray Charles, Carla Thomas, Booker T & The MGs, Bill Eggleston, Phineas & Calvin Newborn, Fred Ford, Charlie Freeman, Gerald Wexler, Jerry Lee Lewis, Waylon Jennings, Otis Redding, Little Richard, Jim Dickinson, Marvin Sease, Bobby Rush, Alex Chilton, and Bukka White.

In time, Booth traveled from his native South Georgia to Memphis, London, Los Angeles, New York and many nameless juke joints to preserve and document the stories and accomplishments of talented American musicians. Booth once wrote: "The blues is subtle; its appeal lies, like most pleasures, beneath the surface." No one describes the nebulous line between obscurity and fame better than Booth.

Sitting at one of Archie's small red Formica tables, drinking sweet iced tea, I thought how appropriate it was to be sharing gator tail appetizer with a man who killed his first alligator at the age of twelve. After all, Stanley Booth still keeps a pistol next to the typewriter.

Irvin Stanley Booth Jr. was born on January 5, 1942. He was the only son of Stanley and Ruby Booth, who lived in Waycross, Georgia, a small South Georgia town sixty miles from the coast and thirty miles from the swampy Florida state line.

Booth's grandfather worked for a Naval Stores Company, and Booth's early youth was spent in a turpentine camp, an isolated world of gum barrels, pine trees, and swamp.

In those swamplands young Stanley began to perceive hidden shadows in "paradise and within myself." At five years old, he witnessed a black man named Frank Porter, a man who worked for his family, attempt to kill his grandfather by stabbing him. Booth would later tell me, "I loved all those people in the turpentine camp—the whites and the blacks—but I soon discovered something else was going on." Booth learned darkness always loomed close.

The swamp's floating islands, which shift with each footstep, earned it the Seminole Indian name, Okefenokee (for which there are 77 different spellings) meaning "Land of the Trembling Earth."

"I loved the swamp country," Booth said, and he later wrote of his childhood there, "At times I was afraid, but nothing in the woods was as frightening as what I would find in the outside world." In a 1969 review of fellow Waycrossian Gram Parsons' old band, the Flying Burrito Brothers, Booth wrote: "Memphis, Birmingham, and Atlanta are Southern, but they are nothing like Waycross: people around Waycross think of Atlanta the way you and I think of the moon—a place that, though remote, might possibly be visited by us or our children." Times have changed, but not much.

Booth also wrote in the same article about the Land of the Trembling Earth: "Men have walked into the swamp—where even the pretty little plants eat meat—never to be heard from again. The people, dealers in, among other things, pine trees, tobacco, peanuts, sugar cane, moonshine whiskey, trucks, tractors, new and used cars, bibles, groceries, dry goods, and hardware; in isolated farms on swamp islands: in turpentine camps deep in the woods, like Dickerson's Crossing, Mexico, the Eight Mile Still; in unincorporated settlements like Sandy Bottom, Headlight, Thelma; in towns like Blackshear, Folkston, Waycross; from banker to bootlegger—all share two curses: hard work and Jesus."

The Booths moved from Waycross to Macon, Georgia, when Stanley was sixteen years old. In 1959, he graduated from Sidney Lanier High School for Boys, where he marched and carried an M1 rifle. That year the Booths moved again—this time to Memphis, Tennessee, where Stanley Sr., was an insurance executive. Booth wrote: "I knew little about the place other than it was on the Mississippi River and had an association with the kind of music I liked. I soon learned that Memphis was, if anything, even more 'Southern' and puritanical than Macon, with no liquor served by the drink and almost no integration. Restaurants, taxis, hotels, parks, libraries, movies, all were segregated. Blacks still sat in the back of the buses. Whites who wanted to hear black music went to an all-white club called the Plantation Inn across the river in West Memphis, Arkansas, and listened to a singing group called the Del Rios or to Lowman Pauling and the Five Royales. My first experience on Beale Street was being thrown out of a Ray Charles concert at the Hippodrome for sharing a table with some black classmates from newly integrated Memphis State University."

In 1962, Booth hopped a Greyhound bus to San Francisco, soaking up works of Jack Kerouac and Miles Davis, meeting Lawrence Ferlinghetti and Alan Watts, and scored his first lid of marijuana.

Booth graduated from Memphis State, where he studied art history, and went on to graduate school in New Orleans at Tulane University, only to return to Memphis without taking a degree. As he put it: "I left school because it distracted me from writing—or maybe because it didn't. I enjoyed living in New Orleans, but lack of money and the bad feeling I had about the racial climate there led me back to Memphis. An ironic move."

In the summer of 1964 Booth returned to Memphis. During this time he became a black belt and began to teach karate. In late 1965, Booth took a position with the Tennessee Welfare Department.

Appalled by the system, Booth quit the welfare department in 1966 and wrote a novel in eighteen days about Memphis' racial disturbances, predicting the act of military tanks patrolling residential streets that occurred two years later.

Then Booth met bluesman Furry Lewis. Booth's friend Charlie Brown ran a club in Memphis called the Bitter Lemon where Furry would sometimes play. Booth got to know Furry and often accompanied Lewis, who worked for the Memphis Sanitation Department, while he swept the streets hours before the city awakened. Lewis was a kind of mentor to Booth. Several years later Booth explained their street level project: "This guy I knew named David Mays and I took an overdose of LSD one night, and we became so brilliant that we developed the War on Poverty: Memphis Area project South Summer Workshops Program. Over the years it cost the government millions of dollars. The first year, I taught writing, and Furry taught music, and made a thousand dollars for working for six weeks, two hours a day, you know. For years afterwards he would say, 'Stanley! What ever became of the guvment?' (Laughs) Because the government money was so good, you know."

Booth's story called "Furry's Blues," published in *Playboy* magazine, won Booth *Playboy's* best nonfiction writer in 1970, when Booth was in the process of writing a book about the Rolling Stones.

During this time, Booth attended the funeral of bluesman Mississippi John Hurt with his girlfriend and Furry Lewis. Unprepared, Furry and Booth were asked to eulogize the great John Hurt. Booth later wrote: "I may have even gotten an amen or two." At the end of the year, Booth and his bride were married by his friend Charlie Brown.

In early 1967, Booth spent time at Graceland with Elvis Presley concerning a story he was writing about the King. The piece was published in *Esquire* and turned out to be the first serious article written on Presley. Booth was so trusted that Dewey Phillips (who either called Booth Birdbrain or Elvis) gave him an overdose of Darvon at Graceland.

Booth later wrote that publishing the Elvis article—whose first line in the original version reads, "Talking about eatin' pussy"—made him a professional journalist, something he never wanted to be.

Soon Booth began writing about musicians working for Stax studios, including Otis Redding and Booker T & the MGs. Booth was in the studio with Redding in 1967 when he recorded "Sittin' On the Dock of the Bay." Two days later, after Booth said goodbye to him in the studio, Redding was killed in a plane crash in Madison, Wisconsin. Booth's extensive research in pain had just begun.

During this period, Booth was keeping time with another freak behind music, Memphis producer-musician Jim Dickinson. He and Dickinson met in Memphis and spent much of their time, as Booth put it, "Talking about music and shining the light of consciousness towards the dark end of the tunnel."

It was Dickinson who gave Booth his first definition of soul: "You hear soul explained in terms of oppression and poverty, and that's certainly part of it—no soul musician was born rich—but it's more than that. It's being proud of your own people, what you come from. That's soul."

Booth then wrote a story for *Eye* magazine on B.B. King, and during one of the last interviews for the article, B.B. and Booth drank bourbon for breakfast—an interview that took place the day after Robert Kennedy's assassination.

Booth would later write: "Having written about Furry Lewis, Elvis Presley, Otis Redding, and B.B. King, I slowly awoke to the realization that I was describing the progress of something, a kind of sexy, subversive music."

Booth's pursuit became an intense path of seeking out and writing about one great musician after another. Booth's definition of the trail he was wandering down was, "As B.B. shows us, the blues' origins are in human need, the desperate cry of a kidnapped and orphaned people, singing in a foreign tongue a sorrow song that proves in the end to be redemptive, transcendent, spiritually liberating in the realest kind of way, ultimately life-changing for performers and listeners alike."

In September of 1968, Booth went to London for *Eye* magazine to write about the Rolling Stones. The story Booth was writing turned out to be Brian Jones' last drug trial. It was suggested by certain publishers Booth should write a book about the Rolling Stones, but Booth was, in his own words, far too "serious and high-minded."

Booth was hesitant to write about the Rolling Stones, not only because "They were rock and rollers, but young, rich, and white." It was, of course, Jim Dickinson who told him the Stones "were bound to be good ol' boys."

Having always been a country music freak, Booth took an interest in the Byrds' classic country album, *Sweetheart of the*

Rodeo, during his London stay. Rodeo was influenced heavily by Gram Parsons—whom Booth had not met—but Booth's mother taught at the same junior high school Gram attended in Waycross. Years later Booth wrote of Parsons: "He'd lived in Waycross between 1946 and 1958; I'd been there for most of those years, but we'd gone to different churches, different schools. Gram's friends were my friends' younger brothers. We just missed each other."

In the spring of 1969 Booth reviewed *The Gilded Palace of Sin,* by Parsons' band, the Flying Burrito Brothers. Booth wrote: "The album's ending somehow summons up a vision of hillbillies and hippies, like lions and lambs together in peace and love instead of sin and violence, getting stoned together, singing old time favorite songs. Perhaps Parsons, coming from the country, feels more deeply than most of the strangeness and hostility of the modern world, but he speaks for us all. Gram Parsons is a good ol' boy."

Stones secretary Jo Bergman called Booth in Memphis on July 3, 1969, to inform him Brian Jones drowned in his swimming pool. From that moment on, in pursuit of the story, Booth plunged into the wicked vortex of the Rolling Stones.

Fall, 1969. Political unrest fills American cities. Cultural lines are drawn. The Stones flew to Los Angeles in October to rehearse for their upcoming tour, and Booth joined them three days after they arrived. Thus began his true adventures with the Rolling Stones.

Booth was at the house the Stones were renting when, in his words, "The back door opened and in walked a gang of men. Tall and longhaired, they stood for a moment in the center of the room as if posing for a faded sepia photograph of the kind that used to end up on posters nailed to trees: The Stones Gang: Wanted Dead or Alive," though only Mick Jagger, standing like a model, his knife blade ass thrust to one side, was currently awaiting trial.

"Beside him was Keith Richards, who was thinner and looked not like a model, but an insane advertisement for dangerous carefree Death—black ragged hair, dead green skin, a cougar tooth hanging from his right earlobe, his lips snarled back from the marijuana cigarette between his rotting fangs...one of the others, with dark hair frosted pale gold and a classic country western outfit from Nudie the Rodeo Tailor, I remembered seeing on the television and record covers—he was Gram Parsons, and he came, so I heard, from my hometown, Waycross, Georgia, on the edge of the Okefenokee Swamp. We had not met, but I reviewed his band, the Flying Burrito Brothers new album *The Gilded Palace of Sin.* I had no idea he knew the Stones. Seeing him here, finding another boy from Waycross at this altitude, I sensed a pattern, some design I couldn't make out, and I got up to speak to Gram Parsons, as if he were a prophet and I were a pilgrim seeking revelation."

The 1969 Stones tour ended with Altamont. the Maysles Brothers—Al and David—filmed a documentary called *Gimme Shelter,* following the Stones from the East Coast down to Muscle Shoals, Alabama, where they recorded "Brown Sugar," "Wild Horses," and the classic Fred McDowell song, "You Got To Move," and then to the disastrous Altamont. Booth makes a small appearance in the film, and escaped Altamont with the Stones on a private helicopter. Parsons and Booth were the last two people to climb on the chopper.

In Muscle Shoals, Booth invited Jim Dickinson to the Stones recording session and introduced him to the band, who needed a piano player on a song called "Wild Horses," which ended up on *Sticky Fingers.* The 1969 tour was successful and groundbreaking tour for the Stones—excluding Altamont. All the while Booth dueled with parasites and agents of all kinds, who made every attempt to distract or discourage him from writing the book.

In the coda of *The True Adventures of the Rolling Stones,* Booth explained: "Following the tour that ended with Altamont, I went to live in England and stayed until, after a certain weekend in Redlands, I decided that if Keith and I kept dipping into the same bag, there would be no book and we would both be dead."

Booth returned to Memphis from England, and his interest in the medicine cabinet increased. He began working on the Stones book—the first draft of the book was uncapitalized, unspaced, uncorrected—and the publishers loved it. Expectations were high, but soon Booth became burdened with distractions.

The experience of being so close to the Stones would come with a price. Jo Bergman told Booth—long after it was too late—that an astrologer advised her that Booth would write his book, and that it would cost him everything except his life.

In early 1971 Memphis law enforcement officers discovered cannabis sativa plants growing in Booth's vegetable garden.

When his home was raided and searched, other substances were found, and seven felonies resulted. If Booth had received the maximum sentence on all seven counts, he could have been sentenced to 140 years in prison.

Fortunately for Booth, Memphis had an enlightened Attorney General who realized Booth was a writer, not a drug dealer. Booth was let off with a fine and a year's probation. After that, Booth went into hiding. For almost ten years, he lived in a log house his parents owned in the Boston Mountains of the Ozark Plateau in Newton County, Arkansas. It was the same area Jesse James and the Younger brothers had hidden in.

During the Rolling Stones 1972 American tour, Booth went on the road with the Stones again, but things had changed. People like Princess Lee Radziwill and Truman Capote were also traveling with the Stones. Booth later wrote of the '72 tour: "It was an ugly scene full of amyl nitrate, Quaaludes, tequila sunrises, cocaine, heroin, and too many pistoleros, and it left me with more material than I could ever use. At its end, I weighed about 100 pounds." Booth then disappeared back into the hills.

In January of 1973, Booth's friend, Charlie Freeman, a Memphis session, guitarist, and founder of the Mar-Keys, died. Freeman had gone on the road with Jerry Lee Lewis and Slim Harpo, and had been the guitarist for the Memphis band, the Dixie Flyers, which also included Jim Dickinson. The Flyers cut records with musicians like Carmen McRae, Ronnie Hawkins, the Memphis Horns, Delaney and Bonnie, Aretha Franklin, Taj Mahal, Little Richard, and Jerry Jeff Walker.

Booth wrote an obituary for Charlie Freeman in *Rolling Stone* called "Blues For the Red Man." Booth published the story under the pseudonym the Okefenokee Kid. At Freeman's funeral, Booth met Fred Ford. Ford—a phenomenal Memphis saxophonist (Ford barked like a dog at the end of Big Mama Thornton's original "Hound Dog')—who often played with Phineas Newborn, became another frame of reference for Booth's writing. Booth remained dedicated to forsaken talents in the mean streets of Memphis, like the Newborn family.

The Newborn Brothers, Phineas and Calvin, sons of master drummer Phineas Sr., could play the entire range of western musical instruments. Phineas, a pianist, could rival the best players around. When Memphis legend W.C. Handy became too old and frail to play the annual Memphis Blues Bowl black high school football game, he passed on his trumpet to Phineas Newborn.

Around the time Charlie Freeman died, Booth's long relationship with his companion of ten years came to an end. Days darkened. Booth later described the personal signpost, noting that he "entered into a deep depression that I would not escape till I had gone crazy, had fits, married two more times and came back to (excessively) robust health." In September of the same year, Gram Parsons died of a morphine and tequila overdose in a motel near Joshua Tree, California.

By 1975 when the Rolling Stones came to Memphis, Booth no longer had the heart to go across town and see them. The Stones book was still not complete. Booth was in the Ozarks the day Elvis died. One of his marriages ended the same day. "I guess she figured it was a no win situation."

On March 24, 1978, Booth, dosed on acid, fell from a north Georgia waterfall. In the fall, he smashed his face and broke his back. In time he became addicted to painkillers. Booth told me of that period: "I never thought I would write again—it was terrible."

On July 3, 1978, Booth's only child, Ruby Eleanora was born. Distractions of fatherhood soon added to his complications. Booth later went to Elvis' doctor, George Nichopoulos (he wrote a chilling story about Dr. Nick called "The King Is Dead! Hang the Doctor!"), who told him, "It looks like you survived a war." Booth later wrote: "After a year I tried to stop taking the drugs my doctors prescribed. I tried twice, and twice had grand-mal seizures, full-scale epileptic brain-fries, blind-rigid, foaming at the mouth, fighting off unseen enemies, screaming, turning into a hydrophobic wolf."

In 1979, starting to recuperate, Booth accompanied Fred Ford and Phineas Newborn to Europe for the Montreaux Jazz Festival and other European shows. Booth lost his most inspiring friend in October of 1982, when Furry Lewis died at the age of 89. He later gave insight to the wicked zone of originality where hipsters and parasites run in: "The night Furry died I saw that fat yellow moon and I knew it would carry him off. The funeral was crowded, lots of TV cameras and speeches by people who never knew him, who couldn't find his house with a police escort. Never mind."

Booth's frustration began to mount. As great talents and friends died neglected, years rolled by, and Booth began to live and suffer in lonely obscurity—much like the poverty-stricken blues musicians he wrote about for so long. With death all around, Booth knew he had to finish the Stones book, as he said, "Because I would rather have died than let go of it before it, not I, was ready. I thought it might be the last thing I ever did, if I ever managed to do it, and I wanted to make it right, or as close as I could make it."

In 1984, Booth's Stones book was published. Much had changed in America during the fifteen years since Altamont. The book survived for years in paperback in spite of confusion concerning its title. The book received good reviews, but sold few copies due to lack of promotion, as Booth explained in the Afterword (a severe literary lesson) of the reprinted edition: "I called the book *The True Adventures of the Rolling Stones* all the (considerable) time I'd been writing it. Some genius at the publisher's got the inspired notion of calling the first hardback edition *Dance with the Devil*. (Editors generally don't give a damn what writers think their books should be called, and in any case are usually frustrated writers themselves, desperate to demonstrate what they sincerely believe to be their superior creativity. Young, unpublished writers should consider yourselves warned)."

"Well, that edition came and, owing to the publisher's excellent marketing skills, disappeared *muy pronto*. Because the book did quite well in the UK under its real title, the American paperback was called *The True Adventures*. The funny part is, a few years later the same publisher put out a novel by the actor Kirk Douglas, and it was called *Dance With the Devil*. Somebody at that publishing house really likes that title and may keep calling books that until one is a big success."

Even Keith Richards said: "Stanley Booth's book is the only one I can read and say, 'Yeah, that's how it was.' Stanley is a lovely guy—he's got an eye. That book took longer to write than the *Bible*."

Booth's parents had retired and returned to South Georgia. Booth waited for the Stones book to be published and then he followed his parents, taking up residence in Brunswick, Georgia.

Now past his toxic nightmares and the Stones book no longer serving as an albatross, Booth began to focus on gathering stories he'd written and known long before he met the Rolling

Stones. He began to compile all the music stories he'd written since he left the Swamp of South Georgia, almost twenty-five years earlier.

Your humble scribe met Booth in 1986. I'd read *The True Adventures of the Rolling Stones* two years earlier as a sophomore in high school in Brunswick, Georgia. I was amazed, having always loved language and music, how the book fused all the aspects of art intertwining with culture, politics, music, literature, and the lives of artists struggling in pursuit of their craft or folly.

I was astonished to discover Booth lived thirteen miles from where I grew up on St. Simons Island, Georgia. It would be like meeting a legend—perhaps it would be possible to even obtain advice for a young aspiring writer. Any mythical notions concerning the craft of writing would soon evaporate.

During this time, Booth began researching a book he is calling *The Pea Patch Murders,* a novel based on actual murders that occurred near Waycross. Booth's great uncle solved the crime. Booth also began compiling and cultivating autobiographical stories he is calling *Alligator Alibis* revolving around a young boy growing up in the South Georgia swamplands.

I've spent many commonplace days with Booth: driving through dangerous neighborhoods looking for the remotest barbecue shack, haggling with crazy women, listening to obscure jazz and blues records, and drinking. Some extremely uncommon days: a 911 call, a Keith Richards concert, a lawsuit, and a savage journey to Memphis.

"Me and him just like brothers," Furry Lewis would say of Booth, who would later write, "but he would never let me forget who the older and wiser brother was." I adopted similar traits of deference. Through the years of keeping time with Booth, I began to understand the cause and curse of an uncompromising artist blessed with talent but dogged by obscurity, demanding revisions concerning terms of success and accomplishment.

In December of 1988, Booth and I drove from South Georgia to Atlanta for the opening night of Keith Richards' first solo tour at the Fox Theatre. Booth hung out with Richards for over a week in Atlanta, Los Angeles, and New York; the interview was published in *Playboy.* The story, "The Devil at 45" was published in *Smart,* an ill-fated magazine, and later in a book Booth was calling *Rythm Oil.*

●●●●●●

While researching a story about the Godfather of Soul, James Brown, when Brown was having problems with the Augusta, Georgia, police department, Booth met the woman who spent extensive time with Brown at the time. Little did Booth know, this woman would later sue him for ten million dollars for the story he wrote about Brown.

In July 1990, Booth was invited by one of his old karate students, Jimmy Crosthwait, to hang a one man show of his color photographs at a Memphis art gallery. The photographs were visions of alligators, gravestones, a naked wife, and desolate swamplands, amongst others.

Domestic tribulation caused Booth's then fiancee to refuse his company on the trip. Booth asked me if I wanted to go instead. I'd never visited Memphis, and what better host for a visit to Memphis than Booth? Knowing Booth's self-fulfilling prophecy—his problems with "police, publishers, and women"—should have warned me of the trouble to come. After an eventful visit to Memphis, he informed me he wanted to stop in Atlanta on the way home to interview this woman for a story he was writing about James Brown. What transpired that week would create complications for years to come.

Booth completed the James Brown story, "The Godfather's Blues," at the end of 1991. The piece took two years to write because South Carolina authorities would not allow Booth to speak with James Brown. It would be this story that stalled the publication of Booth's next book.

Booth's second book, *Rythm Oil*, was published in the United States in March of 1992, which was a year of turmoil. *Rythm Oil* (intentional misspelling taken from a mojo potion sold on Beale Street) is a book of twenty pieces journeying through America's musical south. *Rythm Oil* spans Booth's entire career up to 1992.

Rythm Oil begins at the crossroads with stories about Robert Johnson, Otis Redding, Gram Parsons, Charlie Freeman, Al Green, Phineas Newborn, Stax, Furry Lewis, B.B. King, and James Brown. The journey continues onto places like Graceland, New Orleans, Atlanta, and even a story called "Wiregrass," the name for the territory around the swamp he grew up in. *Rythm Oil* proves a vital resource concerning some of America's greatest music pioneers.

In October of the same year, Booth and Random House discovered the woman Booth interviewed for the James Brown story

19

was suing then for ten million dollars. She claimed the manner she was portrayed in "The Godfather's Blues" appeared demeaning. The woman wanted the story removed from the book, and she demanded royalties from all future sales on the book. The suit was for invasion of privacy, having begged Booth to tell Brown's story, she then sued him when, as she requested, he published it. She told Booth she and Brown were lovers, then denied having told him that. Luckily, Booth had tapes, and yours truly as a witness.

The lawsuit diverted publishers energies for any thoughts on promoting *Rythm Oil.* Legal proceedings and concerns began further straining Booth's personal life. No matter how ludicrous the lawsuit, it was quite real.

A horrific legal desperation gripped Booth. He kept a sense of humor, but his frustration was obvious. Lesser talents seemed to prosper all around Booth while he was being sued for telling the truth. In May of 1993, I gave my deposition concerning the lawsuit, serving as the only witness in the case since I had been present for interludes of Booth's interview.

About once a month, I would return to south Georgia and pay Booth a visit. We'd play music, talk literature, shoot pictures in the swamp, analyze classic movies, indulge in fine spirits, and wait for word on the lawsuit. To keep things interesting, every blue moon we might burn furniture in the backyard.

Booth plodded through all the personal distractions, sequestering himself, focusing on *The Pea Patch Murders, Alligator Alibis,* and research on a collaborative book about Memphis photographer Ernest Withers, as well as various magazine articles.

Booth was still fighting the legal battles of *Rythm Oil* when he agreed to write a Keith Richards biography. Soon after the book was finished, Booth began having problems obtaining contractual advances. Booth wrote the Keith Richards book in forty-four days.

While payment problems heated up on the Keith biography, the lawsuit cooled off. On August 24, 1994, a relieving decision came across in the summary judgement, which stated: "Therefore, notwithstanding the Court's finding the publication at issue was not false as a matter of law, Plaintiff may not recover damages for defamation on the additional ground she has not met her burden of producing clear and convincing evidence of actual malice on the part of either defendant."

Yet another legal battle was in motion, however. Booth was having problems obtaining payment for his Keith Richards biography, which was published in 1994. His agent died, and soon Booth was forced to deal with those in charge of his estate for the fulfilling of the contract. All the while Booth plodded on in austere toil with utmost concern for his craft.

Once asked about the responsibility as a writer, Booth replied: "I think when I was writing about music I was trying to focus on what was valuable and significant in that tradition. And just describing somebody like Furry, and I'm not done, I hope, writing about Furry in a lot of stories, I haven't yet, but if you just describe what somebody like Furry said, you're doing the Lord's work in a sense as far as the music is concerned, because Furry was the music, in the same way Keith is, you know, but even more so. He was completely identified with his musical style, endeavors, ideas, and that's what makes life, what gives life significance. And if you're lucky enough to have talent, it will really give sustenance and meaning to your life, as long as you do right by it. So I don't think it has anything to do with self-aggrandizement or any sort of selfish motive. I think that if you are given the burden of a talent, you have to deal with it the best you can. And, you know, it really doesn't matter what happens to you while you're trying with it as long as you're doing your best. that's all you have to worry about."

In 1995, Booth began researching and writing a book about Johnny Mercer, the Savannah songwriter. During one of his frequent visits to Savannah, Booth photographed and visited Flannery O'Connor's childhood home, and he wrote a sad and sobering tribute to O'Connor called "Crying In the Wilderness." That summer Booth went out on the road for a few shows with the Atlanta band, the Black Crowes.

Booth is a technical master at word economy. His work contains a strong sense of style, and he operates under no illusions. Your humble scribe has become accustomed to his ruthless editorial eye. He once wrote to me: "You have to love your work, to lavish an insane amount of love on it, and time, and care, and vigilance—to eat and sleep and shit with it until you absolutely know there's nothing wrong with it. You must do this because nothing else will suffice."

In 1969, while writing a review of the Memphis Country Blues Festival, Booth wrote an analogy for blues players, but it serves a parable for all the arts: "By now there must be in the world a million guitar virtuosos; but there are very few real blues players. The reason for this is that the blues—not the form but the blues—demands such dedication. This dedication lies beyond technique; it makes being a blues player something like being a priest. virtuosity in playing blues licks is like virtuosity in celebrating the Mass, it is empty, it means nothing. Skill—competence—is a necessity, but a true blues player's virtue lies in his acceptance of his life, a life for which he is only partly responsible."

In 1996, Booth's friend Lee Baker, guitarist for Mud Boy & the Neutrons—another Jim Dickinson band—was murdered. One more sad casualty in a long line of lost heroes.

Several years elapsed in anonymous work. One festering summer evening Booth and I endured a 911 episode that would cause the hair on anyone's head to stand on end—indeed the statute of limitations have not elapsed to reveal such an incident. It certainly was not an evening for the weak-hearted. We had experienced enough craziness together to understand the other's merciless obstacles. It was only appropriate Booth read from the bible at this correspondent's wedding.

In 1998 Booth's publisher allowed *The True Adventures of the Rolling Stones* to go out of print. Booth shed light upon the ruthless business: "Fourteen years later the publisher let the book go out of print, making this new edition possible. In all that time they paid me not a dollar of royalties. I made no royalties on the paperback edition, because the hardback had been published so unsuccessfully. The book sold many thousands of copies and generated a great deal of income, but not for me. Children, beware."

In September of 1999, Booth accepted Gram Parsons' induction into the Georgia Music Hall of Fame, an honor that speaks for itself. In Macon, Georgia, at the Gram Parsons tribute, Booth told a story, with an ironic grin, about how every Thursday Gram was defeated at the Palomino Club in L.A. by a guy in a wheelchair singing Johnny Cash's "I Walk the Line." Booth remains an expert at irony.

Booth's old friend Fred Ford died in November of 1999, forcing him to write another obituary, serving as a witness to one more fallen hero.

Rythm Oil was reprinted (Da Capo) in October of 2000. A complete book waiting on the horizon is another compilation of

22

Booth's essays called *Cowboys, Country Boys and City Slickers.* This book chronicles the lives of : King "Joe" Oliver, Ray Charles, Hoagy Carmichael, Phineas "Little Red" Newborn, Fred Ford, Frank Sinatra, Bireli Lagrene, Jerry Lee Lewis, Waylon Jennings, Miles Davis, Mose Allison and the Black Crowes.

Booth's Johnny Mercer biography is now halfway complete. This book explores the songwriting world of Mercer from his Savannah origins toward his singular niche forever etched in the songwriting and music world. Booth is also working on a Gram Parsons biography, which is due in 2002. In all Booth's work, he uses the miracle of language to breathe eternal life into the accomplishments and circumstances of great American musicians, some who died poor, neglected, talented, and forgotten. Booth serves as a voice for these underdog, or underground, musicians.

Booth's writing remains a cornerstone testimony of Sunday morning gospels, minstrel sideshows, sawmills, scaldcat, funeral parlors, wizard oil, swamp water, shotgun shacks, dirt roads, Mississippi churches, Memphis mean streets, bottleneck junctions, catfish, barbecue woodsmoke, gris-gris, juke joints, railroad tracks, traveling medicine shows, stone cold fevers, voodoo practitioners, mojo dust, soul food, zombie powder, midnight undertakers, whiskey stills, cut-throat wages, chicken yard fiddles, devil's shoestring, spooky field recordings, Civil War songs, fatback grease, black cat bones, and many other redemptions and temptations buried in American music folklore and fact...

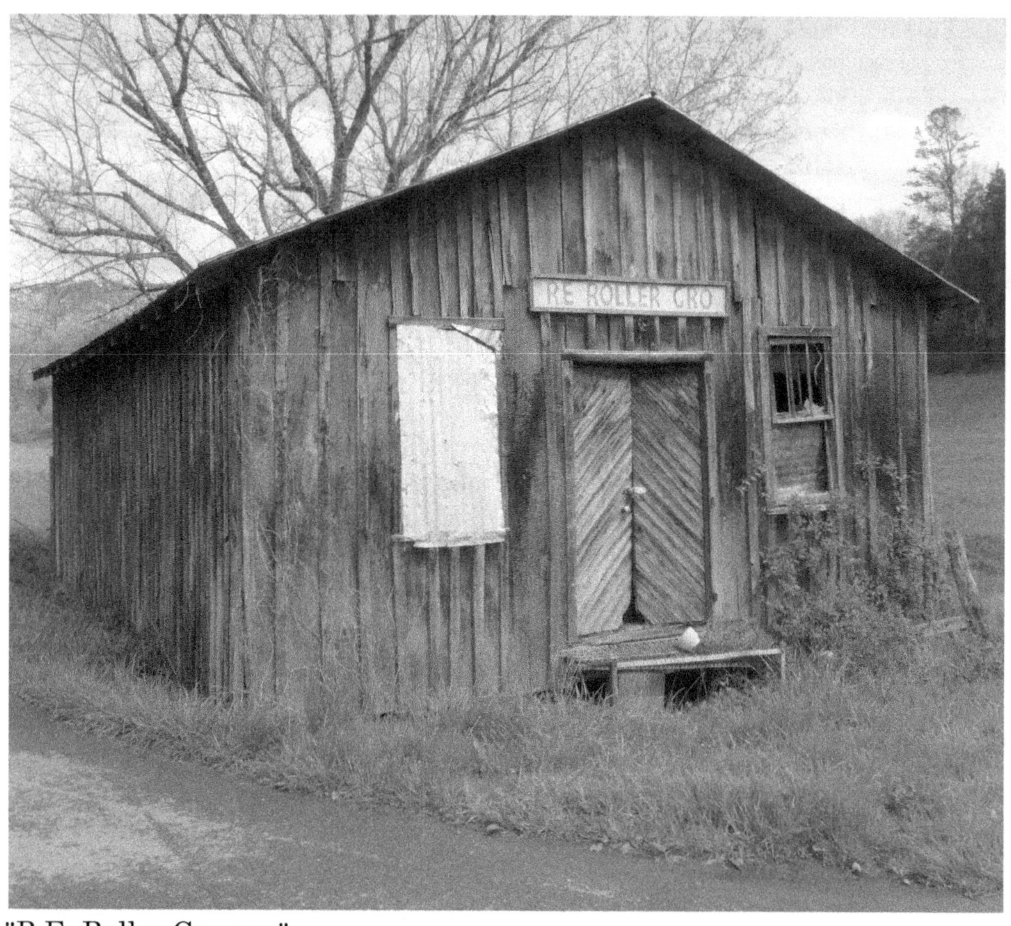

"R.E. Roller Grocery"
Hawkins County, Tennessee

······

Jim Dickinson Interview
Dixie Fried With The High Priest
Of Memphis Mojo

In 1987, Stanley Booth exposed me to the catalogue of Jim Dickinson's music. Booth allowed me to walk into his vast library, pull an album off the shelf, drop the needle and press record. I made hundreds of cassettes. Stanley's equipment was top of the line. In 1990, Booth and I drove to Memphis from coastal Georgia. At the Memphis blues festival we watched the first live performance Dickinson gave with his sons. They were called the Hardly Can Playboys. I think Luther was around 13, and Cody about 10 years old.

This Dickinson interview counts as one of his last. A New York Times writer used a blurb from it in his article after Dickinson died on August 15, 2009. That day I called Stanley. I wasn't sure if he heard the news yet. He hadn't heard, and I broke the news of Dickinson's death. They were old Memphis buddies along with the photographer William Eggleston. Booth got him on the Muscle Shoals sessions that turned out to be the Rolling Stones album Sticky Fingers. I encouraged Dickinson to write two articles for Swampland before he died. One was about his favorite places to eat on the road, and the other was his favorite albums and films. I felt lucky to get all of this on the record.

Jim Dickinson recorded with the Rolling Stones, Bob Dylan, The Replacements, Ry Cooder and many other luminaries that this interviews highlights. Dickinson wrote a memoir before he passed away titled, I'm Just Dead, I'm Not Gone. The book was published in April 2017 from University Press of Mississippi.

"Some people say worried blues ain't tough, If they don't kill you they handle you mighty rough."

— Furry Lewis

Jim Dickinson remains a musical shaman. After 40 years of playing with some of the world's most known and unknown musicians, Dickinson continues making music—rendering him one of the South's most enduring and influential artists. Born in Little Rock, Arkansas, in 1941, Dickinson's musical legacy exists with a long history of potent musical accomplishments such as working with artists such as Sam Phillips, Bob Dylan, The Rolling Stones, Duane Allman, Tom Dowd, Jerry Wexler, Chips Moman, Jerry Jeff Walker, Toots & The Maytals, Big Star, Green On Red, Ry Cooder, Bonnie & Delaney, Mudboy & The Neutrons, James Carr, Albert King, Rita Coolidge, Furry Lewis, Johnny Cash, Aretha Franklin, Carmen McRae, Eddie Hinton, Sam The Sham, Ronnie Hawkins, John Hiatt and a list too long to print in this introduction.

Dickinson provided Luther and Cody Dickinson of The North Mississippi Allstars a formidable musical education. Luther and Cody represent the eighth generation of musicians in the Dickinson family. The Dickinson's influence cast a long and wide shadow in the musical community around their Mississippi hometown. Dickinson's Barn—his home recording studio—serves as a lodestone for artists searching for a real mythical location to absorb and record their music. Jim Dickinson serves as the fulcrum for the musical network around the beautiful and brutal North Mississippi environs located 50 miles south of Memphis, Tennessee.

Dickinson played piano on "Wild Horses" during the fabled Rolling Stones 1969 recording session in Muscle Shoals. Dickinson appears on Bob Dylan's classic *Time Out of Mind* record, which ranks as two heavy resume notes, but he's also played with unknown music purveyors like guitarist Charlie Freeman, jazz pianist Phineas Newborn, bluesman Johnny Woods and the inimitable Dixie Flyers. Dickinson represents a historic landmark or crossroads—where generations meet through space and time, when rock and roll, rockabilly, blues, jazz, country and R&B swirls through his cosmic keyboard—no matter the year. Dickinson forces any music aficionado to dig deeper...to peel back layer after layer of his musical influence, collaborations and lineage...

Sam Phillips—the man who discovered Elvis Presley—recorded Dickinson's original Sun Records sessions. For some of Dickinson's essential work, besides the aforementioned Stones and Dylan sessions, investigate Ry Cooder's, *Paris, Texas,* and the soundtrack, *The Border,* Dickinson's own albums, *James Luther Dickinson Dixie Fried, Killers From Space, Free Beer Tomorrow, Voodoo Jim* and the *Voodoo Tiger, Fishing with Charlie,* and *Other Selected Readings* (Dickinson reads Kerouac-Hughes-Williams), *A Thousand Footprints in the Sand, Toots In Memphis,* Big Star's, *Third* and any number of musical endeavors for an introduction to his talent. Dickinson's a godfather in the music underworld...

Dickinson wrote this insightful Production Manifesto: "The unretainable nature of the present creates in Man a desire to capture the moment. Our fears of extinction compel us to record- to recreate- the ritual ceremony. From the first hand-print cave painting to the most modern computer art, it is the human condition to seek immortality. Life is fleeting. Art is long. A record is a "totem," a document of a unique, unrepeatable event worthy of preservation and able to sustain historic life. The essence of the event is its soul. Record production is a subtle, covert activity. The producer is an invisible man. His role remains a mystery. During the recording process there is an energy field present in the studio-to manipulate and to maximize that presence- to focus on the peculiar "harmony of the moment" is the job of the producer. Music has a spirit beyond the notes and rhythm. To foster that spirit and to cause it to flourish- to capture it at its peak is the producer's task."

In this interview, Dickinson discusses his early musical origins, recording at Sun Records, Ardent Studios, influences, recording on Atlantic Records, the Memphis musical underground, recording with the Rolling Stones, advice from Duane Allman, giving Bob Dylan a tour of rural Mississippi, the tragedy of Eddie Hinton, his influential film soundtracks, upcoming Mississippi musical projects, The North Mississippi All-stars, Luther joining the Black Crowes and what the future holds for this talented keyboardist, producer, songwriter and session man.

Get out the zombie powder, black cat ashes and graveyard dirt for this conversation with the high priest of Memphis mojo

I've been listening to your music for a long time. It's good to finally be able to talk with you...

JD: Well I'm glad somebody was listening.

Your old friend Stanley Booth was a sort of neighbor of mine in South Georgia many years ago. He recorded most all your music for me onto cassettes, which I still have. That was around 1987-88. I always tell this story, but Stanley and I drove to the Memphis Blues Festival

in 1990 where you, Luther and Cody played as Jim Dickinson and the Hardly Can Playboys...they were really young...

JD: That was the first time the family band played together. That was it.

That makes it even more significant for me. That whole trip Stanley and I only listened to three tapes...Blind Willie McTell's, *Atlanta Twelve String,* a bunch of Jimmie Rodgers songs and the song he played for you, which you later covered, called "Billy & Oscar."

JD: (Laughs) Oh yeah....

So, I've been paying attention. You've been busy lately. *Hernando* sounds great...

JD: Yeah, well I just finished a local band called Free World—kind of a Grateful Dead with horns—a hippie band. We've been talking to each other for years. Finally the time came around to do it. Herman Green—he's about 75—an old Memphis horn player—sax player—that Robert Palmer was very into his hippest band—just one old guy and a bunch of kids. I just finished that last week. That was fun. We got...since right after Hernando we did a three day super session with the Allstars, Charlie Musselwhite, Alvin Youngblood Hart and Jimbo Mathus.

Luther was telling me about that...

JD: The combination of Jimbo Mathus and Alvin Youngblood Hart is truly something the world needs to hear. It was really something man. Charlie Musselwhite is the real deal. I don't know why we never knew each other. We were virtually at the same place at the same time, but I guess about six months apart. He was more downtown and I was strictly suburban. I was limited by my suburban environment.

Let's go all the way back. You were born in Little Rock, Arkansas, in 1941. What was your first musical memory?

JD: I never really lived in Little Rock. My father—my parents were from there. I was conceived in Memphis. My mother thought there was something pagan about giving birth in Memphis. We went back to Little Rock. We spent a little time there over the years with my grandparents, but we never really lived there. We moved to Hollywood in the beginning of World War II and then after about nine months we moved to Chicago where we lived until we moved to Memphis in 1949. It was an enormous culture shock for a smart aleck Yankee punk kid, which was what I was. I really hated Memphis at first. I'd go to sleep and think I was going to wake up in Chicago. It got me. It slowly got me. The music played a big hand in capturing me. Now I can't leave. The times I've tried to leave it didn't work. There's something here geographically that I really need musically. My mother played piano in church. I think it's five or six generations of trained musicians behind me, but no professionals. I'm the only professional and I'm untrained (laughs). There was a guy on the radio called Two Ton Baker the Music Maker in Chicago and he was my original inspiration beyond my mother—who was a fabulous player.

I'm sure she gave you a serious musical foundation early in life.

JD: She'd sit down and try. See, she was the music teacher and she tried to teach me and she couldn't. I have real screwed up vision which is probably dyslexia although when I was a kid they didn't know what it was. I have a kind of multi-vision that makes it impossible to read music. She tried to teach me and she tried to get me serious lessons. She wanted me to play. I remember the guy trying to tell me about the dots and the lines. I thought he was putting me on. I thought this was the kind of things grown-ups tell kids and it's bullshit, because I didn't see any dots. I saw a smear. When I got glasses the smear cleared up but I'd still see a multiple image. I can't use a video screen. I can't use a computer. However screwed up my vision, it did something to my hearing. I hear things I firmly believe other people can't hear. Musically, as a piano player I learned to listen and memorize and that's what I do in the studio. Of course, as a session player and the simplicity...when I finally found it in Memphis. Years later an old black man named Dishrag who showed me what my style was based on. He said, 'everything in music is made up by codes.' And I thought he meant like Captain Midnight, and I thought why didn't my mother tell me it was in code! I can't do it (laughs)!

Of course, he meant chords. He said, 'This is how you makes a code (sic). He said you take any note then you go up three and four down. He was talking about keys, not half-steps or whole steps. He was talking about the keys on the keyboard. It was a physical thing I could see. Of course, it works anywhere on the piano. Your thumb ends up on the tonic note and what it makes is a triad. Dish Rag had no idea that's what it was, but it was a code to him. So, with a triad chord in my right hand and an octave in my left, y'know, I kind of taught myself to play. That's what I still do…listen to what I'm playing on "Wild Horses"—I'm playing a major triad or a minor with my left hand and an octave with my right…that's all I play. It's so simple it works in the studio. It creates space and tension and all the things you want a keyboard to do and it doesn't get in the way of the damn guitar because rock and roll is about guitars. So, thank god I've had a career because I play simple and stupid. It really boils down to the simplicity of what I do. I had a friend ask about the Stones session once, he says 'Tell me the truth man, you were holding back weren't you?' I said, 'Dude I was going for it with everything I had (laughs). It's just all I got.'"

When did you really begin playing with other musicians in a band?

JD: In the 50s, even with Elvis in Memphis and the whole thing going on—which was going on in front of my eyes--it wasn't until I went to school at Baylor in Texas that I realized I had seen everything unique. Once I left I thought, 'Well, my god, compared to these musicians that I just met I had all this arcane knowledge. Anyway, in the 50s it wasn't okay to be a musician—and there weren't many. So, it was easy to meet other players. There was one particular guitar player named Stanley Neale When I met Stanley, I thought man I could have a band. Then we played in the talent show with another band where there was a real good drummer and a crappy band—and I had a real good band and a crappy drummer. So, before the end of the night the two became one. That was my first band…Stanley Neale and Steady Eddie Tauber. Then I thought maybe I could do it. In the 50s and in high school I never considered it for a career—impossible. But then I went to Texas because I figured my career was over.

The first people I met in Texas were musicians and they weren't as good as me. I thought wow—but it just kept happening naturally. I studied drama at Baylor University which is kind of a strange thing, but that's what I did. The first thing I did was play drums in a band for Where's Charley? It was just an unavoidable thing I couldn't not do it. It was one of the most fun musical experiences I had playing in that band. It was great. It just seemed like it was happening naturally—I didn't know what the hell I wanted to do. Now I knew I wanted to be an artist, but what? I painted for a while. I tried to write. The music just came naturally. It was the path of least resistance. Then in the late sixties, well into the early 60s and mid-60s the blues festival happened which was a life changing experience for everybody that was there. It all came together. The musicians I was associated with started participating for what would become the golden age of Memphis recording and history.

It works better for me in the studio. The first time I walked in the studio which was Les Bahara's old Meteor studio. I felt at home. I thought this makes sense to me. I don't get off on playing live music. I enjoy it certainly, but I don't respond to the audience the way a lot of people do. In the studio I'm utterly aware of the audience. I can feel them. We're separated by time and space, but I think that's a healthy thing. I've never felt anything for the audience. That goes back to drama. I never felt anything for a live audience other than a mild contempt and I recognized that as being unhealthy. So, I keep it to a minimum. I don't know why that is but I've talked to musicians and actors back in the old days who would talk about this love they felt coming from the audience—I don't feel it. I feel it making the records for certain people, and that somehow they're going to find it and it's gonna work for them.

It takes the visual aspect out of it. On a record you only hear it…

JD: Yes. See, that's the thing. It's two entirely different things—playing live music and working in the studios. I think we make records searching for immortality—fear of death. It's like the handprints on the cave. Here I am motherfucker.

Yeah, like some lost recordings from 80 years ago.

JD: Exactly. I never set out to make pop records. I set out to document a time and place and a feeling. It's like the natives in the jungle don't want you to take their picture because you're capturing their soul and that's exactly what you're doing. That's what I'm there to do. If you're soul is not how you feel in the moment then what in the fuck is it?

That certainly questions any motivation...

JD: Yeah, it's really easy to detect a soulless performance in the studio. There's no lights, no smoke...

It's interesting because a lot of musicians talk about how cold and imposing recording studios can be...

JD: It can be if you let it. It bothers some people. Some people it doesn't bother them at all. That's part of what the producer's job is to control the environment. Sometimes it's all about the sterility. Some people need it. I've got people working in my barn as we speak who are down there because it doesn't feel like a studio.

From what I understand your barn is a place that took many years to cultivate.

JD: (Laughs) Yeah, I've been thinking about it a long time. It represents a lot of trickery all combined...

...A lot of mojo...

JD: Many years ago I wanted to erase the wall between the control room and the studio. It's taken me awhile to do it. Why should the engineer hear one thing and everybody else hears something else? It's just stupid.

It is—I thought it was interesting when Luther talked about recording with John Hiatt, and how Hiatt didn't want any extra people in the studio.

JD: Oh no, I don't either. You're breathing my air man (laughs).

Nobody needs a stranger breathing up the molecules...

JD: That's right. It's all about moving the molecules and if someone's in there, they're taking up space—breathing my air. Hiatt is a very private man...very complicated individual, John Hiatt. He's a reluctant artist as most of them are.

Talk about how you got your first music break.

JD: Well, when I busted out of Baylor I came back to Memphis State to stay out of the draft and stay in school which is about the time I ran into Stanley Booth. I didn't have theater out of my blood. I ran a little summer theater of my own called The Market Theatre on Cleveland Avenue in Memphis. We did folk music as an opening act and on the weekends. The folk music scene...it's 1963. Folk music was really catching on. We got some publicity and I did a show at the Municipal Auditorium with completely unknown folk musicians that packed the place and caused a traffic jam. We got a write-up in the paper and got picked up in Nashville. Bill Justus—God bless his soul—read the thing and he was trying to put a record together of smash party records of instrumentals. In this case he was going to use a vocal group called The Dixieland Folkstyle—a Dixie band playing folk music on Smash/Mercury Records.

So, Justus sees this publicity and one of his trumpet players—this arranger who was George Tidwell, this guy I'd known from high school. So Justus wanted to get in touch with me so Tidwell calls me. I went to Nashville to do this album. He had all the real Nashville cats—Bob Moore, Bill Purcell, Grady Martin—it was unbelievable. The Jordanaires. I was the folk, right? It's amazing how much it sounds like the record Springsteen made a couple of years ago—The Seeger Sessions. It was like corny folk songs—"Michael Row Your Boat Ashore," "Five Hundred Miles Away From Home," that stuff. The hippest thing we cut was

Dylan's "Blowin' in the Wind" with this Dixie band and these hillbillies, the Nashville guys and me singing in this Bob Dylan voice.

That resulted in me getting a contract with Bill Justus to make my first record which was The New Beale Street Sheiks. A jug band record. We actually missed the beginning because my first real music experience was seeing Will Shade and the Memphis Jug Band in downtown Memphis when I was about 10. It was like seeing Martians play music. From that point I really wasn't much interested in much else except finding that. But the racial separation being what it was took ten years for that to happen.

It became more intense for you…how long was it between Nashville's National and Memphis sessions?

JD: The National thing was over in three days. It was just the one record. Everything else I did, I did in Memphis. My first three single records were all recorded at Sam Phillips'. Two of them were recorded by Phillips himself. That, needless to say, was quite an experience. American—Larry Raspberry—from the Gentrys—the first hit Chips Moman had and I knew Chips from just being around. He's a very hypnotic, charismatic figure. A lot of people will talk bad about Chips but I never will. He gave me my break. As far as I'm concerned he's a true genius. In regard to Raspberry and the Gentrys, they had "Keep On Dancin'" as a hit—it was on the charts but half the band was still in high school. So they couldn't go on the road. And Chips wouldn't start making a record until Larry had a whole band. So, Larry calls me one night. My wife and I were living in the Veterans housing on the Memphis State campus. He calls me about 10 o'clock one night saying, Chips is not letting me start recording until I get a band together. Will you go on the road with the Gentrys?" I said, 'Hell no Larry, I don't want to go on the road with the Gentrys.' He said, 'Well man, will you come down here to the studio and tell Chips you will?' I said, 'Yeah, sure man.' So me and my old lady went down to the old American studios. Middle of the night Chips says, 'Hey, will you go on the road with the Gentrys?'

I said, 'Yeah Chips, sure.' I started talking to the rest of the musicians, bullshitting, before I knew what was happening. Chips had locked the doors. We started to record. By the time he unlocked the doors it was noon the next day and we recorded the whole first album and half of the second album. Chips said to me, 'You're too good to go on the road with the Gentrys.' I said, 'That's what I think. Then I had my first job.

Go back and provide a little insight to your experience recording at Sun Records. That's a mind-blowing frame of reference...

JD: It was totally. That's what I mean, in high school I knew Knox Phillips was in my high school. I saw him every day in school, but still...Sun Records—it was like going to Mars, it was unobtainable. I couldn't go down there and knock on the door. Although I could've, I didn't see that. It was just happenstance that caused me to record both of the things I did at Sun. It's just the way things went down. It was a really small community at the time. I was certainly on the fringes of it but Memphis is a fringy place. So, the novelty aspect of rock and roll it runs pretty thick in Memphis. It's the only place in my life where I've even remotely fit in.

The John Fry work at Ardent must have been another interesting experience.

JD: I met Fry—his home studio was less than two blocks from where my wife and I lived. I could jump a fence and go down a ditch and come up at Fry's backyard. He had this studio in his house that was better than American Studios. Chips was there one time and it made him mad. 'Hell, that boy's got better equipment than I do.' I said 'That's why I brought you out here Chips'. I didn't think Chips would even let me engineer. I thought I wanted to be an engineer and I figured John would—that he would teach me. John told me, 'Jim, I don't think you're emotionally unsuited to be an engineer.' Which, he was right about. The engineer has got to try to do it right. It's the producer's role to finish. I sometimes touch the equipment (laughs). I went back and listened to some of my old engineering. Ace Records is going to put a compilation of the early Ardent stuff and some stuff that's never been released. Some of it has. My engineering wasn't too damn bad—a little extreme maybe. I wasn't afraid to turn the knobs.

•••••••

Well, you're still doing it. You didn't miss your mark...

JD: If I had to deal with all this computer stuff—I'd never be able to learn it all. I'm lucky I came along just when I did—I was a good 8 track engineer. This computer thing, I could've never learned it. I use it every day, but I use it with an operator. I can understand what he's doing, but I could never do it.

I'd go into Stanley Booth's massive record collection and get—among hundreds of other things—all those Dixie Flyers albums with Rita Coolidge, Jerry Jeff Walker, Albert Collins, Sam the Sham, Carmen McRae, Ronnie Hawkins and record them all onto tape. That's one of my favorite bands of all time...the Dixie Flyers.

JD: The Carmen McRae record was my favorite.

From that album I love Eddie Hinton's "Breakfast In Bed" and "I Thought I Knew You Well"...

JD: Yeah, man. There's a place where I play...you know I'm a simple player...but I play the beginning of the solo and then I turn it into King Curtis and then King Curtis turns into the New York Symphony Orchestra. Are you kidding me? It's a golden moment. I played that for my mother.

The Jerry Jeff Walker album with the Flyers, *Bein' Free*, is a classic.

JD: That's a good one. That's a good record.

I'm still fascinated with that stuff. I still have my Dixie Flyers 'Greatest Hits' cassette. You can't find any of that stuff...

JD: You're right. It's pretty much vanished. Jerry Jeff bought Bein' Free back and he re-released it as a vanity record. There is a CD available of it. Carmen McRae came out in Japan for about a minute. I've got a copy of it. For me that was my favorite thing the Dixie Flyers did at Atlantic. But that record was crushed by Roberta Flack's manager. The Dixie Flyers were almost a stillborn, which is something that wasn't supposed to happen and the fact that there's any of it around is truly remarkable. They put out this Aretha Franklin outtake thing just a couple of months ago and the worst thing we recorded with her is on there—"My Way"—which you pretty much get the picture.

Charlie Freeman, the Dixie Flyers guitarist, was a real maverick.

JD: Oh man, he was the best.

What do you remember about those days? The Dixie Flyers played with everyone from Duane Allman to Ronnie Hawkins to Albert Collins and beyond...Jerry Wexler made big plans for the Flyers...

JD: Well, it didn't dawn on me—I made the deal and Stanley Booth put it together with Wexler, and what's in Stanley's book is pretty much true, but it didn't dawn on me how geographically dependent we were, and we went down to Miami and went crazy. There's no doubt about it. Tommy McClure was the only one that could play right away. There's something so simple about Tommy that even though he went crazy, he never lost it musically, but the rest of us did. It never came back fully. Leland Rogers told us literally the night before we went to Miami, he said, 'Boys I'm sorry, but I think you already played your best music'. And he was right. We only hit it two or three times where we did the thing we could do. Y'know, we were just rednecks. What the fuck did we know? It was like, I left after six months. We made 14 albums in six months and that's a lot of fucking records. We'd jump from Jerry Jeff Walker to Aretha Franklin in two days— with nothing in between. Other sessions, like Dick Holler—shit that wasn't easy, and we were making an album in five days with sometimes Jerry Wexler, Tom Dowd and Arif Mardin—all there telling us different things. It was not easy, but for me it was like a Master's Degree.

It was beyond a normal education in record making. I already— as Ronnie Hawkins said—been to the mountain and seen the elephant. I worked with Sam Phillips, Chips Moman...some serious people, but six months with Tom Dowd, believe me, was a crash course. It was my job—I was de facto bandleader, and I didn't want to be but it was literally thrust upon me from both Wexler and the band because it was Charlie Freeman's band, but I took all the heat and I ran all the interference which meant arguing with Tom Dowd on a regular basis, which he was literally a rocket scientist. He taught me to compromise and we eventually—years later—became friends and I treasured the friendship, but during the period of time with The Dixie Flyers, it was pretty rough. Like I said, it never crossed my mind that I would get away from Memphis and go crazy, but I certainly did. The first time the season didn't change I thought, 'Man this place sucks.'

When I got a chance to leave, I did. Stanley was right there before it happened—him and Duane Allman. Duane is the one who told me what to do. Things were not running smoothly. Sammy Creason's (Flyers drummer) wife had a publishing company and that was a sore spot. There was a lot of shit going on. Duane said, with Charlie Freeman in the car, riding back from a session one day. Duane said, 'Man you ought to do what I did. Just tell Wexler I'm tired of playing with these rednecks—I want my own band.' Unfortunately, the problem with that was, it was my band, but I did what Duane told me. I quit and I went home and I stopped and talked to Phil Walden on the way home and we—unfortunately—agreed not to work together because we were friends and it wouldn't have worked. It was Duane who basically showed me the door out.

Duane played on a couple of those Dixie Flyers records like the one with Ronnie Hawkins and Sam the Sham...

JD: Well, Duane would show up periodically anyway. He knew when there was a hot session. They would call him on certain things, but Charlie Freeman might be a problem. Duane showed up for different reasons. Sometimes he was just there hanging out. I knew Duane before we went to Miami. I'd known him for years.

So, the Dixie Flyers began to fade before it really began?

JD: Yeah, we cut the Albert Collins albums in Nashville and Memphis was what got us the job. There's another thing I didn't realize Stan Kessler was a big part of that record as an engineer. It didn't dawn on me how much we needed him to get our sound. It's not like Tom Dowd didn't have his hands on the gear. Ronnie Alpert was running the board most of the time and he was 15 fucking years old.

And for someone who recorded with Sam Phillips...

JD: Yeah, I wasn't impressed by Ronnie Alpert. I didn't want him to tell me what it was going to sound like. The Dixie Flyers never experienced stereo headphones. It was a whole different ball of wax in Miami. I think for country boys we did all right.

I suppose Charlie Freeman felt weird about it all.

JD: Well, that came afterwards. Charlie handled it all right. Yet, he and Duane were sort of like me and Stanley...they loved each other but the two of them together meant trouble. That was mostly after I was gone, but it got nasty later. Charlie had bad health and he basically could have died the way he died anytime from when he was 12 years old on. It was like Elvis...it wasn't dope that killed Charlie.

Well, everyone knows the fabled Rolling Stones session in Muscle Shoals when you played piano on "Wild Horses."

JD: (Laughs) Yeah, but nobody knows the truth. Even Stanley didn't tell the truth...well, he told it from his viewpoint.

It's a classic story...

JD: Well, it began my career, that's for sure (laughs)...jump-started it at least. I would have never...well, okay—the world just re-discovered Bettye LaVette, right? I didn't have that much time to wait. That was the best record we made up to that point was the Bettye LaVette record and it only took the world 40 years to find it! No, for me it was "Wild Horses." I didn't find out for ten years why Ian Stewart (Stones pianist) didn't play on the song. What happened, it was the third night and just as they started running down the song, Stu just got up from the piano and started packing up the gear like they were gonna leave. Jagger said, 'I assume we need a keyboardist.' Wexler says, 'Oh baby we could call Barry Beckett.' I'm standing by Wexler and I said, 'I don't think that's what he means Jerry.'

So anyway, I start playing the thing. After we're doing it for about 45 minutes Jagger's in the control room listening and he says to Keith, 'What do you think about the piano?' I thought, 'Well here goes. I'm going home now.' And Keith says, 'It's the only thing I like so far.' God bless him. But I didn't know for ten years why Stu wasn't playing because he played "Brown Sugar" and Wyman played piano on "You Got To Move" because there's no bass on that. Years later…the way you have a meeting with Keith Richards is they send for you. You check into a hotel and you wait for days—literally—and two or three days later, in the middle of the night the phone rings. Somebody comes to pick you up and you're taken to an undisclosed location. That's how you have a meeting with Keith. I was in New York meeting with Keith—trying to get together the Robert Johnson documentary that's never been produced. I was going to do the music and they were gonna put Keith's name on it which was the deal. In the midst of that meeting process I was down in the bar at the Plaza one day…me and Stu—not long before he died.

And I said, 'This by no means a complaint, because my whole career is based on that song, why did you not play "Wild Horses?" And Stu said 'Minor chords—I don't play minor chords.' He said, 'When I play with the lads onstage and a minor chord comes by, I lift my hands (laughs).' I thought fucking all right because "Wild Horses" starts on a big ole B Minor. Stu wasn't having any of that…

You've worked with so many great artists, I just want to throw out some of my favorites. Doug Sahm…

JD: Yeah, I did the last Tornadoes record that they were all on. I only met Doug a couple of times before that but he was a great one. He was very misunderstood, Doug Sahm.

Albert King…

JD:I did three days with Albert King which turned out to be his last session. Never made a nickel for it and I knew sure as shootin' when I stayed home on the fourth day it would all blow up--and it did. I've had a history of problem artists, and Albert was one of them. He was wearing a forty-five. So, you didn't really argue with him.

Eddie Hinton...

JD: Oh, man. Poor Eddie. He was one of the real tragedies. You know, Stanley and I got a theory about going into the blackness...the racially black musical experience. There's something out there and of course the further you go into it...up to a point... it's rewarding. But there's something out there that doesn't want you with it, and I guess Eddie just got too close to that because he certainly was the blackest of all the white boys. Everybody said he sounded like Otis Redding, but to me he sounded like Mavis Staples. Think about that.

I saw him one time at the first Muscle Shoals Sound Celebration, which was the first time they gave themselves awards and patted each other on the back and acted like they really liked each other. Wexler was there and a lot of industry types and it was appropriately in an un-air-conditioned gymnasium. Everybody played—Percy Sledge singing in a tuxedo sweating...it was quite an event. Eddie played with one of his little combos—a guy I can't remember his name, with a left-handed telecaster...Dan Penn called it The Blue Eyed Revue...that was what I always called it, but it wasn't what Eddie called it.

They played sitting down and it was like John Lennon and John Lee Hooker trapped in the same body trying to get out and the music was them trying. It was unbelievable. I looked around at one point and I thought...admittedly I was on psilocybin—but nobody—I mean nobody is getting this except me. It was going right over Wexler's head—the industry dudes and the local good old boys alike...nobody was getting it. It was just too bent I guess. Seeing Eddie Hinton were two or three of the highest musical experiences of my life came from watching Eddie. To me, he seemed to have it all, and he couldn't get arrested with it. By the time I used him on the Toots record, he didn't own a guitar and he was homeless.

He was living in an abandoned trailer. There was nothing left of Eddie but his fingertips, but he was there. He never lost that. Dan Penn—the strange individual that he is—has an interesting theory—I only know this second-hand, but it sounds like Dan to me. Somebody—a mutual friend—asked Dan what he thought happened to Eddie and Dan said Eddie's possessed. And it's almost enough to believe. Something happened to Eddie that was way beyond drugs. I always figured there was some bizarre therapy—some electro-shock or something like that, but I don't know. He might have been possessed. Something happened that's for sure. Roger Hawkins and I talked about it, and he said some people just can't handle failure and Eddie failed every time.

You could hear his heart break if you listen to the Coleman/Hinton project—everything after that has a different sound. That record broke his heart. Yet, something more than that happened to Eddie—he really, really suffered.

It's a sad story and the music is so good...even until the very end, *Hard Luck Guy*...

JD: Yeah, he never stopped being good. He was too crazy to put his shoes on, but he could still play and sing.

Speaking of Mavis, you worked with her, right?

JD: Well, I did the Dylan tribute and I played on her track, but I never met her until later with the boys (North Mississippi All-Stars).

You worked with Furry Lewis...

JD: Yeah, Stanley (Booth) pretty much said all there is to say about Furry Lewis.

Sleepy John Estes...

JD: Yeah, Sleepy John was great. He'd call me up in the middle of the night because he was blind and he had no concept of time, and everybody in his family was mentally retarded so he never had anybody to talk to—he'd call me up in the middle of the night and talk about space aliens. He was out there, Sleepy John.

Talk about the great unknown Memphis pianist Phineas Newborn.

JD: He was unbelievable. He changed the whole way I approached the piano. Just by shaking my hand, it was like holding onto a dynamo. He was unbelievable. When we made that record we started out the first two sessions we did, he wouldn't even speak. He was still at the psychiatric hospital. They were checking him out for the weekends. He would play sometimes without taking off his overcoat. As soon as he saw the piano he would just jump on it and start to play. There were outtakes from that session Fred Ford—he was very protective and sometimes overprotective artistically or strangeness in the cut—he wouldn't let me use it. I heard some playing that defied description that Fred wouldn't let me use.

I met Fred Ford once...

JD: He was a trip. Fred died thinking I owed him money which really hurt me. He just would not accept the fact that somebody did not make money on that record. I gave him Stanley's money and that wasn't easy. When Charlie died...that was Charlie Freeman's project. When Charlie died it just kind of fell to Stanley and me to make sure it happened.

You worked with James Carr...

JD: Oh yeah. The story Peter Guralnick tells about Carr standing on the roof staring at the parking lot—that was on my session. They lost him. They had a bodyguard and a nurse taking care of him. Everybody looked around at one point and realized nobody knew where he was. They found him and he was standing on the roof staring at the parking lot two stories down. They had to go up and get him down...Back up James back up...we'll give you some cough syrup...he had a mental problem though—if a song had a bridge in it he couldn't get out of the bridge. He'd get lost. It was tragic, but that was the greatest R & B voice I was ever in the same room with…I'd never heard Otis in the same room, but I don't know if it could have been much better than James Carr. It was like his voice was coming out of his whole body, not his mouth…it was really strange.

You mentioned Bettye LaVette, I'm sure you've heard that new album, *Scene of the Crime*. You played with her…

JD: Oh yeah, She's still got it man. Bettye was hot. She says now she was 17 when we made that record. She was a helluva 17 I'll tell you that. I took my first cocaine on that record from her. Had I not done that, the next time would have been Keith Richards. At least she prepared me for Keith. Bettye was the real deal. She says she was really scared when we made that record, but she's good.

You worked with Johnny Cash…

JD: (Laughs) Yep. Ry Cooder called me up one day years after we had really done anything and he said, 'What are you doing on Thursday?' I said, not much. What do you have in mind? Would you come to Nashville and play on a Johnny Cash session? I said, 'Yeah, I think so. The great thing that happened out of that session—I can't recall the name of the studio—real old. It was Rainbow…it was off the main beaten path in an old house. We're all sitting around—Steve Earle was there pitching a song, Ry Cooder and his son and the Nashville Bluegrass Band which was the bulk of the rhythm section. Everybody is sitting around waiting for Cash to get there. I'm sinking in the front room with Steve Earle. He was fresh out of prison and even fatter than me. He looked like he weighed 400 pounds and sweating like I don't know what—like a field hand and unchanged. Steve Earle was the same person he was when he was a junkie—it had no effect on his personality.

And here comes Johnny and one of his daughters—not Rosanne—and he's all in black and he's real cheerful, laughing and he's holding this greasy sack. He says, 'I got me some breakfast here. Anybody want a pork chop biscuit?' And everybody in the room was too healthy for that, and me—of course—says 'Sure man, I'm hungry.' I'm sitting there eating my pork chop biscuit and

Cash says—and by this point everyone has kind of turned away from him and his big voice booms out—'Anybody want some coke?' And everybody in the room had the same thought. Everyone turned to look and he's got this liter of Coca-Cola and a big grin on his face. Steve Earle just lost ten pounds...(collective laughter)

You played with Ronnie Hawkins...

JD: Ah, the Hawk. He has the greatest one liner I ever heard. I could work the rest of my life and not come up with the line... you know the story Rolling Stone wrote about him having cancer—the guy's opening question—a real journalistic mind at work—says to the Hawk: 'How do you feel about having cancer?' And Hawk's reply is 'Well, I've already outlived my dick' (collective hilarious laughter). I could think the rest of my life and not think of a line like that. Hawkins is the master. I owe him an un-payable debt.

I have to ask about Bob Dylan's *Time Out of Mind* sessions...it's a classic and you played on the songs...

JD: Well, many things in life are disappointing—rest assured—working with Bob Dylan is not one of those things. It was amazing. I met him a couple times socially which is heavy. He sucks all the air out of the room--there's no doubt about it. Every molecule in the room changes when Dylan walks in. It's like Bob Marley or Elvis. For the session he was in unspoken control over twenty three people, of course twelve musicians on the floor. There were three drum kits...

...Two pedal steels...

JD: ...At the same time...I never in my life heard two pedal steels before. If you took your earphones off, which I eventually did completely you could hear chord tensions in the air that didn't make it to tape. Especially the two pedal steels—Lanois turned it into a kind of string patch. A few months later...I can't really talk bad about the session because it was so great. Let me just say this about the session—months later, I was doing some dates with Levon Helm and somebody was trying to explain to

Levon who I was…I was standing there being humiliated anyway…why should it matter to Levon who I am? Then somebody said I played on *Time Out Of Mind* and Levon kind of perked up and he said, 'Well, they didn't waste no time mixing that one'. That's the way I feel. He didn't waste any time mixing it. I personally feel I can get 40% more out of a record mix and at least three tracks of that album are playbacks from the night we cut it. I went down there an enormous Lanois fan and that part was a disappointment to me.

I know 10 or 11 songs made the record. How many did Bob leave off?

JD: There was only two out-takes. "Mississippi"—which Sheryl Crow eventually covered and a song called "Girl From The Red Shore," which to me was the best thing we did.

For an album, Bob has a knack for leaving off the best songs from a session…

JD: That certainly wasn't the first time. One of the other times I saw him was the night he was sequencing *Shot of Love* and he left out a song about Angela Davis that was by far the best thing, and it's yet to come out. We struggled with "Girl From the Red River Shore". As we walked into the control room for the playback--Dylan was kind of behind me, over my left shoulder, and he said, 'Well, we did everything with that one but call the symphony orchestra'. Or maybe he said, 'If I wanted any more of that, I'd have to call the symphony orchestra.' And he said it, Lanois was right in front of me, to Lanois and if I would have been Dan, I'd have been on the phone. It's not like they have a symphony orchestra—they do. And they would all be there and play for Bob in a heartbeat. I don't know…but that's the only out-take from the eleven days I was there. They were there three days before I got there.

So, it was still a really quick recording process…

JD: Yeah. They also recorded in Oxnard before and Dylan had walked out.

••••••

Talk about when Bob came down to Mississippi to visit you a few years later.

 JD: Yeah—that was great. It's when he was on that tour with Paul Simon. He called up—sometimes he calls when he comes through town. Most of the time he won't, but he did that time and he said (Dylan inflection) 'Hey, I gotta day off. Why don't you take me through Mississippi?' I said alright. He came down here when the boys were still living in the other trailer—I've got two trailers and the barn. The barn is my studio—the boys went over and hid in their trailer and started peeking out the window when they saw Dylan go by.

We talked about Larry Brown. Dylan said, 'You know Larry Brown?' I kind of made light of it, and I said 'Yeah, he's this drunk guy that hangs out at this bar where my kids play.' And Dylan looked at me real sternly like I said the wrong thing and he said 'I read every word he ever wrote.' Oh well, allow me to re-assess my evaluation (laughs) of my good friend Larry Brown.

I've read the novels *Joe, The Rabbit Factory* and *Dirty Work*. I like his short stories better, like *Big Bad Love* and *Facing The Music*...

JD: Yeah, the short stories are great. But I'd been a fan of Bob Dylan since his first record came out. There's no bigger Dylan fan than me. He tried to record with the Flyers. We were set. That was really the beginning of the end of The Dixie Flyers when the Dylan session didn't happen. If it would have happened things would have been different for sure. It was because Wexler and Grossman they were fighting about Grossman's artists on the Woodstock album, which if you'll notice there are none of them there—they were all omitted from the record.

It was Grossman's revenge to blow that session out of the water. It was booked. Charlie and I were sitting in the lobby Monday morning when they cancelled the session. Back then if you were cutting for Columbia you had to have Columbia engineers and there were two Columbia engineers and two body guards that looked like they had machine guns in cases. They thought the session was going to happen. Then ironically, of course, it was done in the same place we recorded *Time Out of Mind*. Same studio—it's the "Layla" room.

Would you and Bob go out for barbecue?

JD: No, Bob pretty much sent for food. He's very particular about what he eats.

Through the years, Cody and Luther played with you on different sessions. Luther played on a Replacements record...

JD: Yeah, that was his first real session. It came real easy for Cody. Luther went out and got everything he had. He worked for it and learned it. Cody, he's still a natural on pretty much any instrument he puts in his hands. But the thing that sets Luther apart—I wish I could say I taught it to him—but Otha Turner taught it to him. You can teach a monkey to play the notes—believe me—many monkeys are out there playing, but feeling the note is something different and you have to learn—it doesn't make sense—but you have to learn to feel what you play. It doesn't come natural. The part of it doesn't come naturally, and Otha Turner taught Luther how to feel what he plays—it's real broad across his whole spectrum—it's not just the blues...

He plays some jazz licks on *Hernando*...

JD: He feels every note, and you can tell it. Cody is a good musician on other instruments—what he does on drums is so special—I wish he got more of a reward for it than he does, but he's constantly looking for something new.

You're a real luminary in that part of the musical geography...

JD: Well, I just knew there was a door when you could get out of which puts me in front of most of the locals. I hope we've done some good. I think we have, Luther certainly has...

I always heard you wanted to produce The Black Crowes. Now Luther is in the Crowes...

JD: Well, yeah. At one point they sniffed around and I sniffed around. Of course their brand of southern rock and roll is my heart-felt thing. I've produced everything from reggae to rockabilly. I could never get enough of southern rock and roll. Chris Robinson has a classic southern rock and roll voice. There's a certain creative tension I sense in the Crowes. When they came down here to the barn to audition Luther, I tried to stay away, but I had to listen to some of it. And I listened to about two and a half songs and I felt myself getting too far into it, so I left. It goes both ways—a lot of what I do as a producer is strictly my physical presence.

I really love your latest record, *Killers From Space*. The songs represent a lot of musical territory you've covered over the years.

JD: I tried to do that. It's a jukebox to me. Hell, I have a different concept of making a record as an artist than what I do as a producer, and I hate producing myself. So, if there's a weakness in my last three records that's it. It was that I didn't have anybody like Tom Dowd to help me stay on the path. I'm more satisfied with *Killers* than *Voodoo Tiger* because there's less of an agenda. It's mostly me singing some songs.

***Free Beer Tomorrow* was a fine album...**

JD: I spent too much time on that. It got a little precious. It was my boys' roots music education—there's about seven years in that record. There's a missing record called, *Topless Bowling* that never came out.,

Will it?

JD: Yeah, I just haven't finished it. It's the stuff I wrote with Ry Cooder and John Hiatt for the movies.

You played on the movie soundtrack of *Paris, Texas*, which is one of my favorite movie soundtracks.

JD: That's the one everybody talks about. We did that in three days fast as we could possibly do it. All the little noises that you can't identify are me. It's an electric piano tuned to a quarter-tone scale and I'm playing it with rolling duct tape reels down the keyboard. Only Cooder would have let me do something like that.

The Border attracted some well-deserved attention...

JD: I got five songs on *The Border*. I made a lot of money on that—I'm all for *The Border*.

There's good reason for that...

JD: There's some really good music on there. It's one of those Sam the Sham things...it's one of my favorite things I did with Ry.

You were around Sam the Sham quite a bit...

JD: Oh yeah, I knew Sam before he was Sam actually. His shtick came from a band from Texas called Big Bow and The Arrows and he'd count off in Spanish. The bass player was the same guy who played in the Pharos. Sam the Sham was the hearse driver with the roadie.

Another favorite movie soundtrack of mine you played on was *Southern Comfort*...

JD: Yeah, they flew Eddie Hinton out for that one. Cooder was always looking for another guitar player. They flew Eddie out and he sat there and held his guitar in his lap for three days. I didn't know Hollywood rules, so there's nothing I could do about it—if it was in Muscle Shoals it would have been different. It pissed Walter Hill, the director, off and sometime later...months later I talked to Eddie about it. I said 'The session got a little strange Eddie, and he said 'Man, that was one of the smoothest sessions I was ever on.' I don't know what he meant by that. He didn't do anything I guess that's why it went so smooth. You can hear him in the main title theme—there's one place you can hear Eddie and that's it in three days that's all he did. The last thing I did with Ry Cooder was Blue City. I think that's right...either *Blue City* or *Alamo Bay*.

Luther told me there were 22 songs on that recent Mississippi session y'all did. Will Cody oversee the Mississippi musical avenues while Luther's out with the Crowes? The Hill Country Band sessions as well as Chris Chew and other members of the music mafia down there should keep him busy.

JD: Yeah, they've rehearsed once and it changes. It's kind of morphing, but what it's going to morph into I don't know. Now he's got Dixie Dan from Detroit coming down. It's going to be interesting. Cody's response to the Crowes situation—I gotta say—I'm really proud of. As a father, I always saw this coming. I knew someday this would happen and frankly I always thought it would be Cody because he was so young and so good that somebody would snap him up. He's not interested in playing anybody else's music. That's pretty heavy I gotta say. Cody is very much his own man. I've worked with drum gods and Cody is one of them. He's one of the five best drummers I've ever heard and that's for sure. Son or no son...

There's always interesting musical activity afoot down there...

JD: Yeah, in this area—Memphis in particular—you have to invent your own work. You can't just sit back and expect to do it like a job because there's no job there. You gotta invent your work and then you gotta keep motherfuckers from stealing it. My boys have seen that their whole lives. I had mixed emotions with Luther as a little child when he had literally no other instruments and Cooder told me—'No, you shouldn't discourage him. A musician can take his instrument and go somewhere else and make a living.' And that's true. The whole industry has changed. Certainly what I have done for 40 years is going away. It never crossed my mind they were going to give the damn stuff away—it seems unreasonable to me, but I guess that's what's going to happen. The studio, through a whole process of making a record, is so important, that I hate to see it vanish, but it really is...

Any immediate projects on the horizon we should look out for?

JD: Man, I don't know. I wish I did. The best thing—I can't say it's new because he's made five or six records, but the best new thing to me is Malcolm Holcombe. Have you heard of him?

I have not.

JD: Check him out on the website—it's crazy I'll put it that way, but it's not savant. There's a craft to it. It's the best new thing I've heard since Johnny Dowd, which that's been a long time ago. I just don't hear anything new that I like that much.

Have you heard The Drive By Truckers, *Brighter Than Creation's Dark?*

JD: Oh yeah. I like some of that a lot. I don't think anything should be that long except *Trout Mask Replica.* I understand why he kept it all. There's politics involved. But yeah, the Truckers record is one I would have liked to make also. It's a concession on my part to like it. It's funny the Muscle Shoals guys were very secretive. They kept their families out of it in a way I never did. That goes all the way back to the Stones session—it was like operating in a restricted area. All of a sudden you're in area 51.

It's the Bermuda Triangle aspect...

JD: Eddie Hinton believed in the triangle between Memphis, Muscle Shoals and Nashville. He said it was a triangle and sometimes—he had an old Plymouth—and sometimes he'd get on the triangle and just drive...

He may have been onto to something...

JD: I know man (laughs). Uh oh, Luther's calling...

Well, I'll let you go. I appreciate you talking. I'll be in touch soon...

JD: Okay, talk to you later.

······

A Celebration of The Life & Work
of Paul Hemphill

I met Paul Hemphill, another hero, in 2007. I'd read about half of his seventeen books before we met. During this time, I operated as the editor of Swampland, and I wanted to interview Hemphill. We set up the interview, but cut it short because Hemphill lost his voice. A few weeks later he was diagnosed with cancer. We stayed in touch through email and I read the rest of his books. Hemphill beat cancer, and I wrote this article after he recovered. Looking back, I feel lucky to cross paths with him. Paul Hemphill died a month before Jim Dickinson—in the same year—on July 11, 2009.

"I was ridin' number nine
Headin' south from Caroline
I heard that lonesome whistle blow."
--Hank Williams

On this clear, mild November Saturday morning at 11AM, I arrived at Manuel's Tavern in Atlanta, Georgia, at the corner of North Avenue and North Highland, to eat breakfast with writer Paul Hemphill. Hemphill, 70, exists as one of the south's most important writers. He remains one of America's last great writers whose work documents some of the most pronounced generational changes in the south. Hemphill worked as a sportswriter, journalist and novelist.

Hemphill earned a Pulitzer Prize nomination for his 1993 book, *Leaving Birmingham,* experienced Hollywood adapt his work *(Long Gone)* to film and over the last 40 years written 15 books with a rare degree of experience about truck drivers, baseball, football, basketball, roller derby queens, stock car drivers, politics, journalists, musicians and bootleggers.

A gaunt, grey-haired Paul Hemphill sat at a table when I arrived at Manuel's Tavern. Hemphill suffered a stroke two years ago, and this spring he was diagnosed with throat cancer. We corresponded over a period of months regarding this article. During an interview in April, his voice kept cracking and he wasn't feeling well, so I suggested we postpone our interview until he felt better. I called three weeks later, and Hemphill informed me he was diagnosed with throat cancer.

I've spent the last 20 years tracking obscure artists with the intention of exposing a wider audience to their work. I always intended to write about the artist while they were still living. In 2004 and early 2005, I'd been in contact with Hunter S. Thompson's agent. Two times I was told Thompson was not in the mood or condition for an interview. When I called in late January of 2005, I was told the interview would happen. I was instructed to call back on March 1. Thompson committed suicide on February 20. I realized I should have acted on the interview much sooner. I did not want this to be another example of delays having dangerous ends.

Fortunately, after a tortuous spring and summer, Hemphill defeated cancer. On this November morning at Manuel's, as we sat down to breakfast, I understood I was in the company of a true southern hero...a real survivor.

Born February 18, 1936 (same day, 32 years before this writer), in Birmingham, Alabama, to a truck driving father and a mother who worked for the government. Hemphill's first love was baseball. The game occupied his most of his time throughout school. Hemphill graduated from Woodlawn High School and received a B.A. from Auburn University. Like most athletic dreamers, Hemphill soon discovered his baseball aspirations would die on the vine. Hemphill told me how he began to realize baseball was not in the cards.

"This was the summer of 54 or 55. I found myself the prettiest girl in town—a strawberry blonde. I had a friend who owned a Pontiac convertible. After the game—sometimes without a shower—we'd go necking with the two prettiest girls in town on the banks of the Neosho River—pure teenagers. I finished my first quarter at Auburn around Christmas and there was an exchange of letters back and forth.

"I decided to hitchhike out to Oswego, and see how things were going. I just finished working with the post office for the holiday. So I hitchhike 800 fucking miles in winter out there in order to dance in this girl's parlor. I was not invited back to play with Oswego the next year. I was able to make the travel squad at Auburn where I became the batting practice pitcher. Nothing ever came of that."

An English professor at Auburn told Hemphill he possessed a way with words and encouraged him to pursue the craft. Hemphill wrote a story called "I Gotta Let The Kid Go" in his book, *The Good Old Boys,* that describes how his baseball coach informed him he was cut from the team, which led Hemphill to become "a writing fool."

"I bought a little manual typewriter, and I taught myself how to write and I began copying other writers—sportswriters. After a while, I would just do the typing of a Hemingway short story. Pretty soon I became a sports editor of the *Auburn Plainsman*—the weekly school paper. That turned out to be the year we were National Champs. That gave me a boost. I wasn't a player, but I worked in the dining hall where athletes lived, so they all knew me. I was there for most of the games."

Hemphill learned the ropes, and he explained his gradual ascent into sports journalism. "I hadn't quite finished at Auburn, so I might've finished in March of 57—but I didn't. Anyway, I was a summer intern for sports at the *Atlanta Constitution.* So, I still had one more quarter to go.

"I didn't have any money to finish school, so I got my first job with Benny Marshall at the *Birmingham News.* He was a hero. I read him when I was a kid in Birmingham. So, in the summer of 58, I moved to the little league (laughs) beat. I was even a bowling editor.

"Then I went to Birmingham to finish up one quarter so I did prep sports. I was pretty damn good. I'd walk up the steps at Legion Field at the Alabama/Auburn game and I felt like a hero because I was covering the high school prep sports game that was always played at Legion Field on Friday nights. So, I was the big guy and that's what I did.

"I got myself a portable typewriter which I used for years for my newspaper work. I'd sit up there in the press box at Legion Field with my binoculars and that's where I learned about writing."

Hemphill covered the Auburn basketball team the year they won the National Championship. Then he joined the Air National Guard to avoid the draft. He was sent to France in 1961 where his grim circumstances brought on a new meat-hook reality.

"That's where I learned a lot of things happen besides sports. We were stationed in Paris. We were over there for the Berlin crisis. That's where I first read Hemingway. It was the first reading I'd done other than sports…that was the beginning."

The same year Hemphill married a girl from Alabama. "She got pregnant when I got her over from Birmingham. We lived in a little courtyard—a little French country place the Nazis used as a headquarters when they were trying to get out of France. I began more reading and I began to put perspective about what happened in the world.

"We did just about a year and then moved back to Birmingham. Just about that time I decided is I was gonna make money I'd better be a sports information director." Hemphill took a PR job at Florida State. "Bill Peterson was the football coach," Hemphill told me, "an interesting guy. It was the year Fred Biletnikoff was a freshman. That was when FSU was announcing they were going big time in football. I liked them, but I realized I made a bad mistake. I was no PR guy. I was a fucking writer..."

In the spring of 1962, Hemphill moved to Augusta, Georgia, employed as a sports editor at the *Augusta Chronicle*. He stayed on for six months and then re-located to Tampa, Florida, for six months. Around this time, Hemphill got his first big break. "My friend called and said, 'Paul here's your chance. Come to Atlanta. They're starting this new newspaper called The Atlanta Times'. I knew it was gonna be Right Wing, but I didn't give a shit because I just wanted to get to the big city. Six columns a week, and I did that for a year and a half."

Then the *Atlanta Journal* called Hemphill for a job he accepted. Hemphill stayed with the Journal for five years. "In 1964, I wound up at the *Atlanta Journal*. It's the biggest paper between Miami and Washington D.C., and I was the star. I was the main columnist—one thousand words a day, 6 days a week. Damn near killed me, but I learned how to do just about everything I needed to do to stay home and write—whether it was books or not. I talked them into letting me go to Vietnam. Part of the stuff I sent to the Neiman people was some of my better Vietnam stuff. I spent two years with them in Vietnam. When I got back, I knew I wasn't long for news papering."

After Vietnam, Hemphill earned a Nieman Fellowship at Harvard University. I asked what the process was for a southern writer to earn such a prestigious honor to an Ivy League school.

"You just submit some of your best work. Give them a bunch of bullshit about a thousand words on why you would benefit by hanging out at the Harvard campus. Give them some of that poor southern boy crap (laughs). And it worked. Harvard just wants to feel real good about having done their work. They're so great just by being there. In those years, I chose exactly what they had in mind about country music."

In 1969 Hemphill started writing his first book, *The Nashville Sound.* He lived in Nashville during this time. Hemphill explained the relatively painless process of writing the book.

"Well, it was pretty easy. The reason it was so easy was because Nashville in those days all the music people lived in the neighborhood between 16th and 17th streets—right downtown. I was friends with Bill Anderson, the country singer and songwriter from Decatur, Alabama. As it happened, Bill just bought a big house on one of the lakes—Old Hickory—I think. He was getting ready to hit the road for one month. He let me stay at his house while he was on the road. It saved me a helluva lot a money."

The Chicago Sun-Times called T*he Nashville Sound,* "The best book ever written about country music." The book provides a clear perspective on the state of country music during that time. Bob Dylan, Gram Parsons, The Byrds, and the Grateful Dead began employing country music into their sound, inspiring longhairs all over the country to seek out country music legends like Merle Haggard, Johnny Cash, Waylon Jennings, George Jones, Willie Nelson, Buck Owens, Lefty Frizzell and others. Hemphill wrote about his ability to penetrate Nashville's inner circle in the Foreword to *The Nashville Sound.*

"To do this book, I lived in Nashville, Tennessee, "hillbilly heaven" for nearly two months, where I saw a dozen performances of the Grand Ole Opry and countless recording sessions and television tapings. I also visited Glen Campbell at the CBS television studios in Hollywood, rode along with Bill Anderson and the Po Boys as they played a string of one-nighters in New England, sat in a tiny dressing room in Bakersfield, California, while son-of-an-Okie Merle Haggard loosened up his tonsils with straight bourbon before singing for the home folks, and sat in an isolated cabin in northeast Georgia, while an old mountaineer played his home-made fiddle the only way he knows how. In all, I traveled 18,000 air miles, interviewed about 150 people and listened exclusively to country music for seven months."

Through Bill Anderson's secretary, Hemphill became longtime friends with some of country's most enduring stars. "She was a super secretary," he told me. "I'd start my day by coming in and she would tell me, 'You need to talk to so and so', and I'd say 'How do I get him?' She'd call him right then. If it was Chet Atkins—who was right down the street, she'd say, 'he's looking for you in five minutes'. So, I'd go out and talk to Chet. It went like that and she had a built in shit detector. She always knew how to play it.

"I got all the basic interviews staying right there in Nashville in one solid month—January of 1969. By March, I had to go to the west coast. I wanted to get Haggard and Glen Campbell."

During this trip, Hemphill became friends with Merle Haggard. "He was perfect—very quotable. Then, unannounced, I got on a bus on Hollywood and Vine and went to Bakersfield. I got off the bus and called Merle's secretary, and she said, 'He and the band are playing at this auditorium for free, with proceeds going for the next year's bowling tournament, but they're right there. I told him to look out for me.

"I heard the first set and the band all disappeared down into the basement and I followed them and there was Merle in a great scene; him sitting there—some teenager getting drunk on his whiskey between sets. I said, 'Merle, this book is called *The Nashville Sound,* but you've never recorded in Nashville. Why is that?' And this kid punches him and says, 'Tell em what you always say Merle.' And Merle said, 'It don't matter where you cut it at, it's what you put in the groove.'"

"About a month later, he was inviting me to the White House because Nixon invited them there. Merle was paying my way up there just to hold hands with him. So, that's how our friendship began. I was done with the book all except a few hundred words before I left Cambridge at the first of June."

During this time, Hemphill decided to quit writing for newspapers. "When I finished the book, I got very little money. It came about November, and I got drunk one night with one of the young reporters. I didn't even have the next day's column done. I was so drunk I could not type a letter to my boss. It took me a couple of hours to type. I wrote 'Dear Mack, I quit. I'm sick of newspapers.' I didn't know what I was gonna do, but I knew it was gonna be better than that."

Hemphill wrote a letter to Michael Korda—a rising new editor at Simon & Schuster about *The Nashville Sound.* A response waited in the form of a letter for Hemphill just before leaving

Harvard and return to Atlanta with his wife and two young children. A week later, Hemphill flew to New York and signed *The Nashville Sound* contract.

"I signed the contract for about two thousand dollars, which I'm told, was not a bad deal then. I finished the book when I get back to Atlanta. *The Nashville Sound* sold well. In the 1970s I wrote for a lot of magazines. I did two or three pieces for *Life,* one for *Reader's Digest,* several for *SPORT* magazine. I had a deal for a column a month. So many major pieces a year. Dick Schaap became my editor there. He was excellent. Then I just up and moved to St. Simons Island. My marriage began to die in a small place like that."

In 1971, Hemphill co-wrote a book with ex-Atlanta mayor Ivan Allen Jr., called *Mayor: Notes On The Sixties*. Hemphill explained the book's origins: "The same guy who was at Simon & Schuster—who was a sales rep there and a friend of mine—he's the one that recommended I mail my proposal for *The Nashville Sound*. Now, he had another idea, he said, 'Ivan Allen is retiring after a great decade. We ought to do a book.' And I said, 'Shit, I love the guy. Sure, I'll do it.' I got the money, but he agreed to do it. It was the beginning of a great friendship. Good book, too."

In 1973, Hemphill visited The University of Georgia as a lecturer. Hemphill always drank, but a gradual literary pressure increased on coastal Georgia. "I drank my way through a couple of years on St. Simons."

Hemphill wrote about this dissolute era: "I was writing books, but I was married to a woman who, to my knowledge, had never finished reading one." In 1974, a collection of Hemphill's newspaper columns were published titled, *The Good Old Boys* which contends as an essential volume in the Hemphill collection.

In the book's Foreword, written in the tone of a fading light for The Old South, revealed Hemphill's instinct: "…But what depresses me, as the South finally joins the Union, is that little of what was distinctive and good as has been retained. The inevitable progress has put us in decent houses and fed our poor and educated us, and even made us more tolerant of black people—however pragmatically—but it also made us talk and act and dress and look just like the people in say, Denver. The good old boys are out in the suburbs now living in identical houses and shopping at the KMART and listening to Glen Campbell (Roy Acuff and Ernest Tubb are now too tacky) and hiding their racism behind code words. They have forfeited their style and their spirit, traded it all in on a color TV and Styrofoam beams for the den, and I find them about as exciting as reformed alcoholics. The book is intended more or less an epitaph to the good old boys."

Hemphill and his first wife divorced in 1975. She took the children and returned to Birmingham. Hemphill's drinking increased. Later that year, Hemphill served as a writer in residence at Florida A&M University.

In 1976, Hemphill married Susan Percy—a Decatur, Georgia, native—and they moved to San Francisco where he accepted a position as a columnist for the *San Francisco Examiner*. Living in California did not suit Hemphill and his new bride. Jimmy Carter was now the president. The south rose from the ashes, and Hemphill decided to move back to Atlanta in 1977.

He began working on a fiction novel about baseball based on his experiences in the minor leagues called *Long Gone*. "It took me four years off and on to learn how to write a novel which was *Long Gone*. But Korda rejected *Long Gone*. He told me he had nothing against short books—which he did. He was getting into that celebrity book shit...paying big money for crappy books. But the same day Sterling Lord, my agent, sold it to Viking. They fell in love with everything they'd seen and I already had the book written."

Hemphill discussed Hollywood's interest in adapting *Long Gone* to film. "When the novel came out, it got great reviews everywhere. One day this guy called saying he was Dustin Hoffman. I thought it was a friend playing a joke and I hung up the phone. The guy called back. It was Dustin Hoffman, but he ended up doing Tootsie..."

Long Gone, a close-to-the-bone story about America's favorite pastime seen in a foretelling business light...almost a prophecy of what was to become of major league baseball. HBO adapted the book to film during a time when they shot a "movie" a month. *Long Gone* served as one of the first films shot for the HBO series. Chicago actor William Petersen (*To Live And Die In L.A., CSI* and *Manhunter*) starred in *Long Gone* as Cecil Cantrell, a 40-year old manager, caught in a minor league conundrum between a love for the game and selling his soul to get ahead. As a longtime fan of Peterson, I asked Hemphill about the actor: "I met Peterson in Ybor City. It was Halloween and he was out all night having a helluva time. He was up at 6 am the next morning on location for three minutes of film. It was the scene they were trying to put the fix in.

"I'd met the actress from *Long Gone,* Virginia Madsen (*Sideways*), over the years and I'd say, 'You'll always be Dixie Lee Box to me (laughs).' She loved it."

Hemphill discussed how editorial surgery was performed on his dialogue for the *Long Gone* adaptation. "What they would do is two takes; first pitch of the game when the kid missed a foul ball. He kicks the ground and said for HBO, 'Remember Cantrell's rule—fuck em, if they can't take a joke.' Then they'd stop and say, 'Let's do one for TV, and he'd say, 'To heck with them if they can't take a joke."

Hemphill expressed disappointments to me, "I get pissed off every year when *Sports Illustrated* or whoever lists the greatest baseball movies ever, and they never mention *Long Gone* because it was a cable HBO movie."

Two years later, in 1981, MacMillan published Hemphill's. *Too Old To Cry*—arguably his best collection of articles. Hemphill feels *Too Old To Cry* is a bit stronger than his other collection of articles, *The Good Old Boys.*

Too Old To Cry contains stories about minor league baseball, Roger Maris, the late Karl Wallenda, dirt racing in places like Waycross, Woodstock, Valdosta, Savannah and Jacksonville; NBA stories, Auburn football, fishing, writing, Merle Haggard, newspaper heroes, hitchhiking, Vietnam, whiskey, moon shiners, fatherhood and other memorable stories.

Hemphill wrote a sustaining perspective in *Too Old To Cry* that may echo many a great man: "Most of my best writing is ultimately sad. It is about lost dreams and excess baggage and divorce, whiskey, suicide, killing, and general unhappiness: a boy who died in my arms, in a bomb crater, while I wrote in Vietnam: an old lady who simply died of loneliness; a young couple with a child, stranded in a bus station; a pathetic kid from Tennessee who messed up a bank robbery in San Francisco."

Meanwhile, Hemphill wrote another fiction novel called *The Sixkiller Chronicles.* The novel takes place in The Smoky Mountains during a time when not every rural home had electricity, but the radio lured even mountain folk to the beauty of technology. *Sixkiller*, like several of Hemphill's great works, failed to fit a Hollywood framework due to its authentic southern quality.

Although, the southern writers—the most difficult to please or impress—wrote praise for Hemphill's work. James Dickey wrote of *The Sixkiller Chronicles*: "Mr. Hemphill's mountain patriarch, Bluejay clay, is a powerful representative of one side of the intensifying struggle for the preservation of the Southern Appalachians and the ways of their people. So convincing is Hemphill's presentation that one almost believes that the contractors who build ski resorts, the mining geologists, and vulgarians who turn his villages into alpine resorts have met their match. Would God it were so."

Pat Conroy wrote of Hemphill's novel: *"The Sixkiller Chronicles* is the crowning achievement of Paul Hemphill's brilliant career. It is a love song to a disappearing America. In the world of American letters, Hemphill now owns that region along the Appalachian Mountains. It is a splendid work."

Hemphill's work classifies him as a literary troubadour. Jonathan Demme, whose work includes Neil Young's, *Heart of Gold, Silence of the Lambs* and *Philadelphia* attempted to film *The Sixkiller Chronicles* into a three part series.

"He (Demme) was one of those who bought the rights and wanted to make a movie. They wanted to make *Sixkiller Chronicles* a three part. Demme was doing the writing and he just couldn't make the third part work. He said, 'We'll have to make a two-parter out of it.' I guess I learned from it about what would and wouldn't work. I wrote that and wanted to get it off because I had my son here at my house. We were waiting to go out on the Appalachian Trail and goddam we finished it. We were on the way to Springer Mountain and we rode by the post office—the one down in Little Five Points (Atlanta) to mail the manuscript to New York."

Hemphill and his son David began a hike on the Appalachian Trail to try and become reacquainted. The arduous trek took a toll on both of them. The seed of this hike served as the fulcrum for Hemphill's next book, *Me And The Boy* (1986). By this time Hemphill quit drinking.

"Then we proceeded onto the trail. I had a lot on my plate. I mean, I had David. We were trying to get to know each other and he was 18 or 19 and I was an old fart trying to get over whiskey."

For a couple of years, Hemphill searched for a worthy writing subject. Hemphill resorted to the wellspring of material from his youth when he went out on the road with his truck driving father. It's essential to understand the relationship between father and son...the south began transforming...times change...he grew older and the south morphed into a generic regional identity. Even amid serious tribulation, Hemphill never failed to pay homage to his family. In honor of his roots, he wrote another fiction novel called *King of the Road* about a 70 year old truck driver named Jake Hawkins who is determined to make one last haul from Alabama to Nevada.

The one and only Johnny Cash wrote this about *King of the Road:* "Jake Hawkins is a lot like my own dad was, and this book took me home. *King of the Road* is a southern masterpiece and one of the finest things I've ever read by any writer. I can't wait to get some copies out to my friends."

To earn respect among one's peers cuts through all the other bullshit some civilian might say about your work. Any real artist knows this. The great writer Harry Crews said this about *King of the Road:* "Here's a tale that starts in the gut but ultimately comes to live in the heart. I love the old man at the center of *King of the Road.* I love his courage, his spirit, and his determination to live his life listening only to the dictates of his own blood. Paul Hemphill is and has been for a long time one of the best reads in the country. Put your money down and pick up this book. You'll not be sorry."

Hemphill continued freelance writing between books. He explained his psychic weather during this time. "Well, by this time, I had to make a living and I got hooked up with Brenau College For Women up in Gainesville, Georgia, and I taught two classes a week. I had to get in the car on Tuesdays and Thursdays. I got pretty good money. The thing I was learning was if I did okay and didn't need the money, I didn't write books. I found that I'd always been like that. I had to write under the gun. I finished one book in eight years because it was *King of the Road.* I did it because I got great money. It was a good advance but then I took leave to take an apartment in Birmingham to write *Leaving Birmingham.*"

Hemphill's book, *Leaving Birmingham: Notes of A Native Son,* documented the city's racial violence...Martin Luther King's letter from a Birmingham jail...four young girls killed in a church bombing. The book was nominated for a Pulitzer Prize. Hemphill talked about *Leaving Birmingham:* "I'd been getting reviews in places like *The New York Times.* It got a lot of good attention. I hadn't been forgotten. It wasn't like I quit writing."

Hemphill began gaining steam in his writing in 1994. He epitomizes the ultimate professional—who regardless what others think of his work or dark personal circumstances, he continues pursuing the vision of his craft. He began developing ideas for his next book, *Heart of the Game,* published in 1996. During this time, Atlanta hosted the Olympics, and an electric air hovered over the city that summer. Hemphill resorted to his first love, baseball, as a subject. Hemphill explained his motive:

"I just started looking around and felt...see, it was 1994 and the baseball strike was coming on and I was pissed. I decided I wanted to write about the heart of the game. I wanted to find out from some kid in the minor league, making a $1000 a month. But the book sold about five or six thousand copies in hardback."

After *Heart of the Game,* Hemphill ended his relationship with his longtime agent, Sterling Lord (who also served as Jack Kerouac's agent). "Sterling was getting old, but shit, he was only 70 (laughs)—he's damned near 90 now and still going. I had an idea over dinner with my new editor at Simon & Schuster—the one who done the baseball book. We started talking about Dixie Speedway and dirt tracks. He said, 'Well, what about the big boys?' I said NASCAR? And I said, 'Well, I don't know.' That's when I got a kick under the table. So, it was a pretty good deal and I wrote that in exactly one year. After I wrote *Wheels,* I never went back to NASCAR."

Hemphill continued searching for fiction ideas. He came across a story about a church burning in Montgomery, Alabama. This story served as the provenance for Hemphill's next fiction novel titled, *The Ballad of Little River.* The writer explained the business circumstances surrounding the book which represents a tale of racial unrest in the rural south: "It was a real bad publishing deal with the wrong people. They didn't do it right. They didn't push it. They were busy solving their own problems, like deciding what kind of publishing house they wanted to be. It's quite different now after all these years they've settled down and became a decent publishing house—but they weren't like that when I did my contract there. It just never worked."

Hemphill's next book, *Nobody's Hero,* told the story of a small-college All-American quarterback who falls from grace and must face the dark reality of a washed-up athlete. By this time, Hemphill went back to his longtime editor, Sterling Lord, but *Nobody's Hero* didn't sell.

"I just fired my editor David Black who made everybody else rich but me. I had the wrong guy representing me. He had no fucking idea what I was about—he didn't know the south or anything. I thought *Nobody's Hero* was a great novel, but it just died. It sold 800 copies."

Another collection of Hemphill's stories, *Lost In the Lights*, was published in 2003 by the University of Alabama Press. *Lost In the Lights* contains 15 stories culled from his best sports writing.

Hal Crowther—author of *Cathedrals of Kudzu*—wrote this about *Lost In the Lights:* "This is a blue-collar, blue highway, blues-in-the-back-of-the-bus side of the American sports obsession. The things Hemphill says about baseball, stock car racing, pro wrestling, and even roller derby are very topical, relevant to the evolution of much of this 'rough South' Sports entertainment. This is the ultimate underdog sports book, by a writer of real gifts and real empathy for these dreamers, losers and oddballs."

During this period, Hemphill directed his writing to his once-again agent Sterling Lord whom Hemphill respected, and allowed the writer to tell his story. "I got Sterling back and he said, 'Give me a couple of pages.' I thought a couple? Hell, my other editor always wanted 100 pages. He drove his clients crazy with those things. I gave him a couple of pages about my Daddy and Hank Williams. He called that afternoon. He told me to write 15 pages and we were gonna go for some big money. I got four publishers interested. Knopf and other people I'd never heard of wanted the book. Finally, Viking co-opted everyone else. They said 'Don't change a word'. Bingo. I got almost one hundred thousand dollars total advance. They got me rights in the U.K. and spoken rights...it was the best deal I ever got."

Lovesick Blues, Hemphill's book on Hank Williams proves a classic. Hemphill provides a concise and insightful biography on the father of country music. Hemphill details parallels in growing up in Williams' home state of Alabama. Hemphill writes about being 13 years old riding with his father on a 1,500 mile truck drive when he first heard Hank Williams.

Hemphill explained how truckers listened to all sorts of radio stations from Nashville, Des Moines, Cincinnati and XERF—a 500,000 watt outlaw station in Ciudad Acuna, Mexico.

The book traces Williams' early years through his famous days at the Opry until his last ride on New Year's Day 1952 in a powder blue Cadillac. I mentioned to Hemphill *Lovesick Blues* earned great reviews. He responded, "Great reviews all over the place. It sold about 20,000 copies which was the breaking point as far as Viking was concerned. They weren't going to put any more money into it—they were quite happy to stop right there at 20,000 copies of hardcover sold. That would earn them their one-hundred grand..."

I watched *Long Gone* when I was 18 and I sought Hemphill's work since then. I tracked down copies of *The Nashville Sound, Long Gone* and *The Good Old Boys*. As the years passed I collected his other works. I decided to write about Hemphill and his work since he epitomizes a true southern artist.

After a tortuous summer, Paul Hemphill defeated throat cancer. He completed a coffee table book this year about Auburn football to be published in time for the 2008 season. We met several times at Manuel's. On this warm November morning, Hemphill informed me he was planning to write a book about his cancer scare. His working title is *Dancing With Joe Camel*.

As the brisk wind blew red, gold and yellow leaves down the street, I tried to nail down the south's transition through the years. Hemphill's been a customer of Manuel's Tavern for 40 years. These Atlanta streets endured much change in the last five decades. After we finished our hearty breakfast, I asked him about the most significant change in the south during his career, and Hemphill revealed to me "I can't believe I'm here to watch the death of newspaper..."

••••••

The Late Great Townes Van Zandt

I met Townes Van Zandt in July of 1995—just before his career resurged. He played a blues club in Atlanta called Blind Willie's. The show was not sold out. Again, I found myself at the right place at the right time. A year later, Van Zandt played Blind Willie's and the place was packed. This story captured my first hand experience of meeting one of America's finest songwriters. I reconstructed the story after Van Zandt died and this version appeared on Swampland.

"There's no prettier sight than a town you left behind."
-Townes Van Zandt

Townes Van Zandt's songs will long outlast his mortal coil of 52 years. Since his death Van Zandt's music continues to reach a wider audience. Tales of his hard living, depression, gambling, collapsing onstage, and songwriting remain legendary. A poisonous legal battle rages between Van Zandt's ex-wife and his longtime business partner over control of the songwriter's legacy. A deluge of Van Zandt's reissues, compilations, tributes, and live recordings have emerged, presenting both parties with a tangled legal web of lost finances while fans must decide what releases to purchase.

Born in Fort Worth, Texas, in 1944, Van Zandt came from a wealthy family. His great-grandfather served as the ambassador to France from the Republic of Texas before the revolution. His great grandfather was a founding father of the city of Ft. Worth. At the University of Texas, Townes Hall is named after his grandmother. Even his father was a wealthy oil man. Van Zandt's parents institutionalized him where he was diagnosed a manic depressive and subjected to insulin shock treatments. He later told his wife Jeanene, "that when he came out, pretty much all of his memory was wiped out. Have you ever heard "Sanitarium Blues? That's the story in song."

Inspired by Lightnin' Hopkins, Hank Williams, and Bob Dylan, he set out rambling across the country. Van Zandt, a definitive troubadour, played haunting folk, blues, and country music. Musicians such as Doc Watson, Merle Haggard, Willie Nelson,

Doug Sahm, and Emmylou Harris recorded Van Zandt's songs. Some of his greatest albums include *Live At The Old Quarter, Flyin' Shoes, High, Low, and In Between, The Late Great Townes Van Zandt* and *No Deeper Blue.*

Your humble correspondent met Townes Van Zandt in July of 1995 for the first time at Blind Willie's Blues Club in Atlanta. I'd been talking to the club owner, Eric King, about how I loved Van Zandt's songs, and King suggested I go back and say hello. I hesitated, well aware of Van Zandt's reputation, but after further encouragement, I walked through the dressing room door. The Man sat alone in the small dressing room.

"Hello Townes. Eric said it was okay to come back and say hello."

"Oh, yeah? We'll you better go get him…"

"Sorry," I began retreating to the door.

"Hey man, come back here. I was kidding. I wanted to see how you'd react. Here…"

I stepped forward and took the flask from the man Steve Earle proclaimed, "Townes Van Zandt is the greatest songwriter on earth, and I'll stand on Bob Dylan's coffee table in my cowboy boots and say so." After a hearty pull, I handed the flask back to him, stared into his dark eyes and asked,

"Is that scaldcat?"

"Vodka."

I sat down in the metal folding chair next to him. Townes took my pocket notebook and began drawing pictures: one of a cactus near a desert highway that later became an album cover. Then he picked up his guitar and began strumming. He told me to never get discouraged as a writer, and that I was young and things would take time. When asked if people with far less talent enjoyed undeserved spoils ever bother him, Van Zandt revealed, "I never really wanted to be famous…like Mick Jagger or someone like that; I was content in playing the smaller places."

We talked until they called him out to perform his first set. That night he dedicated "White Freight Liner Blues" to this writer. The following summer I met Van Zandt again at Blind Willie's. Six months later he died, on the same day as Hank Williams, on January 1, 1997.

Currently, the condition of Van Zandt's estate remains in turmoil. No clear resolution lingers in the near future. Last year, Van Zandt's wife released *In the Beginning,* lost songs from his

first Nashville recording sessions. On the other side of the bitter
dispute, Harold and Kevin Eggers, recently released Acoustic
Blues, a stark live compilation, including some of Van Zandt's
final songs recorded three weeks before his death.

The soul of his music resonates long after it's heard, including
lyrics from his old song "Lungs":

"Salvation sat and crossed herself
Called the Devil partner
Wisdom burned upon the shelf
Who'll kill the raging cancer
Seal the river at its mouth
Take the water prisoner
Fill the sky with screams and cries
Bathed in fiery answers."

Although his music catalogue hangs in legal lockdown, his act
remains difficult to follow. Since his death, Townes Van Zandt's
songs now appear a far cry from dead.

••••••

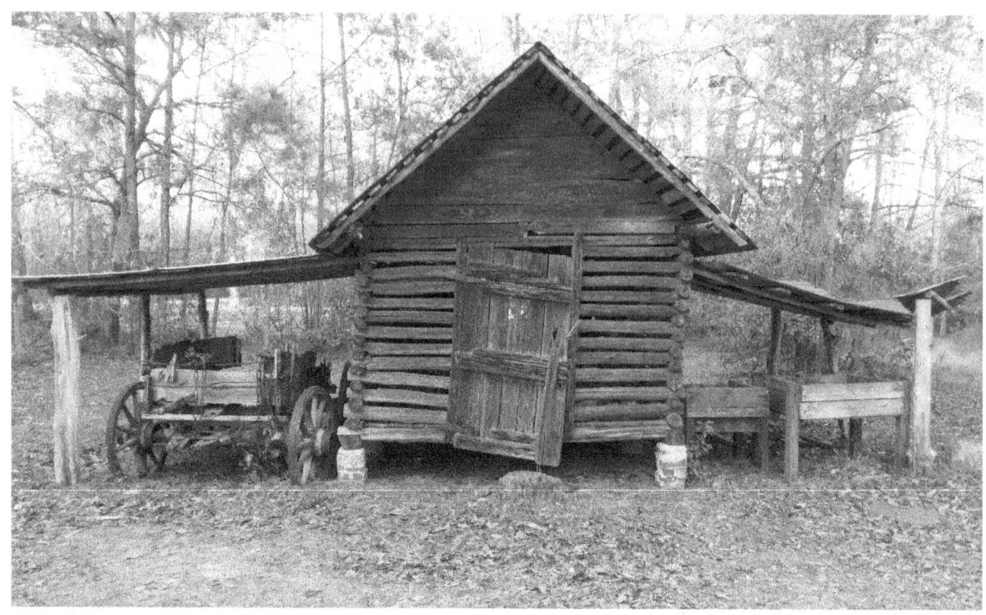

"Sunbury, Georgia"

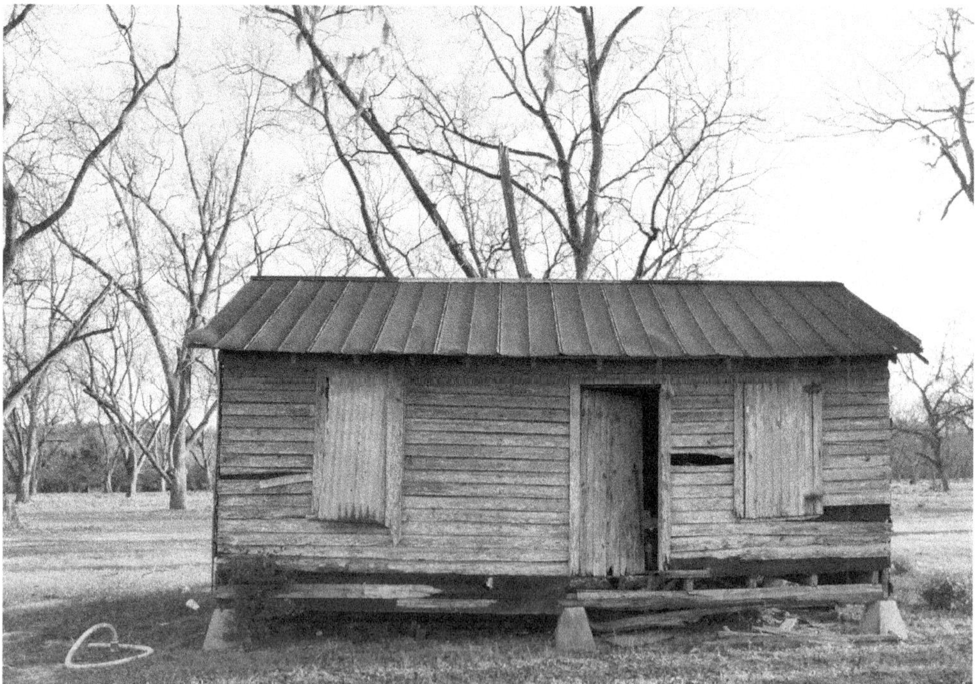

"Stockton, Georgia"

Steve Cropper Interview:
The Master Song Craftsman and Rhythm King

Steve Cropper remains a musical luminary. This phone interview transpired in 2008, a time that proved a period of extreme transition for your humble scribe. I met Cropper years later in person on Sea Island, Georgia. Most people have heard a song Cropper played on whether they know it or not—from "Sittin' On The Dock of the Bay" to "Green Onions." Steve Cropper is still out there laying it down...

> *"He could play the guitar like ringin' a bell..."*
> *- Chuck Berry*

Very few musicians stand as an influential songwriter like Steve Cropper. Cropper served as the nucleus of the STAX Records empire. Cropper wrote a hit record at 16. By 19, he started a band that later evolved into one of the greatest bands in southern music history, Booker T & The MGs. Cropper collaborated with luminaries such as The Mar-Keys, Otis Redding, Wilson Pickett, Rufus Thomas, Sam & Dave, The Bar-Kays, Isaac Hayes, David Porter, The Staple Singers, Carla Thomas, Aretha Franklin, James Burton, John Lennon, Bob Dylan, Neil Young, Jeff Beck and Levon Helm.

Cropper led The Blues Brothers Band across the globe many times. His studio produced numerous chart hits, and he's well-respected among his peers. Cropper continues making vital music. His latest record, *Nudge It Up A Notch,* hits the streets on July 29. A soul album he recorded with Guy Sebastian went triple platinum in Australia, and will come out in the States early in 2009.

In this interview Cropper discusses his early musical days, friendships, hit records, the fall of STAX, the tragedy of Otis Redding, timeless collaborations, backing Bob Dylan, touring with Neil Young, his latest projects and a few unknown facts about his incandescent musical journey. He's one of a kind. It was a thrill to conduct this interview. Of course, we could have talked for days regarding his accomplishments and there were many more questions I wanted to ask, but this interview provides a clear insight into one of the world's finest guitarists... and songwriters.

•••••

SC: Hello James...

Hello Mr. Steve...

SC: I was just calling you on your other line...

How's it going?

SC: Pretty good.

You got a little time?

SC: I can take a little bit (Laughs). Tell me about Swampland...

Well, Swampland is a comprehensive field guide to the South. We cover music, literature, food, film, sports and news that can be weaved into a story about the culture of the country's southern region. Of course, you play a vital role in southern music...

SC: Gotcha...

A few recent interviews of mine have been Charlie Louvin, James Burton, Charlie Musselwhite...Jim Dickinson...

SC: Yeah, I know some of those guys. Where are you?

I'm in Atlanta. You know an old friend of mine, Stanley Booth. He was a neighbor of mine in South Georgia. He made me a bunch of tapes of all your music about 22 years ago. He was around with you and Otis...

SC: Absolutely he was around. I remember him well. I've seen him since then of course. He's a good guy. Good writer too. That's great...

Well, let's take a quick journey through your past. You were born in Dora, Missouri...

SC: Dora, Missouri. Actually, if you want to be technical, I was born several miles from there in a little town called Willow

••••••

Springs. We were living on a farm in Dora and what happened
was my dad was over there doing something and he dropped my
Mom off. I was about two weeks late of the predictions and he
had business over in Willow Springs and he was going to drop
my mom off over at my aunt's and she went into labor while she
was there. So, they got a hold of my dad and all that and there I
came. When we were able, we went back to the farm, which was
in Dora. Kind of like being born down the street...

Did you have a musical family?

SC: No, none whatsoever. I had one uncle by marriage that
played piano and a little bit of fiddle. He had a guitar in his clos-
et that he never played. I don't know if it belonged to his uncle
or somebody. He played country fiddle, piano and sang in the
church. I used to get that guitar out and just play with it like
a rubber band just to feel the vibration. That's where I got the
first taste that I liked guitar. Then I was taken to some shows
and I got to see some good players. It inspired me a little bit—it
was more country. I didn't gravitate so much towards country,
but it's what I grew up on. I was ten years old when we moved
to Memphis. That's when I first heard gospel music. Of course,
a little rock and roll too—but I heard gospel and it was 'Wow'
what is this?

Charlie Musselwhite said Memphis radio...

SC:...was happening. I mean it was unbelievable. We didn't have
electricity on the farm. I was too young. My dad was in the Navy
so we were stationed in Oakland. After he got out, he took a job
in St. Louis for a while—but I was too young to remember any of
that. So, at the farm, we didn't have electricity until about 1948
so I would've been about 7 years old, and 8 before we had electricity and had the radio. I studied by coal oil lamps (Laughs).
Mom cooked on wood and coal oil...kind of interesting.

You got your first guitar at 14, right?

SC: You got it.

An electric?

......

SC: No, it was a Sears & Roebuck flat-top round-hole acoustic. It was about the cheapest one they had in there. I think it was $17. I told my dad what I wanted. He didn't say he didn't have the money—because he did—but he wanted to make sure I was serious. I mowed lawns, set bowling pins and whatever odd job I could do and save my allowance, which was about fifty cents a week. I saved up my $17 for that guitar. My mom loved to tell this story. She'd say, 'Well, if it wasn't for me he wouldn't be a musician. She said when they brought it out—I waited all afternoon. I knew it was coming on a Saturday, and I waited all day. Finally the truck rounded the corner. She'd tell the whole story of them pulling that guitar off the truck in a cardboard box. Then they said there was a twenty-five cent delivery fee. I said, 'Hey Mom!' They wanted that twenty-five cent delivery charge. She said if she hadn't lent me twenty five cents I would've never been a musician (Laughs).

I'm sure it didn't take you long to figure out the instrument. Would you say very early you possessed an innate, god-given talent for the guitar? Or did you love it so much that it didn't matter if you had that innate talent because you were going to play it anyway...

SC: I don't think it mattered. The thing was I had seen a guy that I was older than me in high school—he was a senior and I a freshman—playing one of the school shows. A guy named Ed Bruce turned out to be a pretty famous country star and a TV star and all that sort of stuff. He had an electric guitar and he played a song called "Bo Diddley"—speaking of the late, great Bo Diddley. That was one of the first songs I wanted to learn. I went backstage, and I said, 'Man, that was fantastic.' I don't remember exactly what I said, but I remember what he said—basically, I asked how did you learn to play like that? Really all he was doing was playing rhythm guitar—but it was just so cool. He said, 'Well son—if you want to play like that you got to get a guitar and learn how to do it.' So I did (Laughs). You just gotta learn how to do it. So, I had some buddies that played...a great friend of mine, who's no longer with us anymore—Charlie Freeman. He was already taking guitar lessons from a jazz guitar player. So, I would wait over at Charlie's house with my guitar after school until he got home from his lessons. I'd be there on the front porch when he and his mom pulled up. He would show me what he learned that day. I'd help him because I'd play rhythm behind him playing. So we started a little band—that's how it all started…the two of us doing songs. I was in the tenth grade.

What I was going to say earlier, when the guitar came out of the cardboard box, the bridge was not on really tight, but I had to get a book to learn how to tune it—it had the strings on it, so it had the gauge on it but I learned all that. I had a friend of mine that played a little guitar that tuned it up for me. I just started banging on it, learning it and I guess it stuck. But with Charlie, the first song I learned was Bill Doggett's "Honky Tonk." That was the song to learn in those days if you wanted to be a rock and roll musician. It's funny that we all kind of passed it around and learned it in the key of E. Then we found out—by horns and all—we didn't think too much in terms of keys because we weren't piano players—we didn't take piano lessons. When we had horns years later, they informed us, 'You guys are in the wrong key because it's in the key of F' (Laughs), which is a half-step up, but so what. So what we used to do was learn the song in E the way we played it—learning Billy Butler's licks and all that, then when the horns came in we would modulate to F. That's the key the record's in. But we were ready to go…

How far along from that did you and Freeman startup the Royal Spades?

SC: Well, that was originally Charlie and I and a friend of ours named Ted. He thought we were pretty good—he'd come over and hear us play and all of that. He said, 'I've got this friend that's a disc jockey and he ought to hear you guys play.' In my opinion we were probably horrible by my standards today—I'm sure we were the worst. Anyway, we went down and they guys name was Keith Sheriff. He was originally from Canada and he was a disc jockey in Memphis and had a great show that all the high school kids and everybody listened to…he played a lot of the teenager records. So, he told our friend to bring us down to his show. I think he came on in the evenings…at 7 O'clock or something. I remember going down there to the station. We went and introduced ourselves. He said, 'Well I'm in the middle of my show'. He said 'Why don't you guys take your guitars and set them up out there—is it just the two of you? We said, 'Yeah'. So he said set up and that he had a microphone out there. He said, 'during my show, when I'm playing records I'll open the mic up and when I point to you and you guys start to play. I had a Gibson and Charlie had a Fender Telecaster.

Two classic tones...

SC: Typical. So, he pointed and we started playing. After we were finished, he said, 'You guys come on in here. You guys are pretty good.' About that time, the phone rang from the request line. He said, 'What do you boys call yourselves?' I said, 'What are you talking about? Oh, uh, well, we've been playing as the Royal Spades.' That's because we played poker. So, anyway, somebody heard us and what we didn't know the DJ liked what he heard and he hit a button and he put us out on the air. All of a sudden the phone started lighting up with people calling in— 'Who are these guys? They're pretty good.' I didn't know what was going on. We were barely 17. So, he said, 'Do you guys have a band?' And we said no. He said, 'I do these sock hops every Friday night'. We were like--we know. He said if you guys get a drummer and a bass player I'll put you on my sock hop. So we started looking through school asking around and we could not find a bass player anywhere. So we found this kid in the 9th grade—Charlie and I were already in the 11th. We found this kid that played drums—his name was Terry Johnson. He'd been taking lessons. His daddy had a country band—a three or four piece country band and Terry played drums with his dad's band. He said why don't y'all come over to rehearsal one night. We did and we played some country stuff. We started working with Terry and so we called Keith and said we had some stuff worked up and he said, 'Okay, I'm going to put you on the sock hop.'

We played at the Memphis National Guard Armory—that's where they used to keep the Memphis bell—the one they made the movie about. We played that sock hop with two guitars and a drummer (Laughs). It went over pretty good. Then Duck Dunn wanted to play guitar and we tried to teach him a little bit, but he was a little slow on it. He didn't catch the licks as fast as Charlie and I did, so he was a little frustrated and I tried to help him a little bit. Then he didn't show up for a while. Then he shows up and he's got a bass. He was the bass player from then on. We had two guitars, bass and drums. We called ourselves The Royal Spades.

In the Memphis backdrop—all this music was happening...Elvis...Rockabilly...The Blues...

SC: Absolutely. Elvis. Jerry Lee. Carl Perkins. Of course, Johnny Cash had already been through there—all these different guys that Sun Records was recording. The next step in how it all transpired was real simple. This kid came up to me in school one day and he says, 'Hey, I hear you guys got a pretty good band. I'd like to join your band.' I said, 'Well we're not looking for anybody. We're pretty happy with two guitars, bass and drums— we're not looking for anybody, but what do you play? I thought he might be a keyboard player. He said, 'I play saxophone.' I said, 'Oh well, we're not looking for any horns.' So, I was just curious—'How long have you been playing?' He said, 'I've been taking lessons for three months.' I said, 'Really (Laughs)' Then he said his uncle had a recording studio. Actually it was his uncle had some recording equipment in his garage. I said 'Could you show up at rehearsal? We rehearse every Saturday morning at 10 o'clock at our drummer's house.'

He shows up. We started playing something...there were some pretty good records out—I think Bill Justus we knew from Dick Clark, and I had written a song he did on the flipside of his third release. So, when I was 16 I had a flipside of a number three record in the nation.

Not many 16 year olds can say that in the last 70 years, or longer...

SC: Yeah, it's kind of weird. Anyway, Packy turned up at the rehearsal.

The incredible Packy Axton...

SC: He turned out to be a half-decent saxophone player. Charles "Packy" Axton. His mom and Jim Stewart wanted to advance the recording studio. He thought we were terrible, and I'm sure we were. He was a country fiddler and he had a pretty good ear, but he thought we were awful and would never make it. Mrs. Axton mortgaged her house and borrowed the money for him to buy this new property to build a bigger studio. She wanted a record shop. So she put a record shop in the front of the studio. We used to go out there on weekends—usually on Sunday when there wasn't anything happening and rehearse, play and record our songs. Like I said, Jim never thought we would amount to a hill of beans—I don't think he wanted us to, but because Mrs. Axton's son is in the band she kept pushing us. When this opportunity came she wanted to move closer to town anyway because we were out in Brunswick, Tennessee, and she didn't have many customers out there. They got this opportunity to take a lease on this theatre where STAX was and where the museum is now. So they did whatever they could do or had to do with the bank because Jim worked at the bank—he was able to figure things out. We went over there and started to help build that studio. I remember Packy and I on weekends we were down there knocking bolts in those theatre seats. We helped with the baffles, curtains and all that sort of stuff.

By then you had your own sound. Were you listening to many blues records?

SC: Very few blues records other than Jimmy Reed. I love Jimmy Reed. I listened to Chuck Berry, Bo Diddley and of course Billy Butler with the Bill Doggett's band. We loved that stuff. I got influenced by some jazz players from Tal Farlow to…you name it. The guy that really influenced me—a guy that played guitar for The Five Royales—was Lowman Pauling. Duck and I got an opportunity to go to a show they played. We were underage, but we figured out how to get in there. And we got to see Lowman and the Five Royales and man that changed my whole life. That was it for the rest of my life. He had this long strap hanging down to his knees—much like when Chuck Berry lets his strap off and plays down by his knees and dances across the stage. Lowman was doing it, but he had this long strap. And I thought man that was the coolest thing I've ever seen in my life. I could not wait to get home and put two belts together and made me a long strap (collective laughter). I played that way forever. There's a picture of me playing after we had "Last Night" in 1961 at the

Royal Peacock Lounge in Atlanta with my guitar between my legs. That's my logo for the *Play It Steve* record (laughs). That was the summer of 61, so I was still 19.

That's when the MAR-Keys started up.

SC: Well, the story I just told we were on tour with "Last Night". The Mar-Keys kind of happened before that. Very simply—we came up with the song that Chips Moman's piano player Jerry Lee "Smoochy" Smith—he went by the name of Smoochie and was a helluva piano player. He's still alive today and he's great. He came up with this little riff, and so Packy and I went into the studio with him and we came up with the "Last Night" riff. So, Chips Moman heard it and he thought it was a hit, and he heard Smoochie play it and anyway he put together—with our trumpet player—Wayne Jackson. I just did a session today with Wayne Jackson playing on a T.G. Shepard record today that he's doing with a whole bunch of people like Engelbert Humperdinck, B.J. Thomas, George Jones, Maurice Gibbs, Delbert McClinton—it's going to be a helluva record. Anyway, that's what we were doing this afternoon. But it was Wayne and Gilbert Caples. Floyd Newman and Packy Axton played on "Last Night" and of course Don Nix played on the road. It was the three of them—Wayne, Don Nix and Packy—Chips didn't want a guitar on it. I don't know why, they always said I didn't play on it because there was no guitar, but if you listen to the record, you'll hear a sustaining whole note—a C note—that's being sustained during the organ solo and I was the one holding that note down. When it came time for the organ solo, I'd hold that note down. So, I was on the record.

How long was it during all those sessions that Chips Moman left STAX? It wasn't too long...

SC: No, it wasn't too long. Chips was a really good writer and a really good guitar player, but he wanted so desperately to be an engineer and a producer. I'm not sure because Jim Stewart really wanted to engineer—he did *Green Onions* and a bunch of other things. Stewart did about half, and Chips did about half of it. I don't think they came to an agreement on some things—I don't know if it was over money or whatever—but Chips just said one day, 'That's it. I'm out of here.' That was okay. That was fine. He started American Records and he did quite well. Chips has one of the greatest ears in the industry. He cut all of B.J. Thomas' hits…Neil Diamond and Elvis—you name it. So Chips went the op route, and we went the R & B route. That's kind of the way it is. He had Neil Diamond and we had Otis Redding. He had Joe Tex, and we had Sam and Dave.

You were the nucleus there at STAX…

SC: Yep, young kids that basically were forced on the system because nobody else wanted to work for that cheap (Laughs). When it came time to sweep the floor up or came time to put up tapes or whatever it was, I didn't mind doing it. I was there to volunteer.

Where was Charlie Freeman at this point?

SC: Charlie elected while we had the band…Charlie had been moonlighting a little bit playing with this guy named Macy Skipper. Macy was from a little town in Arkansas and Sam Creason (The Dixie Flyers) a very famous drummer who's no longer with us anymore either. Charlie was in that band so he started playing with them from time to time. Macy Skipper—I think I got that right—and maybe Charlie Hines, but it seems they got an offer to go tour and do some stuff in Canada. Charlie elected to do that. All of a sudden that leaves us short of a guitar player, and my old buddy—we started the band together. By then we already had horns so we had a good singer and a keyboard player, bass, drums and so for a while we did it that way—we continued on and Charlie was still out there somewhere when we did "Last Night" so he was still out there somewhere when we did "Last Night" so he wasn't in on that.

When did you first meet Otis Redding?

SC: I first met him when he first came up with Johnnie Jenkins and the Pinetoppers from Macon, Georgia. They had a little bit of a hit called "Love Twist," which made some noise. Atlantic and their manager—he might have known Phil Walden but I don't think Phil actually booked Johnnie Jenkins—maybe he did—but anyway through Atlantic and Jerry Wexler and they

••••••

all thought since we were so well known for hit instrumentals that they'd bring Johnnie there and give him another hit instrumental. Otis was his singer—we didn't know that at the time. I thought Otis was his driver because he'd drive up in front of the studio, get out of the car, go to the trunk and started getting amps and microphones and all that. I walked over and said, 'Hey you don't need to bring in microphones and all that. We're a recording studio—we've got our own mics. He was bringing the stuff in like they were setting up for a gig. He just looked at me kind of dumbfounded. We all set up. Then we had the band there for the session.

During the session Al Jackson came to me, and he said, 'You know that guy drove the car that came in with Johnnie? I said 'Yeah'. He said, 'Man that guy's bugging me to death.' I didn't see this going on. He said, 'Every time we take a break and y'all go into the control room to listen, this guy comes over and he's driving me nuts to hear him sing. I keep saying I don't have anything to do with that—Steve Cropper is the guy to talk to. We're busy right now, but I'll ask Steve.' So he mentions it, and I said, 'Well, if we have time after the session I'll listen to him.'

So, after the session, Al came to me and said, 'You told me you'd listen to this guy. You got time?' I forgot about it, and I said, 'Oh, okay.' Everybody's breaking up their equipment and leaving so we can pick up the next day. I said, 'Bring him down to the piano.' I said, 'What do you do?' Otis said, 'I sing a little bit.' I said, 'Do you play piano?' He said, 'I play a little gut-tar, but I don't play piano.' He said, 'Give me some of those church chords'—he meant those triplets—dut-dut-dut. I started playing in the key of B Flat. Otis started singing "These Arms of Mine."

I went 'Holy Moly.' The hair on my arm stood up about four inches. I looked around at everybody and said, 'Somebody get Jim Stewart in here right now (Laughs)! I said, 'Jim, listen to this guy.' Jim said, 'We got to put that down.' Duck said I came out—all these guys had night gigs so they had to go home and leave the session at a certain time. They probably went onstage around 8 O'clock or something. Anyway, we get Duck on bass, Al Jackson on drums, Johnnie Jenkins on guitar and I played piano—we recorded "These Arms of Mine." The next day at 11 o'clock, instead of cutting Johnnie Jenkins—we cut the flipside of "These Arms of Mine." I think it was "Hey Baby," a Little Richard kind of thing.

You've worked with Wilson Pickett, Eddie Floyd, Sam & Dave, Aretha Franklin, Rufus Thomas, Carla Thomas, but Otis was really the big one.

SC: Yeah, we were so successful with Otis that Atlantic decided… it was Jerry Wexler that asked me if I'd heard of Sam & Dave, and they had them come in. Wexler asked, 'Have you heard of these guys from Florida?' I said no. He brought them in and it was an instant click. They'd been out there for a while. They'd been trying to get a hit record without any luck. Wilson Pickett didn't have any real luck. He sang with the Falcons on "I Found a Love" that was a pretty big record but they couldn't get any real rock and roll going on it. So Wexler brought him down and we sat in a hotel room all night long and wound up with "In the Midnight Hour," "Don't Fight It" and "I'm Not Tired." All three of those songs went up the charts at different times, but we cut all three of those songs the next day, and all three were hits.

Wilson Pickett reminds me…did you ever cross paths with Duane Allman?

SC: I did not, unfortunately. Duane died before I really knew who he was, but Gregg I've seen many times. I've done shows with Dickey Betts, and we've hung out.

The STAX compilation they released last year proves a formidable collection. Many of those songs you played on.

SC: Yeah, it was at least a couple of artists a week. We'd cut for two days—mainly in those days we didn't have to worry about projects so much. We didn't worry about cutting ten or fifteen sides—we just worried about cutting two or three singles. You'd cut two of your best songs and then you'd cut a couple of back-ups. You might cut four songs. Usually it was three song sessions. Out of that you would pick which one would be the single, and then you'd have two to pick from as the flipside.

Things happened at STAX at a pretty fast rate. At what point did Otis want the MGs as his full-time band?

SC: We did a STAX/Volt tour in 1967 in the month of April and May, and that was prior to the Monterey Pop Festival. So they had Frank Fenter and Phil Walden through Atlantic-Europe set up this tour. I was under the impression—I think this is true—I don't really know for sure that Otis had been over there just for a little bit and he had a major following in England. So we realized he was so much bigger in Europe than he was the States because we were never able to get him off the R&B charts—it just hung in that region and that's about where it was. We could never really break Otis into pop. He was R&B. Of course, after his death everyone knew who he was and then of course "Dock of The Bay" came out. Then it's all over with, and it's too bad that didn't happen when he was around.

So, we decided to take the band over there because we could do this package. So there you had Booker T & The MGs, The Mar-Keys...we've got "Green Onions", "Last Night" and all these other hits. There we are backing Sam & Dave, Otis Redding, Arthur Conley and we had a pretty good tour going. The feeling was—it was so successful—we get back to the States and Otis was like 'I don't think I can work with my band again. I've got to have you guys.' We were saying 'Otis you can't have us—we've got too many artists we've got to provide music for and we've got to get back to the studio. We've been gone now for four weeks and it's nuts because everyone is waiting.' Of course, the other thing was everybody came back with a totally different attitude. We all left equally as guys that wanted to play and we go over to England and the fans all make us superstars. We came back with this attitude that we're greater than thou. Then all of this bickering started—'I'm this and you're that...I don't want to produce staff anymore...I want my name on the record'...and it just went into havoc. I have always said when people ask me what was the reason STAX went under. What was the demise? Well a lot of it was business and all that, but it started they day we broke up the production pool.

That's my opinion and I'm sticking to it. The day we broke up that team that all worked together for the same purpose. The day we broke that up was the day we started going downhill. We still had a lot of success. Right after that I think I was nominated as producer of the year because my name was on seven records on the charts. That's a lot. It was a neat thing to get, but still it changed. Then we split up as a band—as a backing band because we all had these responsibilities to these other artists. Also, the timing was so bad because Atlantic decided they were going to sell and make all this money from this corporation in New York and they didn't want us to be part of that finance—they didn't want to split any of that money. They cut us out of the deal. There we were making all these hits for Atlantic Records—if it hadn't been for us they wouldn't have got the deal in the first place. They can take that to their grave—most of them are gone anyway except for one or two that's still left. But that's exactly what happened. There was always bitterness about it. Jerry Wexler—God bless him—I love him to death. And Jim Stewart—he was a mentor to us and it was heartbreaking when they didn't include us in the deal. They reneged on Sam & Dave… they said they owned all the master tapes and we didn't. They left us high and drive. We had to start all over from scratch. So, they owned all the past masters on everybody and all of a sudden we're sitting with nothing.

So then we made a deal with Paramount—we weren't going to do it and then Jim Stewart said we really need to and we had to work a lot harder. We signed with Paramount. The industry was changing and all of a sudden instead of making hit singles, like we had been doing for eight or nine years—they stuck us right in the thick of things and they wanted us to make all of these albums. So Booker had to make all of these albums, Isaac and David had to make albums…and Al, Duck and myself had to make albums. So, instead of working on two or three songs for an artist—I was working on ten to twelve songs for an artist. It was a workload that was totally uncomfortable. I think a lot of music suffered. We still had good songs—a lot of great songs came out of that. There was a lot done. Like I said, we had a lot of chart records, but in the long run I think it started downhill.

A hard lesson…a warning for all aspiring artists…

SC: When you break up that team—one guy doesn't win a basketball game or football game. I don't care if he makes the last 3-pointer in overtime—how did he get there? It took a whole bunch of other guys playing together to get him to that shot. Otherwise, they would have lost. That's what I'm saying—that guy may get all of the glory, but takes teamwork. I've always preached that. I've had more people say, 'Do you think that STAX wave could ever be duplicated?' Probably not. I'm not saying it can't happen, but those conditions are gone. It will never happen like that again.

Was "Dock of The Bay" one of those last great sessions?

SC: Well, a lot of people like to think it was, but "Dock of The Bay" was cut during the last recording sessions of Otis, but it wasn't the last great session. We'd had that thing in the can for a couple of weeks. We talked about what we were going to do with it. Otis and I both felt it could use some background. I was producing the Staple Singers and I wanted to get them to come and sing on it, and Otis thought that was a great idea, but we didn't have time to do that, and I ended up putting ocean waves on it and seagulls.

I don't know even if it's important. I know what the last stuff that was cut. Most of it was done by Ronnie Capone, me and Otis. We cut a song called "Champagne and Wine," we cut another one called "Direct Me." and another one called "Ton of Joy." I think we did another version of that with the band as well. There was a lot of recording going on. The last time I saw Otis, he popped his head in the control room and I was setting up to do guitar overdubs on some stuff we cut and also "Dock of The Bay". Otis said, 'I'll see you on Monday.' I said, 'We got a gig tomorrow night.' That was Friday afternoon he was leaving on a plane to fly up to Nashville to do a show. That's the last time I ever saw him. He had three shows—Friday, Saturday and Sunday nights—one show at a college in Indianapolis. I believe we did a show with the Isley Brothers and Jimi Hendrix was playing that show.

I remember we were sitting on the runway at 7 o'clock the next morning—all iced in and we couldn't fly out and we had to wait. Duck and I looked at each other and said if we could get a hold of—I think his name was Dick—Otis' pilot, he could get us out of here.' Little did we know, they were already going down...

It's sad. And we missed the flight. We got into Indianapolis, but we'd already missed our connection to Memphis so we had to wait for the next one. David Porter was singing with us in those days when we did colleges—we didn't have enough instrumentals to do a whole show so we carried David to sing. So David said 'I'm going to go call my wife and let her know we'll all be on the next flight and when we'll get in.' So he comes back white as a sheet, like he'd just seen 900 ghosts. We asked him what was wrong. Was he sick? He said, 'My wife just heard on the radio that Otis' plane went down and he died.' That's how we found out—Sunday, about mid-day.

An end of an era...Let's skip ahead a bit. You've got a new record coming out.

SC: Yeah, it's coming out July 29.

It's called *Nudge It Up A Notch*...

SC: That's right.

Oh, recently I got an email requesting I ask you about touring Australia with Guy Sebastian. Last year a soul tribute album went triple platinum in Australia, but it won't be out in the States until early 2009.

SC: It's a great record. Guy has been in town since about a week ago to write and we've written a couple of things. I've had him writing with Blue Miller, David McCloskey and Joanna Cotten. I don't know who else he might write with because I'm leaving for Paris tomorrow with The Blues Brothers. I'll be gone for a couple of weeks. Guy has to be back on July 9, so he can only stay a few more days.

***Nudge It Up A Notch* has a different sound...it's not what people might expect. But your playing sounds unmistakable. Felix Cavaliere is on it...**

SC: It's interesting. We started most of the writing at Jon Tiven's studio in Nashville. Some of the things we finished were at my studio and some of it we finished in Felix's studio. We mixed it at a place called the Sound Kitchen with David Z. I think we made a pretty decent record. We didn't start this to make a record—we started it just to write some songs and have some fun to see where it would take us. We just kept going…we were having so much fun. All of a sudden, we're looking at each other and we've got 8 or 9 tracks. We felt like we should just keep going and turn it into something. Then we got it and we said are we going to finish this or what? So, Felix took it home and started working on a lot of the vocals. Some of the ones he wasn't comfortable with… but somebody—Concord or Tiven—why don't we turn these into instrumentals? So in the final hour that's kind of what I did—I went in for some overdubs and made them instrumentals and put two or three on there. Originally, like a year or so ago—before we really thought about shopping it, we thought we'll just put it on the Internet and if people want to download it—great, we'll do it that way.

When Concord decided they were going to activate the STAX label, Jon Tiven knew one of those guys there and I was not familiar with anybody, but I knew what was going on with STAX and the museum and all that. They wanted to reactivate the old STAX label. I thought, 'How interesting is that?' They asked me what I thought, and I said, 'It's kind of like Hurry up and wait. Let's wait and see. If they can pull it off I think it's a great thing if it can happen. If they do it with the same passion we did it with, it might be successful.' There are so many young ears out there; they're not going to know what the STAX label is…if you're just going to make another record label, you're just going to be in competition with everybody else. If you try and keep it rooted music that is the way we made music years ago…not this polished merchandizing crap.

Before I let you go, I'm going to throw out a few names…

SC: Okay. Go…

Bob Dylan.

SC: A good friend. I think the peak of our relationship probably came during his birthday celebration. On his 50th Birthday celebration at Madison Square Garden—I think Duck and I played on 27 different songs. There was more in the show, but we played on 27 different songs (Laughs). It went by like a rocket. We were just tossing chord changes and go on to the next song. What came out of it was pretty good. We've always been fans with Bob. We never really worked with him. He came to us. We were playing in Europe and he came backstage, and he said, 'Hey, they're going to celebrate my 50th birthday and I'd like the MGs to be my back-up band.' We said give us a call and he did. We decided to do it and we had a lot of fun. That really got us.

Neil Young.

SC: It's funny. The first time we met Neil was at the Rock and Roll Hall of Fame and we did Bob's "All Along the Watchtower". They called and asked for permission to release that as maybe a single for airplay and we said fine. Duck and I were on tour in Australia with the Blues Brothers when we got the call from Booker and he said, 'I talked to Neil's manager Elliot Roberts and he said this is what Neil is offering and here's when he wants to go out on the road. He wants us to go out to his ranch and rehearse for two weeks.' That was in January or February of 1993. We started the tour that summer. Duck and Booker later did a record with Neil *(Are You Passionate?)*, but I was on tour with the Blues Brothers.

Keith Richards.

SC: A great friend. What can I say? I used to see Keith more often when Belushi was still alive because he would hang around in New York and he came to the club. They had a blues bar in New York and we used to go down and Keith was there. He's always said nice things about me. He'd be a close friend if he was around more. I just don't see him much these days.

James Burton.

SC: I first met James Burton on *Shindig* in 1965. I've got a picture of two skinny guys out back at ABC Studios where they filmed that and I found out he was from Shreveport, which made him a southern boy. I knew he played great. Then we lost contact for a few years and then all of a sudden he shows up as Elvis

Presley's guitar player. James was playing with Ronnie Tutt—we were pretty close friends. Tutt's fantastic. I have a lot of respect for James Burton. To me, he's family—he's like a brother.

What did you think of The Black Crowes' version of "Hard To Handle"?

SC: They threw it off time by half a beat, but that's okay. We did a show with The Black Crowes in Norway at a festival. I always thought they were good—they had a lot of passion and a lot of energy. They did a good job. Anytime I hear a remake of a STAX song and it does well, I'm a happy camper. Most people don't know that Duck Dunn's son—Jeff—was the Crowes' sound guy for a tour. They not only had a passion for the sound, but they had someone who grew up with the sound on the road with them—that can never hurt.

Well, I only have about another thousand questions to ask, but I know you're pressed for time...duty calls...

SC: If you have any more questions just call me. I leave for Paris tomorrow and I won't be back until July 15—we're playing France, Italy and Spain with the original Blues Brothers band that's been playing for 20 years. They're killing me (Laughs).

Well, Godspeed out there Steve. You're a hero to a lot of folks...

SC: Thank ya man.

We'll cross paths again...

SC: Okay James. Have a good one. I appreciate it bud...

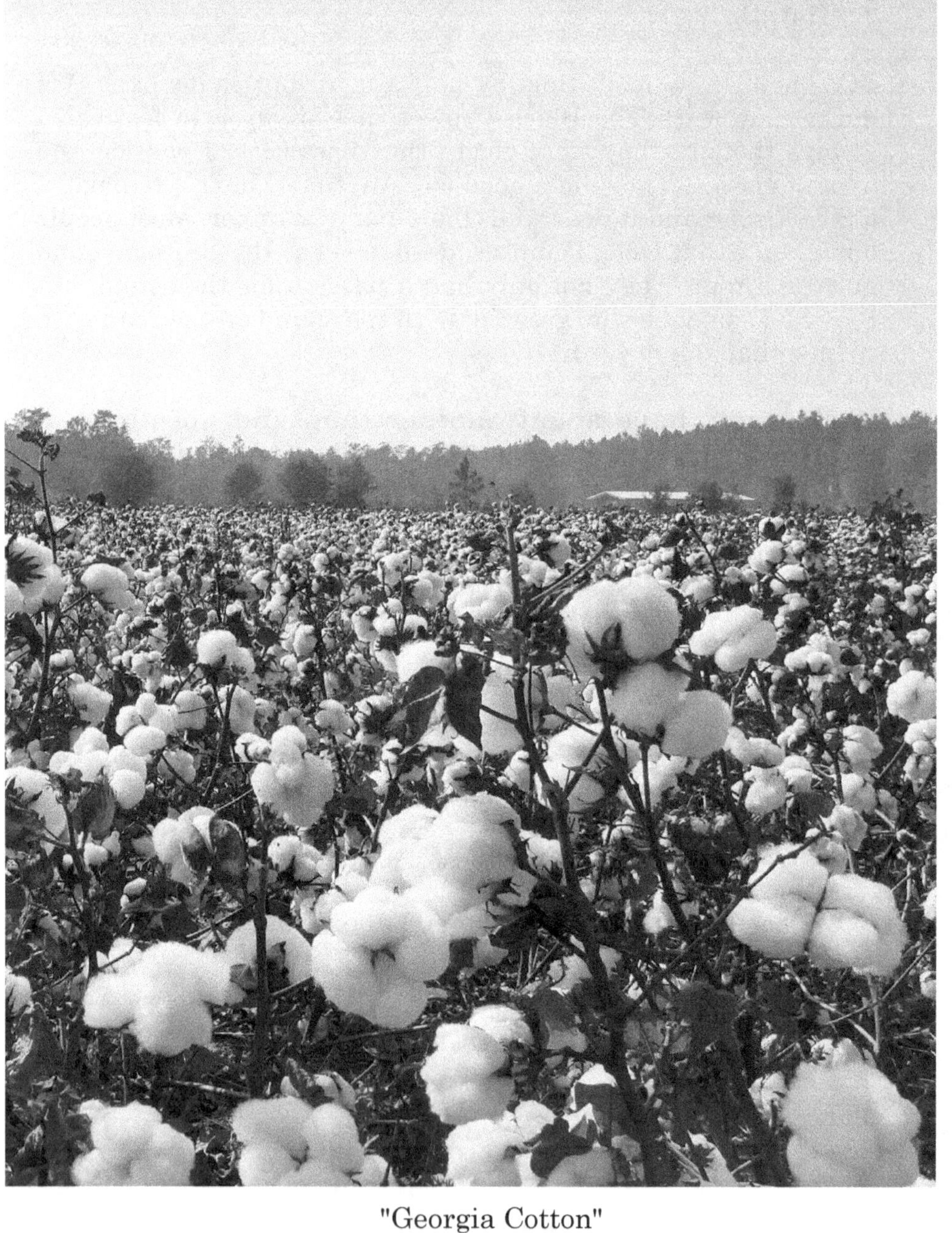

"Georgia Cotton"

••••••

The Georgia Sea Island Singers: Preserving Coastal Music Traditions

I conducted this interview in the spring of 2006 with Mrs. Frankie Quimby. She grew up on the Georgia sea islands. Her ancestors were traced all the way back to the Foulah Tribe in Africa. This interview captures vital American music history.

After four decades, Frankie and Doug Quimby continue to travel the world as the Georgia Sea Island Singers, sharing the Gullah culture with audiences from presidents to preschoolers. The group's performance history includes prestigious gigs such as the 1968 Mexico City Olympics, the 1994 Lillehammer Olympics, the Inauguration of President Jimmy Carter and the 2004 G8 Conference, as well as engagements in Africa, Spain, France, Germany, Nova Scotia, and Canada. Now, for the first time, the venerable Georgia Sea Island singers have released their own record, entitled *Seh Deh De Cumin.* This inimitable collection illuminates the lyrical Gullah language, spiritual songs, games, and redemptive shouts passed down from the slaves on Georgia's southeastern coast.

Over 250 years ago, plantation owners began importing slaves from West Africa to the coasts of Georgia and South Carolina. The slaves endured extreme hardship and injustice on the rice plantations where they were forced to labor. Isolated from the mainland on the humid, mosquito-ridden islands, however, the slaves were able to freely preserve their ethnic traditions. The blend of language and culture that survived and evolved is known as Gullah.

Frankie Sullivan Quimby was born and raised on Georgia's Sea Islands and can trace her ancestry back to the Foulah Tribe, who once resided on the banks of the Niger River. Although her husband Douglas was born in Baconton, Georgia, near Albany, his grandfather spoke in Gullah dialect, as many members of his family once worked on coastal plantations before being sold to inland landowners.

The Quimbys are the second generation of slave descendants to perform in the Georgia Sea Island Singers. The history of the group goes all the way back to the early 1900s when Lydia Parrish, wife of Maxfield Parrish, began her own "folklife studies" on St. Simons Island, where she lived. She would pay men and women who lived on the island to share their songs and memories, which she documented. Around 1920, Parrish sponsored the formation of the Spiritual Singers of Georgia, who performed for guests at the Cloister Hotel. Bessie Jones, a young woman from Dawson, Georgia, who had moved to St. Simons Island with her husband, joined the choral group in 1933.

In 1942, Parrish published *The Slave Songs of the Georgia Sea Islands,* a collection that, although it was compiled by an amateur, nonetheless remains an invaluable source of history. The other significant documentation of the group came from famed folklorist Alan Lomax. He originally visited the island in 1935, accompanied by author and fellow folklorist, Zora Neale Hurston. They met Parrish and Jones and experienced the Spiritual singers. Lomax returned in 1959 and 1960 to conduct extensive recordings of this group.

Bessie Jones shared with Lomax her desire to take this heritage to the people, to "teach the chillun," as she told him. The two worked together to solicit bookings and it was agreed the group would now be called the Georgia Sea Island Singers. The members at that time, song leader Jones, community leader Big John Davis, Peter Davis, Henry Morrison, Emma Ramsey and Mable Hillery, toured together for almost a decade.

Douglas Quimby joined the group in 1969, after having sung with the Sensational Friendly Stars, a well-known gospel group, for six years. One by one, the original members either stopped performing or passed away, and the Quimbys embraced the mission to share the Gullah culture, which Bill Moyers calls "a heritage so rich no price tag can measure its value." Tony Merrell, a lifelong resident of Brunswick and master of the djembe and talking drums, joined the Quimbys in 2001.

Frankie Quimby once said, "I'm a firm believer that you can't know where you're going until you realize where you've come from. We have dedicated our lives to trying to preserve that rich heritage and culture that our ancestors handed down to us." The 18 songs in the *Seh Deh De Cumin* collection serve as a direct link to the original source of slave songs that preserves a vital insight into African-American history. With honor we present this recent interview with Mrs. Frankie Quimby.

How long has your family lived on St. Simons and Brunswick, Georgia?

FQ: Oh, well over a hundred years. See, John Davis and that generation were my relatives. Those are relatives of mine. I'm a Sullivan by birth. The Sullivans, The Davises and the Ramseys that lived on St. Simons were all brought to St. Simons from Africa.

Explain the origins of the group changing their name to the Georgia Sea Island Singers.

FQ: (The name changed) when Alan Lomax came back and recorded us. The old singers began to travel because they were singing at places like the Cloister and The King & Prince and for Lydia Parrish at her house on St. Simons. In those days it was Emma Ramsey, Henry Morrison, John Davis, and Bessie Jones—all of them singing. They all sung together for Ms. Parrish, but when Alan Lomax came…that's when they began to travel off the island.

Were you and Mr. (Doug) Quimby already married by the time y'all joined?

FQ: Yes. John Davis had stopped going out with them by this time—so that's how we started with Bessie Jones, because they weren't traveling. She needed someone to sing, and she heard Doug singing in a quartet in a church and she asked Doug if he would go—that's how we got started with her.

So, this is the first recording of the Georgia Sea Island Singers record in the last forty years.

FQ: Well, they did an album with Alan Lomax called *Southern Journey*. That was their first recording. John Davis called them the St. Simons Island Singers—he even called them the Coastal Singers in those days, but they had made another album. You know, Bessie Jones did some recordings. One was called *So Glad I'm Here*. Then she recorded an album with some children's games—that was 1975.

••• •••

Explain the title of the new CD, *Seh Deh De Cumin*.

FQ: That's in Gullah. In English, it means Yonder Comes Day. They way they sang it on the mainland was "Yonder Comes Day." On the island, it becomes Gullah language—it was "Seh Deh De Cumin." On the new album, song five, "O Day," is the same song. See, black people will say five or six different phrases and mean one thing. In Gullah it's "Seh Deh De Cumin." In English it's "Yonder Comes Day", and it turns out "O Day". The slaves spoke in coded messages. They communicated with rhythms using their mouths, making music using their bodies as rhythm instruments.

Storytelling and explaining underlying meanings of some songs plays an integral part of your performances. Talk about Harriet Tubman and how slave songs corresponded with the "underground railroad."

FQ: We had our underground railroad from here when the Seminole Indians would hide us in Florida, near Tallahassee, and that area, but with Harriet Tubman…they would go to North and South Carolina and when she got back, they would get out in the fields and they begin to sing in a coded message: "Way down In the Old Tar River." The slaves on the surrounding plantations would hear him and understand that was a code when Harriet was back in the area. In those days, your voice would travel because there wasn't pollution in the air and they would answer back because they were excited since they knew someone was gonna start the northern count to freedom that night, and they'd sing "The Old Tar river is black and dirty…" to fool the slave owners who thought they were talking about some regular river, but they were really talking about the underground movement with Harriet Tubman.

On other songs like "Moses," "Liza Jane," and "Little Sally Walker," you demonstrate differences between how the mainland slaves sang, and how the Gullah sang these old songs. What are your favorites off the new CD?

FQ: I think "Moses" is my favorite. It was recorded in Brunswick—they did a beautiful job.

These songs obviously transfer well to live audiences...

FQ: Yes, besides the Gullah language, we can always talk about slave games and dances—we do sharecropping dances and shouts from the Georgia and South Carolina coasts. There's a lot of history there to cover.

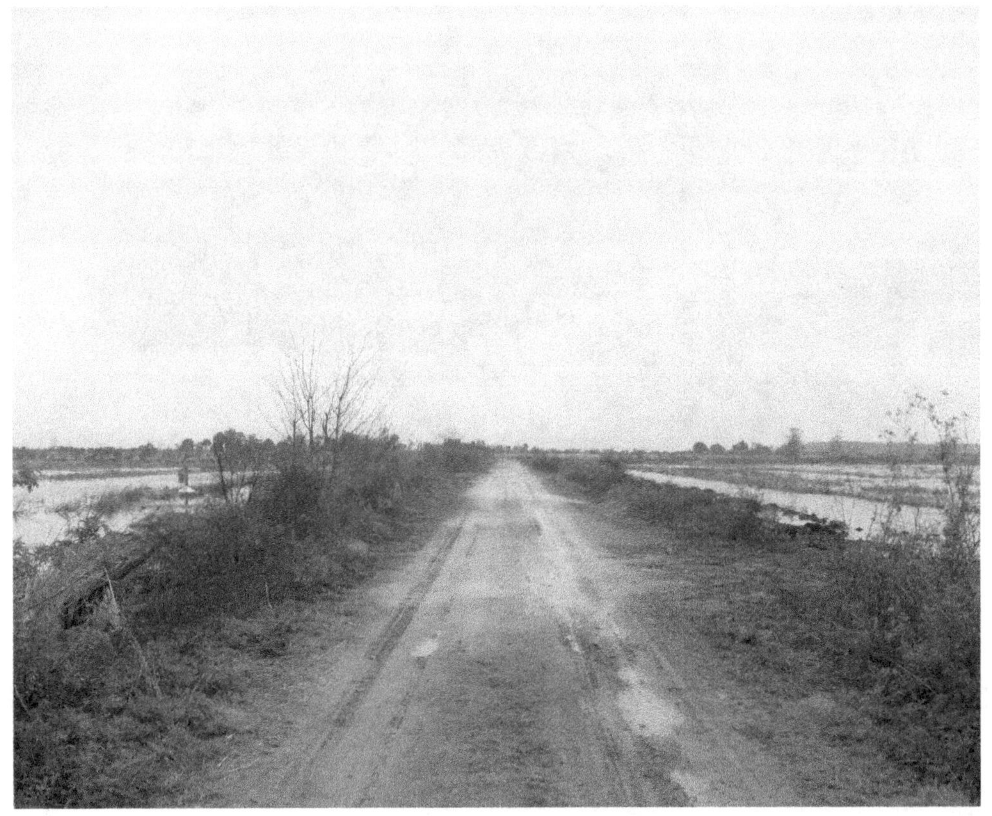

"Low Country Dirt Road"

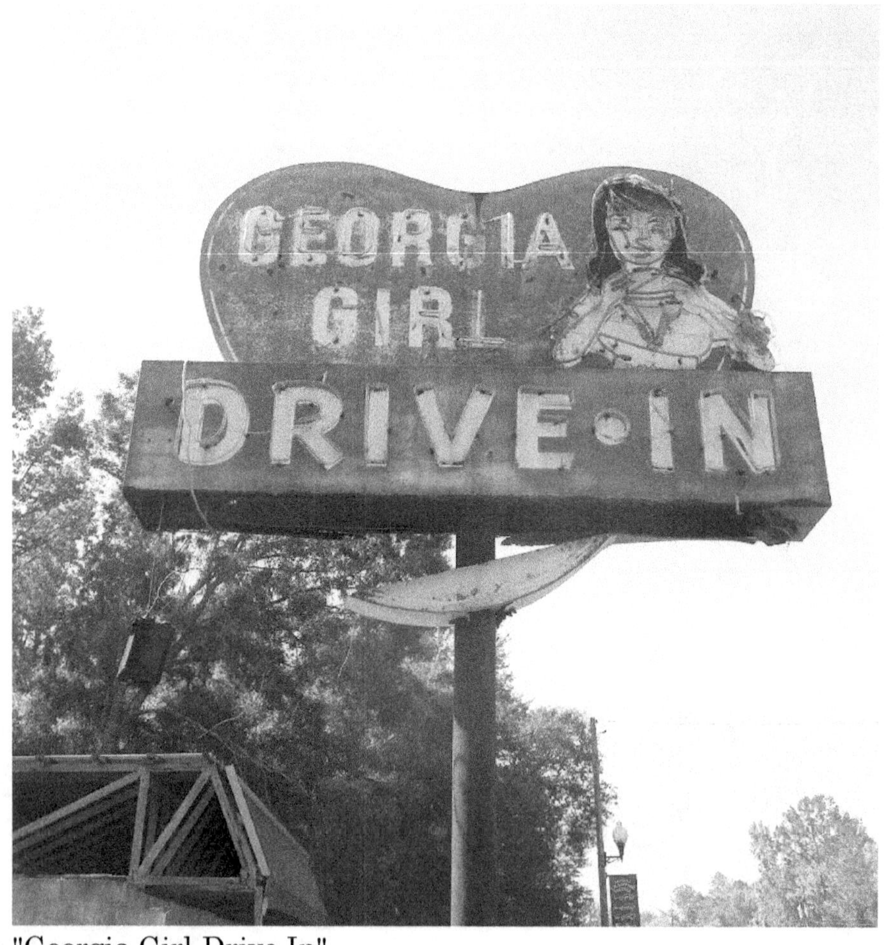

"Georgia Girl-Drive In"
Woodbine, Georgia

••••••

Way Down South with John Sayles

The John Sayles film, Honeydripper, inspired me to seek him out for an interview. This Q & A captures a portrait of the film-maker at the time Honeydripper showed in theatres. Honeydripper revolved around Alabama blues musicians. Honeydripper counts among my favorite Sayles films such as Sunshine State, Brother From Another Planet, Matewon, Eight Men Out, Passion Fish, Lone Star and his role in the movie, In The Electric Mist.

He's twice been nominated for the Academy Award twice. His Bruce Springsteen videos such as "Born In The U.S.A," "I'm On Fire" and "Glory Days" command respect the in the music video pantheon. In this interview, Sayles came off as I expected—wry, sharp and insightful. His two films after *Honeydripper* include *Amigo* (2010) and *Go for Sisters* (2013).

Sayles' films command respect. His latest film, *Honeydripper,* takes place in Alabama during the 1950s. Honeydripper counts as Sayles' 16th film which contains a stellar cast and homage to southern blues music. *Honeydripper* includes the strong line-up featuring Danny Glover, Stacy Keach, Charles S. Dutton and musicians Dr. Mable John, Keb Mo, Gary Clark Jr. and Howlin' Wolf's saxophone player Eddie Shaw.

Sayles began his career working with the great Roger Corman. Later, Sayles earned the prestigious MacArthur Fellowship given to individuals with rare originality. Some of Sayles' great films include *The Brother From Another Planet, Passion Fish, Eight Men Out, Matewan, Silver City, Lone Star, Sunshine State, The Howling* and a script called *Night Skies* that served as the provenance of Steven Spielberg's film, *E.T. the Extra-Terrestrial.*

Sayles serves on the board for the Austin Film Society. The National Film preservation Board of the United States decided Sayles' film, *Return of Secaucus 7,* would be one of the 25 films selected in 1997 for preservation in the Library of Congress National Film Registry.

Spielberg commissioned Sayles to write the script for *Jurassic Park 4.* Sayles' cinematic scope casts a wide penumbra on diverse subject matter. Sayles' film Baby It's You was the first film ever to feature the music of Bruce Springsteen. Sayles also filmed Springsteen's videos "Born In the U.S.A," "Glory Days," and "I'm On Fire."

Sayles' *Honeydripper* tells the story of a family dealing with domestic, cultural and musical changes. Danny Glover's character, "Pinetop" Purvis, an old piano player tries to save his juke joint by recruiting a hotshot guitar legend for one last glorious night which will make or break the establishment's future. Stacy Keach plays a cantankerous sheriff. The film's house band includes Gary Clark on guitar, STAX legend Dr. Mable John (who served as a Ray Charles Raelettes), Henderson Huggins on piano and Howlin' Wolf's saxophone player Eddie Shaw.

In this interview we discuss his latest film, southern culture, filming in Hank Williams' hometown, Flannery O'Connor, southern literature, the all-star musical cast of Honeydripper and other gems from one of America's great filmmakers.

Your cinematic geography never stays in one place. You've filmed in Texas, Florida, Louisiana, West Virginia, and many other locations, but with *Honeydripper* you've finally filmed in Alabama:

JS: Yes, this is the first time I would say we've worked in the traditional Deep South.

In *Honeydripper,* Keb Mo's character is not the Devil, but a very mischievous spirit. Discuss your intention with that fabled character...the blind, bottleneck slide player who seems to know the musicians' secrets...

JS: The way I explained it to Kevin (Keb Mo) Moore that he was kind of a spirit to the music and very mischievous. So, for Danny Glover's character...only two characters can see the blind guitarist, and they're both musicians. For Danny Glover's character he's really the ghost of Christmas past. This spirit reminds Glover's character of this murder he was involved in and this dogs Glover's character in his mind. Then for Gary Clark's character, he's really the guy who makes sure he gets there for his date with destiny. He kind of pushes the music forward. So, yeah, he's not the Devil at the crossroads, but he really knows that guy.

Yeah, like he says...the Devil has the first guitar, and this guy has the second one.

JS: Exactly.

The economy of dialogue in *Honeydripper* is excellent. Southerners are militant about how they are portrayed in film and I think this movie does not shame southerners.

JS: I spent quite a bit of time in the south as a kid. I had relatives in southern Florida and in Jacksonville. They even lived in Georgia for a while. So I remember coming down and just soaking up the language. One of the things you realize is that any state has three or four accents.

You play the liquor man in the film.

JS: Yeah, I just went and hung out at the Piggly Wiggly and it all came back to me.

You were the meanest guy in the movie.

JS: Just about. It's one of those things where I kept asking myself...I'm 6'4 and Danny is 6'2, and I felt like without pushing it too much, I thought it might help a little bit.

Talk about filming *Honeydripper* in Hank Williams' home town.

JS: We really didn't know until we settled on the place and started talking to some of the people who run the town. We just liked the look of it. We knew we were going to be shooting in Greenville, which is about ten minutes north. We scouted both Arkansas and Alabama because we needed cotton and a decommissioned army base because we needed barracks still standing that we wouldn't have to build. As we looked around for the main street of the town we found Georgiana (Hank's hometown). It's one of those towns where most of the new stuff is not on the main street. You might have a shopping mall, but it's a couple of blocks away so that those railroad tracks were still there. Two of the four were still active so we had to work around the trains. We had to have warning from the CSX when to get off the tracks. Then we started getting Hank stories from all the local people. He's very popular there now, but I think when he was around he was considered a sort of juvenile delinquent.

The hometown syndrome?

JS: Yeah. A lot of stories of driving Hank unconscious from the honky tonk and parking him asleep in his car in the church parking lot because he promised to sing a church song the next day. Ten minutes before he'd sing, someone would wake him up, and he'd come in and sing at church. In *Honeydripper* I tried to get some of that duality. There were people who were just church people and some were just honky tonk people, and some tried to do both. Hank was somebody who throughout his life those were two strands of his music that were very important to him and very popular.

In *Honeydripper*, Glover's wife, Delilah, walks a fine line between those two worlds.

JS: She's somebody who says in the film, 'I sang in those bars, and that her first redemption was meeting him' (Glover) and he got her out of drinking too much and feeling bad about herself. Now she's heading for her second redemption. If you think about those people who pick cotton—and it was white people as well as black people. Everybody we met under 50 in that part of Alabama had picked cotton when they were a kid. For a lot of those poor sharecroppers and itinerant pickers, Saturday night was where you transcended that tough life that you're going to go back to Monday. Then if there was a revival tent and they often stayed for a whole week—that was like the circus coming to town. That was not just religious transcendence, but it was entertainment. There was music and you got to dress up and see your neighbors and get into the spirit of things. Delilah is trying to wrestle with this thing—she's hearing the preacher and things at church that her husband might be a bad man, but she knows in her heart that's not true. She's trying to figure that out.

In some ways, she's the hero…

JS: I think so. What I told Lisa Gay Hamilton (Delilah) there's a Reverend telling her the Lord is telling you where you've got to be, and then all of a sudden the Lord tells her where she's got to be, and…

…It's by her husband…

JS: Yes, by her husband. As much as he's pissed her off by stealing her daughter's money or whatever, she understands him and understands how important this situation is because he's not just fighting for the juke joint. He's a black man in 1950 in Alabama who is his own man. How did that happen? What does that mean to him? Or the community? That's what he's going to lose, not just the four walls of the club.

Stacy Keach really did a great job in portraying a rural southern sheriff.

JS: Well, you know, Stacy is from Savannah originally, so he came up down there. He was saying when I hired him the first two movies he shot were in Alabama. *The Heart Is A Lonely Hunter* was shot in Selma. He made a movie called *The Traveling Executioner* that was shot in Alabama. He's spent a lot of time down there. His way of controlling people in the town is to keep them off balance. So, sometimes he's humorous, sometimes he's friendly and in the same sentence almost he can turn on you and get right up in your face.

…One minute he says his wife's cooking is awful…

JS: …And in the next he's arresting you for vagrancy and selling you to the highest bidder as an unpaid county laborer. So, he's corrupt and he's racist in a kind of paternal way, but he's not a sadist or murderer. He's a guy who—I think—controls his town fairly well by knowing as much as he can about people. So, his scenes with Danny Glover's character are loaded. He hasn't figured this guy out yet. He bemused—sometimes mad—and amused because this guy pushes back. What gives?

...An intense atmosphere for Alabama in 1950...

JS: It was always personal. People know each other as mothers—they know the other's history. So they had no mercy on anyone from the outside. So, this kid guitar player who comes in on the train, of course he's going to get picked up by the cops, and thrown onto the chain gang. There's no history with him so they don't owe him anything. Whereas, those towns—the racism was there, but those people also kind of took care of each other and they certainly knew each other. People with the same name—some white—some black—and they knew how they had the same name. it was extremely personal.

It must have been thrilling to have Mable Jones—one of Ray Charles' Raelettes—in *Honeydripper.*

JS: Oh yeah. It was one of the things that was the most fun in the movie. First of all, I got to steep myself in the music of that moment. Some of the point of the film is all these people were listening to each other. There's gospel, there's jump, there's swing, there's old fashioned steel guitar blues, there's pop ballads, and there's country western. I used a Hank Williams song—you know—in the movie "Move It On Over," which if you listen carefully is "Rock Around the Clock." It's rockabilly before anyone was calling it rockabilly. Then to get these good musicians—Benny Shaw used to play with Howlin' Wolf for many years. Mabel, of course, had her own career as a singer. She ran the Raelettes for Ray Charles. Gary—the guitar player—is a phenomenon. We got lucky. A fellow we know who runs the South By Southwest music festival, the minute he heard what we were doing he said, 'He might be too young, but you've got to check this kid out. He was born and raised in Austin, playing this music since he was 14. To get them all together on the stage is what you hear in the movie—except for Danny Glover, who's faking the piano. Although he took lessons, his hands are in the right place...everything is live. A solo was different on every take. They were just listening to each other, jamming on a general theme we gave them.

How long did it take to film *Honeydripper?*

JS: We have a very ambitious movie on a relatively low budget. You plan a lot and then shoot very little. We only had five weeks to shoot. We only had Danny Glover for three and a half weeks because he had a movie before us and a movie after us, so the shooting was very intense. We were in Alabama a couple of months planning things and making sure the locations made sense—working out the schedule to get the actors in the same room at the same time. There's a couple of shots where Danny is looking at Keb Mo and they weren't there together, which is kind of appropriate because Keb Mo is a ghost. Danny didn't have to work too hard. He didn't have to talk to anyone. We had a couple curve balls thrown at us. You wake up in the morning and the cotton field we were going to shoot had been picked overnight because they were afraid there was gonna be rain. The machines pick the cotton so fast, so we'd have to have an emergency scouting report and find some more cotton we could shoot in. the people in the towns were really nice. That revival tent scene—The New Beginning Ministry—those 8 people singing are the best of their singers and all the people in the congregation sing as well, so that was tough picking eight people who get to sing the gospel. Albert Hall was the actor who plays the reverend—you might remember him from *Apocalypse Now*—he was the captain of the boat...

...They called him Chief...

JS: ...That's right. He gets the spear in the chest at the end. He's from Bessemer, Alabama. So he remembered the revivals because he went as a kid. The call and response from the people was the whole thing. We'd just say, 'You're going to have church for a while. He's going to repeat the sermon a couple of times.' We tried not to do it too often, but we got such energy from the local people. Like everywhere I've filmed—on Amelia Island, Texas, Louisiana—and hiring 15-20 people for smaller parts, they've got the accent. They understand the story and we didn't have to fly them there. It's a nice bond with the community.

The music from *Honeydripper* will appear as a soundtrack, right?

JS: Yeah, Rhino Records will do a soundtrack that will come out in early February when we go wider with the movie.

I think Danny Glover rises to the occasion in this film.

JS: He's the guy having the crisis. This character grew up with music. Blues doesn't go back that far...it goes back just before 1900 in the Mississippi Delta. He's 50 in 1950. So, he's somebody who's grown up with the music. He's played in New Orleans with Buddy Bolden and was at least around when they were playing. Then he went through the jazz into swing—his big era with the touring bands and still plays boogie woogie—and traditional blues and now there's this new thing on the horizon. A subplot to the movie there was this brief battle in the early fifties between the guitar and the piano for a struggle of dominance. The minute they got the solid body guitar and amplifier that went with it, the piano player's' days were numbered in rock and roll. Y'know, Ray Charles, Jerry Lee Lewis, Fats Domino and Professor Longhair held out and still had careers, but I think it was just portability. You think of a poor kid who can get that four dollar Sears & Roebuck guitar in the mail...

...And get on the train with it...

JS: Yes, exactly. You can't take a piano on a train. Those garage bands in the sixties until the electronic fold-up keyboards you could put in the van came out it just wasn't portable. So kids stopped learning how to play the piano. The saxophone wandered off to jazz. The Muscle Shoals sound kept those instruments around. Later Bruce Springsteen brought it around with Clarence Clemons, but the guitar really took over and I think that's what this character is sensing. He knows there's a place for him in the music, but he's not the lead guy anymore.

It's a changing of the guard.

JS: Yeah, you know it happened in the movies when they went from silent to talkies. I just think about the guys in the negro baseball leagues in their 30s and their 40s when baseball integrated. They know they weren't going to get called up when they had Jackie Robinson. The negro leagues died within four years of integration. But, I'm always interested in those big sea changes. Who are the ones who can jump on this new thing? Who are the one's who stay behind?

Like walking a tightrope between cultural boundaries…

JS: Yes. For example, Bob Dylan could've said, 'Hey, I'm a folk musician. I'm not playing electric guitars'. But he saw, 'My God, what could I do with that thing?' It was a good decision for him.

You're a formidable fiction writer, what are your feelings about the writing of the southern writer Flannery O'Connor?

JS: She's unique. She's one of those people that I'm a big fan of. There's such a strong tradition of fiction writing in the south. Flannery O'Connor is one of those southern writers who are absolutely unique—a different way from looking at the world. Her stuff is very spiritual in a way and very strange in a way. I think she's in the same tradition as Eudora Welty. Harry Crews is a guy I really like. Of course, Faulkner, but John Huston made Flannery's *Wise Blood* which was a nice little movie within that literature. She's not adapted many times I think because she's so unique and poetic. You hear traces of those writers music in Lucinda Williams.

I also think The Drive By Truckers…

JS: True. Lucinda's father was a professor at LSU of literature. I met her one time and she met Eudora Welty at a University class. A lot other imagery, fun and darkness really come out in her music.

Have you seen Cormac McCarthy's, *No Country For Old Men?*

JS: I haven't seen it. I'm a friend of the Coen Brothers, so I'm looking forward to it. Somebody told me they were going to make *Blood Meridian* which is the goriest, scariest book I've ever read. So, I don't know how they are going to pull it off. He's an intriguing writer—he's a little bit more on the Texas side of the southern writers these days.

Back To *Honeydripper*, I think Glover did a fine job singing Howlin Wolf's "Goin' Down Slow."

I asked Danny if he played any instruments when I first met him and he said no. But being an actor, when we told him he was playing a piano player, he started taking a bunch of lessons. So, we took the guts out of a piano and he was just banging away. It's physical that playing. A lot of clubs were so small; they had to learn to play standing up because there was no room onstage for a piano stool. Nobody is a boogie woogie piano player who starts playing past the age of fifty.

So, *Honeydripper* hits theaters in New York and Los Angeles December 28?

JS: New York and L.A. to qualify for an Academy Award. Then it will open wider basically starting on Martin Luther King Day. In Atlanta we're doing a big thing down there. Generally, it will open in February. For us, it's a small independent movie when you start you hope to grow from there. We'll hit about 40 cities and hopefully wider. I know we're going to Savannah and Memphis and Atlanta. We're doing a big thing with Hands on Atlanta. You're in Atlanta, right?

Right.

JS: I lived in Atlanta for a little bit in the early seventies right when they were tearing everything down (laughs)…expanding the city. There was a joke at the time, if Atlanta is the Athens of Georgia, then what's Athens? Its hip there, they've got a lot going on.

Well, good luck with *Honeydripper* and thanks for your time.

JS: Thanks James, it was good talking with you.

••••••

James Burton:
An Original Six-String Journeyman

James Burton ranks as one of America's finest guitarists. A true heavy in the business. Burton served as Elvis Presley's guitarist as well as Gram Parsons, Ricky Nelson, Merle Haggard and many others revealed in this Q & A. He's recorded with all the greats. This interview covers his entire career up until 2008. His resume exceeds all the standards of excellence. Burton is a spiritual person. The James Burton Foundation continues to raise money for underprivileged children. In October 2016, Burton appeared on a TV show called American Supergroups.

Born in Shreveport, Louisiana, on August 21, 1939, guitarist-extraordinaire James Burton began playing music professionally at 14. He recorded the inimitable solo on Dale Hawkins' hit "Suzie Q" at 15. By the time he was 16, Burton operated as the guitarist in Ricky Nelson's band. Burton played in Nelson's band for eight years. In 1964, he started the Shindogs—the houseband on the TV show *Shindig*—with Delaney Bramlett.

To even seasoned guitar legends, James Burton's sound remains unmistakable. Burton went on to record with over one thousand artists, some of which included, Herb Alpert, Buffalo Springfield, Hoyt Axton, J.J. Cale, Johnny Cash, Judy Collins, Nat King Cole, Willie Nelson, Frank Sinatra, Ray Charles, the Everly Brothers, Elvis Presley, Merle Haggard, Gram Parsons, Emmylou Harris, Waylon Jennings, Jerry Lee Lewis, Billy Joe Shaver, Bobby Darin, Joni Mitchell, Phil Ochs, Buck Owens, Glen Campbell, George Jones, Dean Martin, Randy Newman, Sammy Davis, Jr., Frankie Lane, Burl Ives, Charlie Rich, Duane Eddy, Townes Van Zandt, Henry Mancini, Leon Russell, Hank Williams, Jr., John Denver, Ronnie Hawkins, Ry Cooder, Ronnie Milsap, Del Shannon, Jimmie Dale Gilmore and many others.

The great southern music fan and Rolling Stones guitar legend Keith Richards inducted James Burton into the rock and Roll Hall of Fame in 2001. James Burton's guitar style inspired the "chicken-pickin'" sound. Burton's spirit and talent remains a graceful presence on any music scene.

From March 31 through April 2, 2007, James Burton will host the second annual James Burton International Guitar Festival in Shreveport, Louisiana. The purpose of this festival serves to provide local kids with musical instruments and opportunities. Some of this year's guests include Dickey Betts, Ed King, Chris Isaak, Rick Derringer, Lee Roy Parnell, The Cox Family, Doyle Dykes and Rick Vito.

In this interview, Mr. Burton discusses his early musical aptitudes and various career moves leading all the way up to his latest Guitar festival.

What was your first guitar?

JB: Well, my first guitar was actually an acoustic guitar. I'm not even sure the name of it. Unfortunately, I don't even have it. I didn't keep my first guitar. It was something like a Regal. A Silvertone Regal. It was in that category. I've got some old pictures at home that I think I have with that guitar.

How old were you then?

JB: Oh, I started playing when I was 12 or 13. I got my acoustic when I was 12.

At 15 you were already recording the solo on the Dale Hawkins hit, "Suzie Q."

JB: Yeah, I actually started playing when I was 13. My mother and dad bought me my first electric—Fender Telecaster—a blonde body, a beautiful, two-pickup, Telecaster.

Do you still have that one?

JB: Oh yeah. They bought me my first guitar and I started playing. I went professional when I was 14.

How did you land the Dale Hawkins gig?

JB: Well, it was just a blessing from God I guess. It was like he just put it in my hands and said 'Here, play.' It was just incredible. When I was in school, I won a couple of talent contests. Then I went out to one talent contest that they had in Bossier City at a nightclub. So my dad drove me over there and walked up to the guy and said 'My son plays guitar and he's 13 years old.

Is it okay if he plays the talent show?' The guy said sure. I won first place that night. I won first place in three talent contests and then I went to cutting records when I was 13 and 14. I think I played on Merle Kilgore's first record. Then when I recorded "Suzie Q" I was 15—around 1953 or 1954.

I'm sure "Suzie Q" opened a lot of doors for you.

JB: It did. Well, when I was working with Dale Hawkins in a blues band we cut "Suzie Q" and a few others with him.

What were your early musical influences?

JB: Oh, you know—the old blues stuff like Chuck Berry, Lightnin' Hopkins, B.B. King, Bo Diddley, Elmore James, John Lee Hooker...stuff like that. Country music was my first love. I learned from those old country albums.

I interviewed Charlie Louvin two weeks ago. Did you listen to the Louvin Brothers music?

JB: Yeah. I loved the Louvin Brothers music...Charlie and Ira...

So, "Suzie Q" got your name around...

JB: Yeah, and when I was 14 I played guitar on the Louisiana Hayride at the Municipal Auditorium in downtown Shreveport, Louisiana. I was playing with guys like Floyd Cramer and Jimmy Daze on steel guitar. I played behind guys like George Jones and Billy Walker—all the great music acts that came through there. Then I went to work with a guy named Bob Luman. He had a pretty hot band. I cut several records with him, and we played on the Hayride as well. But I didn't play the Hayride the same time as Elvis. Elvis would come and play the Hayride and our manager—Horace Logan—would send us off on tour. When Elvis would go on tour we'd come back and play the Hayride. I knew all those guys. You know, D.J. Fontana—the drummer—is from here in Shreveport. I met Elvis in 1969 when I put his band together. But I knew Scotty Moore, D.J. Fontana, Bill Black and all those guys. They used to come and sit in with us. Bob Luman and I toured with Gene Vincent, Jerry Lee Lewis...ah, there's so many...

••••••

You've played on, last I could check, at least 400 artists albums. Is that an accurate count?

JB: Well, it's a lot more than that. I've got a discography some place at home where the list goes forever. I've played with artists like Nat King Cole, Ray Charles, Frank Sinatra, Dean Martin, Sammy Davis Jr., Frankie Lane, Burl Ives…the list just goes on. That's not counting the Monkees, Glen Campbell, Charlie Rich, Buck Owens, Merle Haggard, Elvis, Emmylou Harris, Hoyt Axton-I played on almost all of his albums…

Like the Louvin Brothers, I discovered your playing through the music of Gram Parsons. Could you talk about him a little bit?

JB: Well, Gram…I played on a Byrds record. Gram was a singer in the Byrds. Gram and I were good friends. We used to go out to the Palomino Club in North Hollywood and jam. He'd always call, 'Man, I'm going out tonight. I need you to come play guitar with me.' We'd go out and play and he'd get up and sing. One day I got a phone call from Merle Haggard. Merle said, 'Do you know this guy Gram Parsons?' I said yeah I know Gram. He said, 'Well, is he an okay country singer?' I said yeah, he's a good singer. Merle said would you be interested in co-producing a record with me on him? I said, Well, sure, I'll do that. Then about two weeks go by and never heard back from Merle, so one day Gram called me and said 'James'—he jumped through the phone man—'I got a deal. My manager Ed Tickner got me a deal on Warner Brothers.' He said, 'We're going in the studio.' So, we went in the studio and started cutting. We cut a couple of albums real fast. That's where I met Emmylou. Then when Gram passed away then Ed Tickner took over Emmylou and got her the same deal with Warner Brothers. So we went to the studio and started recording with her. It was a hot band. Did you see that Gram DVD?

Oh yeah. It was great to see you play that riff to "Ooh Las Vegas". You covered some ground before meeting up with Gram. Nat King Cole and Ray Charles are heavy company…

••••••

JB: Oh yeah. I did the Andy Williams show with Ray Charles. I've recorded with so many artists it's frightening.

I'll throw out a few names of other artists you've performed with such as Ricky Nelson. You were all over his music...

JB: Yeah, I met Ricky when I was 16. When I went to work with him—I guess I was with him for about eight and a half years. I think I was with him up until about '64 or '65. Then we did a TV show called *Shindig*. That was me and Delaney Bramlett—we were the Shindogs—me, Delaney, Julie Cooper, Chuck Blackwell and Glen Hardin.

I'll throw out another favorite of mine you played with, Townes Van Zandt.

JB: Townes Van Zandt, yeah I cut records with him. I remember Townes Van Zandt real well. He was a good writer. I played a lot of Dobro stuff in his music. He was a sad writer. He kind of reminded me of Hank Williams.

They died the same day, January 1. Talk about working with Johnny Cash.

JB: Well, Johnny called me to do a TV show and that's when I made my exit from Ricky because that TV show happened to be Shindig. So, I went in and did the very first show with the pilot for *Shindig* and the producer Jack Goode was a huge fan and he said, 'Man, I want you on the show every week.' So, that's when he said let's put a band together. So we formed the Shindogs.

Another great guitar player you've worked with is J.J. Cale.

JB: Oh yeah, J.J. is an old buddy of mine. He's a good writer, a good friend of Leon Russell. I knew J.J. for a long time. I also recorded with him on some stuff. We did an album called *Shades*.

How about Leon Russell? I've always loved his music.

JB: Oh man, Leon and I go way back when he was 18 years old—Russell Bridges. I met Leon when he first came to California. He was playing out in the valley at the Sun Valley Ranch with Sonny and Al Jones who is actually from Shreveport-Bossier City. Their sister is Billie Jean Horton now who was married to Hank Williams and then when Hank died she married Johnny Horton.

You played with Ronnie Hawkins...

JB: Oh, Ronnie Hawkins. Crazy guy. He's doing pretty good. He was really sick for a while, but I think he's doing better. Ry Cooder and I overdubbed on an album for him in California—he came to California. He tried to get me to Canada several times to do some stuff with him but I was always so busy. He called me to ask if I could come in and overdub on an album because they already cut the tracks and everything and they just wanted me and Ry Cooder to overdub on it. Ry Cooder is another good buddy of mine.

Your playing fit in well with Buck Owens' sound.

JB: Well, pretty good. Don Rich was a good friend of mine. Of course, Buck and I played with a guy from North Hollywood—Jimmy Schneider—and the steel guitar player Tom Bromley. Tom Bromley went to work with Buck. Yeah, I did a few sessions with ol' Buck. Actually I also did a production for him on his son Buddy Allen.

So, of course in 1969 you began playing guitar for Elvis Presley. How did that come together?

JB: Well, in '68 Elvis called me for the comeback special. That's the one where he wore the black leather suit. I couldn't do it because I was doing an album with Frank Sinatra with Jimmy Boyd producing. So I couldn't do the Elvis comeback special on NBC. It was 1969 and he called me and we talked about three hours on the phone. He asked me if I'd be interested in putting a band together for him because he wanted to go play Vegas. He got tired of doing movies. He wanted to do some live shows.

112

••• •••

Was that when the one at the International Hotel was re-corded?

JB: Yeah. At the International Hotel, that was the very first show we did in the August of '69. The first guy I hired, the piano player in '69, was Larry Muhoberac. He knew Ronnie Tutt from Dallas, Texas; they worked together. Ronnie wanted to move to L.A. So, when I set up the rehearsals and when Elvis came in we actually had Larry on piano, Ronnie Tutt on the drums, and me. Glen Hardin couldn't make that one, but Jerry Scheff was on bass. Jerry and I worked together on a lot of record dates together. I always loved his playing. He always stuck in my mind when bass players' names came up.

You've been in the middle of some serious musical en-deavors, playing with very well-known artists and you've always maintained a sense of professional and personal balance. Do you think being able to go out and do your own thing between other artists' sessions kept you from getting bogged down. For instance, like a musician who has been in the same band for years and feels trapped?

JB: Well, it was always smooth for me. Elvis and I became real good friends. His music was great. He was a great entertainer and it was like doing my show. When we would go play Vegas for a month, and after we played for a month, I'd go back to my home in L.A. in Burbank and record sessions with all my clients and different artists. When we'd get through recording, I'm back on the road with Elvis. Then, also, during that time with Elvis I was also working with Emmylou Harris. We started back in '74, I think. But from 1969 up to 1977, I played on everything Elvis put out. I was on everything. Nine years with Elvis. It was a cooking band...

At one point, I heard somewhere you were so busy you began giving people Glen Campbell's number for work.

JB: Here's the deal. I met Glen Campbell when he first came to California. I was playing a club out there with a guy who was a stand-in for Elvis. He was actually a friend of Elvis,' named

Lance Legall. We had a blues band. When I wasn't out working with Ricky Nelson I'd go play the blues clubs. Glen came to town and one night he came to the club and sat in and played. He sounded real good and everybody really liked him. So, Glen and I became real good friends. I played on his first record for Capitol Records when he got his record deal. Ricky Nelson didn't want me to play on other recording sessions back in the early days when I was with him because he always said my sound was his sound and he didn't want me to go out and play with other artists. So when I went and did the TV show that was kind of an exit for me to go out and do a lot of studio work. I gave Glen my recording sessions. I would tell my clients who called me to call Glen. Of course, I always played on Johnny Burnett records and Roger Miller—my old buddies.

You played on various occasions with Hoyt Axton and Jerry Lee Lewis...

JB: Oh yeah, a lot of Hoyt Axton records. God, you name it. Unbelievable. A lot of Jerry Lee Lewis... "Rockin' My Life Away"...

You've played with Carl Perkins...

JB: Yeah, he's a good friend of mine, Carl.

Talk about playing with Merle Haggard.

JB: I played on a lot of Merle Haggard records. The first one I played on with Merle was "The Bottle Let Me Down." He wrote a song and he loved that style of playing. I played on Ricky Nelson records, the name of that record was "You Just Can't Quit." I did a guitar lick on it and it blew him away. So, he called me and said, 'Man, you got to play on my records.' I did "Working Man Blues." "Mama Tried"...

Since Macon, Georgia, is just south of here, did you ever get to play with Duane Allman?

JB: I never met Duane. They got real hot there for a while. I invited Dickey Betts up to the show. I hung out with him on his bus one night. He's a great guy.

You played on Everly Brothers records.

JB: Yeah man, two or three albums. They're good friends of mine. Phil Everly lived a few blocks around the corner from me in Burbank, California.

How many albums would you say you've played on?

JB: Oh, it's up in the thousands. It's unbelievable. I probably got a record of it all. I used to keep up with it pretty good in L.A. doing studio work, but I kind of got out of it when I started traveling a lot.

When did you move from Louisiana to California? Your home base is in Louisiana these days, right?

JB: I still have my home in Toluca Lake in Burbank—we always rent it out to nice people. We actually moved back here in 1988 or 1989, maybe '90.

I know there are so many, but what are some of your most vivid moments in your career?

JB: Oh, there's so many. I don't know. Of course, some of the moments we talked about, but I did an album with Mama Cass. I played on Mamas and Papas records. The Beach Boys—going up to Brian Wilson's house up in Bel Air, California and playing all weekend. The Monkees' Mike Nesmith did a three-day recording at RCA and he wanted us to come and stay the whole weekend. He didn't want us to go home. He said, 'Stay here. We've got catered food—we've got everything you need here.' We recorded for three days straight. Many, many great moments—especially with Elvis—like the satellite show *(Aloha from Hawaii)*; millions of people saw that one. I've done some great projects with Johnny Cash. I cut all Michael Parks' records with him. I played with Judy Collins, Buddy Emmons, Henry Mancini...

Charlie Rich...Del Shannon...Jimmie Dale Gilmore...

JB: I saw Del Shannon two weeks before he committed suicide. He was a good buddy of mine. Danny Gatton, he's another old buddy.

115

Let's talk about the James Burton International Guitar Festival which takes place at the end of March.

JB: It's something I've always wanted to do. I've always worked with so many great artists and I never really had time for myself. I was cutting records at Capitol Records with folks like Wanda Jackson, Wynn Stewart...you name it. It gets mind boggling to talk about it. I can't remember all of what I've played on. There's just so many sessions. Every now and then I'll talk to someone and they'll mention stuff I played on that I forgot about, but I've always wanted to do my own show. The first one was in 2005.

That was the year you began the Foundation?

JB: Yes, in 2005 we started, and we called it the James Burton International Guitar Festival. I realized that calling and inviting my friends to come like its 'James & Friends'. I invited all these wonderful people—they're all friends of mine. This is a perfect opportunity—I wanted to give something back to the kids because they're going to continue our music. I thought it would be great to donate money to the kids for musical instruments, music theory and do a scholarship. The first show was great, it worked out so well. We did it on my birthday weekend of August 20-21. My birthday is the 21st that's why we did it that weekend. That's when I displayed my new signature guitar. I'll have to send you one of these books, you're gonna want one. A good friend of mine, Steven Seagal, was invited and he said, 'Don't take my name off the list.' He was in Romania and couldn't make it. He was doing a movie. He did a great DVD for me to play at the show, which I did, and it was great. That year we had Johnny A, a great guitar player out of Boston—great friend of mine. Jeff "Skunk" Baxter with the Doobie Brothers, Matthew & Gunnar Nelson, Jeff Cook with Alabama, Johnny Rivers, Johnny Hiland—great guitar player—lives around the Nashville area—a knock-out player. Greg Koch came, he works for Fender, he's a great guitar player. He brought some good guys to play with—Roscoe and Jerry Donahue. We had Seymour Duncan...Sonny Landreth. This was the first part of the show. After a 15-20 minute intermission, then Eric Johnson and his band played, Doyle Dykes, Dr. John, Steve Cropper, Steve Wariner, Brad Paisley—it was a great line-up.

You are a guitar player that even guitar legends look up to for your tone & style...

JB: Well, I appreciate that. The great thing is this show is James & Friends. We all love each other. It's just a blessing from God. We're all so close, like a big family.

What are some your latest musical activities besides this benefit. Have you appeared on any recent records?

JB: I've been traveling over in Europe a lot. We do this 'Elvis on the Big Screen' show. It's all Elvis live with the original band—singers, everything. We go to Europe a lot. We just did a tour in Australia. We all got monitors—Ronnie, our drummer, wears earphones. We all have count-offs for the intros. It's a great show. It's just like Elvis being there. I just got a call from a friend of mine who wants me to go back over there in November and December—my wife said no, but he already booked the shows. Man, I need a vacation (laughs)!

So, with the festival coming at the end of March, I'm sure you're gearing up for that in a big way.

JB: We're very fortunate. We have some wonderful people on board and it's a lot of work putting a show like this together. We have so many wonderful volunteers and we still get calls from people who want to do everything they can. We don't make a dime from this. All the money goes to buy instruments for the kids. We just went to Shriner's Hospital and put over twenty guitars in that hospital. My first show that we did in '05 we made enough money to furnish over 600 guitars to the schools for the kids and actually buy a music program. We're looking to go to Saint Jude's and now there's a lot more—the other Shriner's Hospital wants to talk about us doing some stuff with them.

Talk about the movie filmed at your bar.

JB: Yeah, we gotta talk about that. We did a movie with Kevin Costner. Kevin came here to film *The Guardian*. After he filmed *The Guardian,* he stayed over in Shreveport and did another movie called *Mr. Brooks*. In *The Guardian* we actually used my club—The James Burton Rock & Roll Café—downtown. In the movie they called our place Maggie's Hanger. When you see the movie and you see the front of Maggie's Hanger—that's my club. They covered up Elvis, Ricky and Roy Orbison, and made it into a Coast Guard looking place—with the ropes and helicopters… anything that had to do with the coast guard. It's a great movie. You'll see me onstage with Bonnie Bramlett—she's such a great singer—and she played Maggie in the movie; she did some acting and sang a couple of songs and I played guitar with this band from Chicago.

Talk about your signature guitar series.

JB: I've been with Fender since the '50s—we go back to '56-'57. Leo Fender had been giving me guitars since then. Leo and I were real good friends. Me and Jimmy Bryant—a great guitar player—we're probably the first two guys to play the Fender Telecaster. Jimmy was the first and I was the second. After CBS bought Fender and then it went back to the Fenders, when CBS got out of it, I had a great idea—I thought it would be great to have a signature guitar. I wanted to have my own James Burton Telecaster, so I did, and I was playing a Paisley Pink one with Elvis—but I'd been talking to Fender for 20 years about doing a signature model. Well, when Dan Smith came to Fender when he left Yamaha, him and a guy named Roger Baumer, we started putting it together. We came up with the idea of what I wanted which was to do a three pickup telecaster with a paisley pattern. Not the pink paisley, but do my own design like the black & gold paisley design. We did a black and red paisley, and then I did one with a solid red and solid white pearl. Now, my newest guitar has flames on it with the paisley pattern—it's a pretty hot one. So, anyway that was my idea to do the signature models. They make and sell them everyday. I did one in blue, kinda like a blue flame. The pink one, even though it wasn't my signature guitar, became famous because I played it with Elvis. I played it with a lot of different artists. I'm really glad we did that.

How many guitars do you own?

JB: Oh, god. I don't know. I guess I should get a count. It's a lot. I don't really keep them at home. I keep them in music storage places. I only travel with one guitar and the most is two for a backup. I'm playing my black and red paisley now—the one with the flames—I'm playing that. It's a three-pickup, five-way switch with an overdrive.

What's been the main thread of solace throughout your career?

JB: I think the interesting thing is being active. Just staying busy, working with so many different artists is great. It's good for you.

What are your plans after this Foundation show?

JB: I'm going to Sweden and Copenhagen to do some shows with a band over there, the Cadillac band and some friends of mine. We'll do a few shows and I'll come back and do some shows. The rest of the year is unbelievable—back and forth to Europe.

When will you announce this year's line-up for the Foundation show?

JB: Probably in the next two weeks we're going to make some announcements of all the artists coming. The dates are March 30, 31, and April 1. When you see the line-up, you'll have to get down here for the show. Keep your fingers crossed, and say a prayer.

Thanks for taking the time to talk with me...

JB: Hey, you're welcome. It was my pleasure. You'll enjoy all the talent coming to the show. Look everything over, and if you need anything just give me a call. When you come, bring your camera because you'll want to get a picture of my statue and Elvis' statue right next to one another...

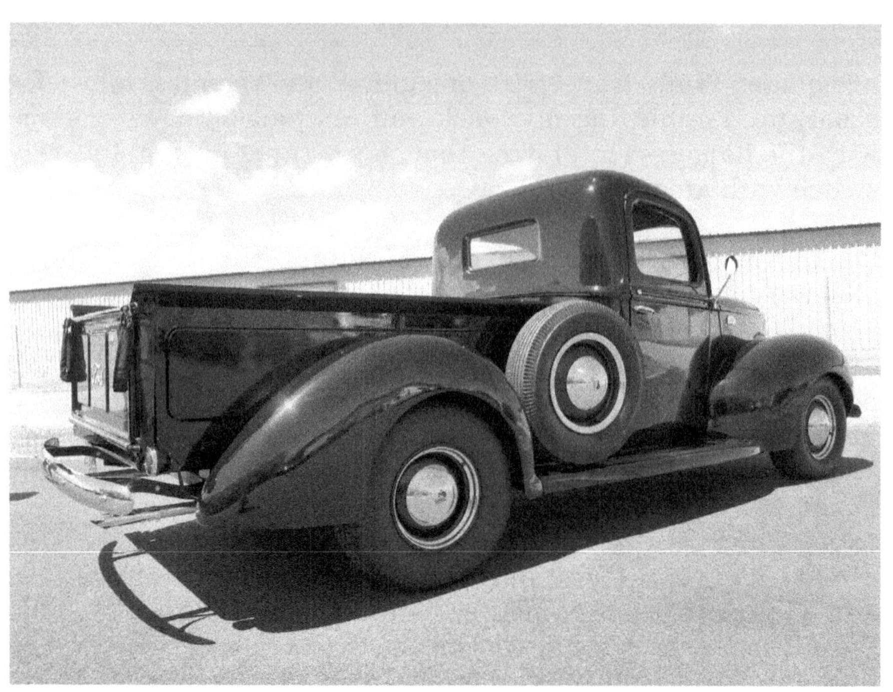

"1940 Ford"
St. Simons Island, Georgia

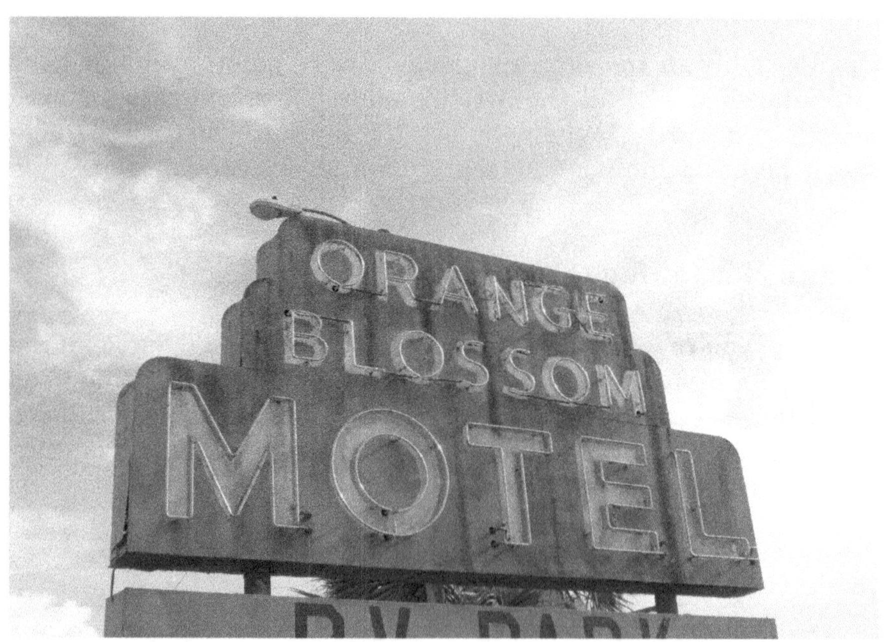

"Orange Blossom Motel"
Citra, Florida

Bloodkin's One Long Hustle

This story tells itself. An introduction in this case isn't really necessary. This article counted as one of the last longform articles I wrote for Swampland. In 2014, Bloodkin appeared on five spoken word pieces we recorded at Mark Neill's Valdosta, Georgia, studio for my fiction book The Local Stranger. The spoken word collection can be found on ITunes. I've read a few times with the band in the last couple of years. Bloodkin's catalogue provides compelling evidence they are first rate songwriters. In November 2016, Daniel Hutchens suffered a stroke. Luckily, he's on the mend.

"Every generation learns to dance/Across that floor they steal their moments..."

"Orchard"
- Daniel Hutchens

I'm standing in the Georgia Theatre in Athens, Georgia. I stare up at the high ceiling. The place is empty. Bloodkin, one of this city's long time bands, perform their sound check onstage. An accidental fire gutted the Theatre a few years back, and like a phoenix, this resurrected Athens music institution proves a fitting backdrop for the tonight's performance.

Between place, band, and time, tonight captures a moment of mystical convergence for me. I used to stand in this place often over 20 years ago when I attended the University of Georgia and a young Bloodkin was just picking up steam, but I have only been back to the "new" Georgia Theatre a few times since it was rebuilt. I was here last December for Bloodkin's tribute to the Rolling Stones called "Exile On Lumpkin Street" when Stones saxophonist Bobby Keys played with the band. In August, I attended the tribute to Michael Houser, the lead guitarist for Widespread Panic who died of pancreatic cancer in 2002. I'm here tonight for Bloodkin's release of their 5 CD box set *One Long Hustle* and a celebration of their 25 year anniversary.

The Bloodkin story is not for those weak at heart. In some ways, this is a story that is glorious to tell, but gritty to live—it's a story of survival. It's a tale about sacrificing everything for your art. The catch is the work must transcend time. There is no doubt the music of Bloodkin will endure. Daniel Hutchens and Eric Carter constructed a mighty songbook, and they are still out there writing songs and playing shows. They're originals. They haven't achieved global acclaim or riches, but they should...and hey, they're still writing, recording and performing, so you never know. They've played gigs all over the country—mean dive bars, festivals, living rooms, juke joints, porches, backyards, sold out coliseums and various other so-called stages. In one song, Danny summed it up when he sang in "Another Lost Son of Gypsy Rose Lee," "We earned some dead blue kisses and a ringing in our ears."

Bloodkin's new 5-CD box set—*One Long Hustle*—contains 88 song recordings covering the scope of their entire career. It's an amazing collection and testament to their music and how far they've come. It has not been easy. Everything is just as meaningful now as it ever was with no one is getting any younger. Knowing Bloodkin all these years—the friendship, the brotherhood, tragedies, heartbreaks, accomplishments, failures and, God knows, laughs—their story is really that of any hardworking hero.

I've served as a witness and comrade in Bloodkin's rock & roll crusade. We have been close friends throughout most of the years that *One Long Hustle* spans. Bloodkin is truly family to me. I was about 22 when I met them. I lived with Danny and Eric for four and a half years in the DaVille Apartments when the rock & roll atmosphere of Athens, Georgia, was at a zenith in the 90s. I've seen the dark underbelly of rock & roll, shady deals, rock & roll illusions and glory of Bloodkin first hand... things that cannot be forgotten.

I really haven't written in depth about the band in years because it's a fine line. Ernest Hemingway said you should never write about your friends because it softens one's ruthless perspective. You take it easy on them. So as a storyteller telling a tale of songsmiths, I have the luxury and the curse of blurring the lines between art and friendship after 20-plus years. In this great unknown, I intend to do just that...

"Voodoo can't touch us/ We're too fuckin' mean..."
"Birthmark"

Daniel Hutchens was eight when he met a six year old Eric Carter through a neighbor in Ripley, West Virginia. The boys connected immediately sharing an interest in comic books, baseball, and rock & roll music. A few years later their fascination in music expanded as Hutchens began playing guitar, and Carter started out on drums. "He was a good drummer—then his parents bought him a guitar, and the drums sort of went out the window," laughed Hutchens.

They were crazy motherfuckers with a wicked sense of humor, and they were deadly serious about songwriting and playing music. In their early days in West Virginia Eric and Danny began writing songs. I remember being told it was the younger Eric who actually turned Danny onto the Rolling Stones and Bob Dylan. Eventually, in their own way, Danny chose the Dylan's troubadour path as Eric seemed to align with Keith Richards' rock & roll lineage. They called themselves The Black Market Babies and before they were called Bloodkin, a name Danny took the from a short story by William Goyen titled "The Faces of Blood Kindred."

The insulated nature of their home state made our heroes restless. I remember them telling me stories of growing up in West Virginia and the classic social perspective locals always have of longhairs who read books. I understood having been to West Virginia all my life. My 99-year old grandmother still lives there. Still, they honed their chops in their home state. They already wrote almost a hundred songs before they left the state. They played shows around West Virginia including one in 1984 when Danny and Eric backed up beat poet Allen Ginsberg in 1984. Of course, Ginsberg was close friends with William Burroughs, Neal Cassady, and Jack Kerouac. Danny showed me a Xerox copy of the check once. Like Ginsberg's friend Kerouac, the road beckoned, and they knew they would have to leave town.

Compared to Huntington, West Virginia, Athens, Georgia, home of the University of Georgia, served as a lodestone of culture when our heroes arrived in 1986. Danny wrote in the *Long Hustle* liner notes this about their geographical move:

"We wound up in Athens mainly by chance—we'd heard about the music scene just like everyone else in America, and we thought we'd move there and give it a try. We never thought we'd wind up staying twenty-plus years. But Athens delivered on all the things Huntington hadn't, and then some. To this day, there's not a better place in the world to start up a rock & roll band. I'm not exactly sure what exactly makes it such a great place for music—I don't think anyone's ever really been sure. That's part of the magic; you can't put a finger on it."

Athens contained everything they wanted. Athens was hip—it wasn't West Virginia. It's a college town. There were plenty of bars and girls in Athens. They were having a blast. They began playing gigs and trying to get a solid lineup. They did the struggling musician thing, working jobs in restaurants such as Gus Garcia's and Harry Bissett's that didn't interfere with their gigs. Athens allowed them complete artistic freedom. In those days, the Bloodkin line-up settled into Danny and Eric backed with the rhythm section of Barry Sell and Aaron Phillips. Bloodkin also fell in with the right crowd—musically speaking. In those early Athens days Bloodkin kept company with bands like Widespread Panic, the Dashboard Saviors, Pylon, Flat Duo Jets, Vic Chesnutt, Kilkenny Cats, White Buffalo, Hayride and a long list of other musicians. They were already originals amid the crowd. Athens was deep with hippie roots and certainly alternative ones, but Bloodkin really were the hard-core rock & rollers. They established themselves with their Bob Dylan/Rolling Stones combination in that late 80s period when Athens was being defined worldwide as a hotbed of alternative rock & roll by bands like the B-52s and REM.

As a mean rock & roll band that didn't prescribe to hippie musical ethics or alternative pop aesthetics, Bloodkin honed their song craft during those early Athens days. They were deadly serious about doing things their way without selling out. As a testament to their vision, the Black Crowes' Chris Robinson asked Eric to join the band around this time. Eric declined to join that emerging Atlanta band--opting to stay with Danny. Foreshadowing Danny and Eric's longer story, the Crowes went onto sell 25 million albums, and Bloodkin took their first step towards operating on an obscure tightrope. Danny wrote about this first moment that captured the essence of Eric Carter in the *One Long Hustle* liner notes and how Eric's ethic proved to be destiny:

"Eric willfully turned his back on being a rock star, but he certainly could have achieved that goal if that's what he had wanted deep down—his options certainly weren't limited to me. He turned The Black Crowes down flat when they were starting out; he considered them too derivative. I told him to go earn some cash and gain some celebrity. But he was too pure, too proud, too stubborn. And those same qualities are part of what makes his guitar playing so great. He may have passed up the full blown fame and fortune, but he nailed the Art. As the recordings attest."

Our heroes were too young to be deterred as Bloodkin musical diamonds continued to shine in the Athens scene. Their songwriting efforts bore fruit when a few of their songs got into the hands of members from Widespread Panic whose regional touring popularity had them as the next group from Athens poised for flight behind R.E.M. Panic loved Bloodkin's music and championed the band from the start. In fact, they loved Bloodkin's music so much that they decided to record "Makes Sense To Me" on their breakthrough second album *Mom's Kitchen* in 1991. Things were looking up for Bloodkin. It seemed they began operating on the threshold of exposing a wider audience to their music. It was around this time that I met Bloodkin.

"I stole the kisses when the bride was young/A razor blade beneath my tongue."
"Paying What I Owe"

I grew up on St. Simons Island, Georgia. Like Danny and Eric in West Virginia, I started early on my writing journey from my coastal Georgia home. As a longtime literature and music nut, I discovered the writer Stanley Booth lived across the causeway in Brunswick, Georgia, when I was 17. Booth wrote the definitive book on The Rolling Stones called the *True Adventures of the Rolling Stones.* The book revolved around the 1969 Stones tour that ended with Altamont. Booth would turn out to be a significant musical and literary influence upon this writer.

Booth was born in Waycross, Georgia, but he lived in Memphis for 25 years. Always a hub for American music, Memphis became an essential rock & roll city during the 50s and 60s with Sun Records (Elvis, Jerry Lee Lewis, Sam Phillips), Stax Records (Otis Redding, Booker T and the MGs), and Hi Records (Al Green, Willie Mitchell). As a writer there, Booth knew Otis Redding, Gram Parsons, Steve Cropper, Duck Dunn, B.B. King, Furry Lewis, Duane Allman, Jim Dickinson, Jerry Wexler, Phineas Newborn, Charlie Freeman, Lash LaRue, Furry Lewis, Al Green, Carla Thomas and a long list of others. Booth served as a literary mentor to me giving me a hard dose of truth about what it meant to be a writer. Booth also exposed me to books and albums I would've never heard about if not for him and his vast collection. Booth was a serious frame of reference. His music and literary collection rivaled most small town libraries. I recorded hundreds of jazz, blues, country, and rock & roll albums at his house.

Today, my friend Griffin Bufkin serves as the proprietor of St Simons' famed Southern Soul Barbeque, but in our youth Griffin and I used to ride the school bus together. We shared a love for music back then. Years later, I made my friends cassettes of obscure music often culled from Stanley Booth's collection. Mixed tapes like these were gold as this was before CDs—much less Internet or cell phones. The tapes contained esoteric songs from known and unknown artists or undiscovered gems. Years later in 1990, Griffin was booking a bar in Valdosta, Georgia called Ashley Street Station. He had one of my tapes playing over the system when Bloodkin arrived to play the club. That particular tape happened to contain a Bob Dylan song called "God Knows" that Danny or Eric never heard. They asked Griffin who made the tape. Griffin told them about me, and a couple months later I met Danny at the Roadhouse Bar in Athens. I remember Danny giving me the cassettes called "Start From Scratch," which became Disc one on *One Long Hustle* box set. A few days later, I met Eric. The cosmic friendship began...

After high school, I lived in Valdosta, Georgia, for a few months before moving to Athens, Georgia, and eventually graduating from the University of Georgia. Around the same time period I met Bloodkin, I took a pilgrimage to Memphis with Stanley Booth when he was writing his second book called *Rythm Oil* (sic). Booth and I visited Sun Studios, the Peabody Motel and the Lamplighter Lounge. We saw the Dickinson Family (Jim with sons Luther & Cody, who later formed North Mississippi All-stars) perform together for the first time at the Memphis Blues Festival billed as Jim Dickinson & The Hardlycan Playboys.

From Booth I learned about the literary craft and some hardcore artistic business facts. Luckily, Booth's influence evaporated any illusion I operated on regarding artistic bliss. I learned there is a severe price to pay for your art. This knowledge would become invaluable as I began my time with Bloodkin as their friend, witness and creative compadre.

When I moved into the living room of their two-bedroom apartment in early 1992, it was a productive time for Hutchens/Carter. It seemed like they were writing new songs almost every day. I'd hear Danny in his bedroom playing the same song over and over. It got to the point where I learned the songs long before they were recorded or played live. Sometimes I'd fall in love with that original version before it would be changed around for its officially recording. I got Danny a job at Dial America, and we had fun with that for a while. We'd hang out, talk, play music, watch TV and cop a buzz. I carried a lot of guitar cases and amps for them in those days. I'd jump in the van and travel with them to shows. It was really all about fun as long as the craft was involved. All sorts of Athens music locals came by the apartment. Panic's Todd Nance and his wife were regulars along with Todd McBride, Mike Gibson, John Donley, Jackie Jasper, Greta Bettis and a cast of other local characters.

1992 was an interesting year. The Rodney King riots were exploding. Grunge was taking over. Widespread Panic were already on their way after Phil Walden chose the band to be the flagship group on his resurrected Capricorn Records. A Georgia music legend, Walden had managed Otis Redding and later Duane Allman. Walden created Capricorn Records as a vehicle for the Allman Brothers Band. Before its bankruptcy in 1979, Capricorn had been one of the most successful independent labels of the 70s and now Walden had his mind set on re-creating the Capricorn/Allman magic with Widespread Panic.

As Panic continued to achieve success on Capricorn, people were getting used to Bloodkin's association with Panic. Phil Walden facilitated Danny's songwriting with potential Capricorn artists such as Jerry Joseph. There was a high sense of anticipation in the air surrounding Bloodkin as they prepared to record an album of their own. Disc two on *One Long Hustle* is a good representation of material that was being played around the house during this time. Disc three on the box set contains some of my favorite songs that never saw the light of until now

such as "Misunderstand," "Devil Without A Disguise," "Hand
Right In Front of Your Face," and "Paying What I Owe."

As a staff producer for Capricorn Records in the 70s, Johnny
Sandlin recorded with the Allman Brothers, Cowboy, Eddie Hinton and a long list of others. In the early 90s, Sandlin became a
musical link between the two Capricorn eras since he was now
serving Widespread Panic's producer as well. Panic had always
championed Bloodkin's music and did everything they could to
expose Bloodkin's music to a wider audience, so it was decided that Bloodkin would record their debut album, *Good Luck
Charm,* at Johnny Sandlin's studio in Decatur, Alabama. In late
92, they began to travel to Decatur to record with legends—hardboiled professionals like the legendary bass/drum duo of David
Hood and Roger Hawkins from the Muscle Shoals Rhythm Section (aka "The Swampers"). Bloodkin's lineup now consisted of
Chris Barrineau on bass and Jack Dawson on the drums. This
core band would be featured on *Good Luck Charm.* Compositions for these sessions included old standbys like "Preacher-
man," "Quarter Tank of Gasoline," "Privilege," "Can't Get High,"
"Success Yourself" and "End of the Show". Every member of
Widespread Panic played on the album.

In the summer of 1993, Danny traveled to Europe to play bass
in Moe Tucker's Band. Tucker served as the drummer in the
Velvet Underground. Danny got a taste of how to travel with the
real rock & rollers. I remember he suffered heatstroke that summer somewhere in Europe while Eric and I held the fort down in
Athens. One evening I asked Eric to show me some things on the
guitar. It flashed an insight into his character, and his ability to
cut truthfully right to the matter. I already knew some chords,
and could pluck around but there were a few things I wanted
him to show me. After a lick, I mentioned, "I can't really use my
pinky finger that well." Eric looked at me and grinned with cigarette smoke obscuring his face, "Then you're not really serious,
are you?" Rest assured, I began practicing with the pinky finger.

I wrote the liner notes for *Good Luck Charm,* and when the
record was released in September of 93, I read some poetry at

the release party at the Nowhere Bar in Athens with the band playing behind me. That was the first public outing for what we called 'The Fandango Brothers." We's sit around, and they would play guitar around pieces of lyrics, poems or stories I'd written--much like they'd done with Allen Ginsberg. A lot of of personal ground was covered in these days. Everyone became familiar with the other's tendencies and proclivities. This was a serious song-crafting period that would last for several years. Widespread Panic recording the Bloodkin song "Henry Parsons Died" for their *Everyday* album allowed even more exposure for Bloodkin. It seemed rock & roll dreams were at their fingertips, and they were ascending...

"Good luck, I think you're gonna need it / When you cut out in the storm..."
"Wet Trombone Blues"

1994 was an interesting year. Now, Bloodkin had a record to promote. They hit the road with a vengeance. A taste of the rock & roll dream dawned. I began writing *The Bloodkin Chronicles*— which is now book length—and documented the daily notes I'd make when they would play shows, or even practice. The downtown Athens camaraderie really began to accelerate. There were a lot of late night activities. A lot of music was played. A lot of songs written. Mysteries and lore of the art reigned supreme around Apartment C6. We began recording Fandango Brothers numbers around the house more often during this time. The core of our friendship always revolved around the work of our heroes and how we tried to follow the old traditions. They were musicians who were well-read, and I was a writer who heard a lot of music and tried to tinker on instruments myself. Tastes of Panic excesses would spill over as far as exposure, friends and benefits. Danny did another tour with the Velvet Underground and operated as Lou Reed's guitar tech in Europe. Danny cultivated a friendship with Sterling Morrison that continued until Morrison's death.

Despite all the good vibes around the record, *Good Luck Charm* had been released on a label started by John Bell of Panic and Johnny Sandlin. Their faith in Bloodkin notwithstanding, these were the days before the Internet—no iTunes, music downloads, streaming music, YouTube, etc. It was essential the record labels have good distribution to get your record into record stores and then might to get your songs heard on the radio. The Sandlin/Bell label could not do this effectively, which hampered Bloodkin's progress. I once heard a story that Capricorn was pursuing Bloodkin, but somehow the deal didn't materialize. A deal like this could have made all the difference.

Still, things were going pretty well, and fun remained the main source of everything that was undertaken. Bloodkin still seemed poised for a wider exposure due to Panic's growing success. After Panic recorded "Henry Parsons Died" on their *Everyday* album, they covered Bloodkin's "Can't Get High" on the *Ain't Life Grand* CD making it a single. Unfortunately, the video for "Can't Get High"—the Bloodkin song Panic recorded on their *Ain't Life Grand* album—was never delivered to MTV by the Capricorn rep, which stunted the chance of massive television exposure. The song still hit #27 on the Billboard charts, but that setback seemed to linger in some strange way. Panic was beginning to soar, yet that was the first faint trace of Bloodkin falling between the cracks.

All along, I watched first-hand the types of people who warm their hands around a rock & roll band. Some folks have a legitimate reason to be there, and some don't. It's a sad case in some respects that attracts people like hustlers, crazy women, drunks & addicts, big talkers and sick egomaniacs with terminal identity crisis and no real form of self-expression other than ranting, raving or making a scene in a bar. They come and they go. Having said that, in Bloodkin's case—for the most part—the people around them I love more now than I did then. Lifelong connections I'll never forget, and I'm happy they continue.

"I live in a rotgut midnight town my home/Rotgut midnight town I call it home."
"Rotgut"

By 1995, things were getting a little crazy. We were all running pretty hard, and it was the earliest signs of threads wearing thin. In preparation for what would become their second album *Creeperweed,* Danny and Eric were playing and recording a lot of songs in our kitchen—Apartment C6. Tunes like "Black Jacket," "All Dolled Up," and "Asked For Water," were some of the tunes. But, there were so many songs I heard and loved that never saw the light of day—songs like "Absolutely Nothing"—until *One Long Hustle.* A lot of songs on the box set were written during this period.

Chris Barrineau played a vital role in the energy, music, and personal camaraderie during these days. We were all close. Our apartment became the rock & roll headquarters. All kinds of folks were coming over, and after awhile it got a little strange. We were flirting with dark shadows out on the fringe. Living together, we all became accustomed to the others phrases and expressions and soon we all adopted the same phrases so in some cases it might be difficult to ascertain who actually thought of it first.

Around this time, Danny and I wrote a song called "Early Grave." I wrote the verses and he wrote the chorus. Maybe one day the version we recorded will see the light of day. However, the *Creeperweed* recording sessions stand as a real glorious time of music, telepathy, magic and serendipity. Danny wrote this regarding *Creeperweed:*

"In 1995 we made *Creeperweed,* which wound up being one of my favorite recording experiences. I knew two things going in: One, I wanted to make a record that was more spontaneous and less "polished" than *Good Luck Charm;* as valuable an experience as working with Johnny Sandlin had been, *Good Luck Charm* is very much Johnny's vision of Bloodkin, and now I wanted to create something a little closer to the band's original heart. Two, I wanted the record to be made entirely with "acoustic" instruments. I use the quotes because some of the acoustic instruments were variously equipped with electronic pick-ups and plugged into amplifiers, or otherwise affected during the recording process. But I wanted the flavor of those basic instruments: acoustic guitars, dobro, acoustic bass (not upright, but just Chris Barrineau's hollow-body acoustic bass guitar), drums, harmonica, fiddle. The only "electric" instrument used was John Keane's pedal steel. I heard this record in my head before we ever made it; of all our records this was was definitely my baby. It was no easy task to convince Eric Carter not to play any electric guitar on an entire record."

The album was recorded mostly at Doug Stanley's house, but Widespread Panic's old rehearsal space served as the magical location where they recorded the stellar instrumental "Mercy Train To Bogart" in one take. They stripped their sound down to acoustic instruments. Danny played guitar with his back to me. Todd Nance sat on Danny's right. Eric was sitting to Todd's right. Mike Gibson was on Eric's right. Barrineau to his right—all in a circle. I sat at the empty keyboard seat. And under those circumstances, it may stand as one of my most memorable musical moments. There was a weird light in the dimmed place that night—king of a blue-ish green aura. Three minutes of pure timeless reflection for your humble scribe. After these sessions, the rock & roll habits became more evident on everyone...and things became a bit darker and weirder.

During this time I met Patterson Hood. His father David Hood, the Muscle Shoals Rhythm Section bassist who had also played bass on *Good Luck Charm,* remains a legend having playing on records by Aretha Franklin to Bob Dylan to Traffic. Patterson was the sound guy at the High Hat Blues Club. He had not formed the Drive By Truckers yet, but his emergence on the Bloodkin radar during this time provides another glimpse of foreshadowing. Hood would later play an important role in the band's history, but it would take more than a decade.

Bloodkin remained the undiscovered Athens band. *Creeperweed* was released in September of 1996, but it had the same "lack of a record label" problem as *Good Luck Charm.* Still, the evening Todd served as the drummer when they played the release party at the High Hat Blues Club that counts as one of my favorite Bloodkin shows of all time. The show represented a zenith musically for me because the performance captured the full force of their songwriting and the raw power of these four guys playing music. Straight to the source. Close to the bone. There were many, many great memories to come, but that night was pure magic.

I began to feel things were changing a little bit. By October of 95, after the *Creeperweed* sessions, I could feel the shifting sands of time descending on everyone. I was getting antsy...a little nervous. People close to us began overdosing and going to jail. I began spending more time in Atlanta, and by the fall of 96 I moved out of the DaVille Apartments. I felt a foreboding sense of change that maybe the band didn't during that time after the *Creeperweed* sessions. It was the end of an era for me...

"That's what happens when a war is on
You keep your gun clean if you ever wanna see home."
"Lifer"

With a renewed sense of rock and roll vigor, the band released *Out of State Plates* in 1997. Danny and Eric had cultivated a friendship with Athens sound guru David Barbe. Soon, they began making plans to record at Barbe's Transduction Studios. Today, Barbe serves as the Drive-By Truckers producer dating back to their breakthrough *Southern Rock Opera* in 2001 and also heads the University of Georgia's Music Business Program. Back then, Barbe was a young engineer/producer who had played bass in the band Sugar. Barbe also worked with the other Athens sound guru, John Keane who recorded various Widespread Panic albums. Barbe and Bloodkin both shared the need to get back to rock and roll basics that defined *Out of State Plates*. Songs like "Lifer", "Taboo" and "Tennessee Williams" rotated for some time during live shows. Danny wrote "Tennessee Williams" with bassist Chris Barrineau. Older songs such as "Yeah" and "Wet Trombone Blues" emerged on this recording.

The sense of rebirth also came from the group's new manager, Zac Weil. Zac was a champion for Bloodkin. He was an accessory to whatever endeavor was transpiring at the time. *Out of State Plates*—once again—suffered from a lack of record label, but Zac was not deterred. He set up some gigs in Colorado playing with Gov't Mule. He looked for anything and everything to keep the creative momentum based on *Out of State Plates* moving onward. Zac was a great figure in the Bloodkin camp. He championed their music, but at the same time he enabled and shared some of their self-destructive habits.

In 1998, Widespread Panic played a free show in Athens, Georgia. Widespread was covering at least a half dozen Bloodkin songs by now. Bloodkin played the after show party along with Gov't Mule at the 40 Watt. Another glorious evening. Panic earned the Guinness Book of World Record for attendance of an outdoor CD release party for *Light Fuse Get Away* when 100,000 people showed up in the streets of Athens. The next weekend Danny served as one of the groomsmen in my wedding. This was an intense time of transition for the band. Barrineau departed the group. I was living in Atlanta and felt a little distant from it all. Panic had now reached a level of success that transcended the musical community of Athens. Eerie realities loomed. There was a changing of the guards.

Things began to fray a bit in 1999. The group was wearing and tearing and a slow burn of deterioration emanated this era. Disillusion. Panic reached a level where their success kept them on the road, and they were rarely home in Athens.

I was now married and working a job in Atlanta while writing for various magazines such as *Hittin the Note, An Honest Tune, PASTE, The Woody Creeker, Gritz* and the *Georgia Music Magazine.* Zac began to become a little lost. He came to grips with certain rock & roll illusions and realities. I remember him telling me he was moving to North Carolina to pursue a computer job. He died a week later in April of 2000. I was at his house the morning the paramedics carried him away. I wrote an obituary for him.

In the fall of 2000, Bloodkin recorded a show at Smith's Olde Bar in Atlanta that later emerged as an out of print record called *All Dolled Up.* I read the introduction to this album onstage, and wrote the liner notes. Change again floated in the air like smoke, but we were all still here. My daughter was born the next month. *All Dolled Up* really captures the live spirit of Bloodkin, but it soon went out of print. It was another example of a dirty deal regarding a label that pandered to the jam band scene, and Bloodkin became caught in the proverbial record company legal hassle. Professional frustration seemed to begin appearing at every turn. Danny explained the situation in liner notes for *One Long Hustle:*

"...We recorded and released a live CD called *All Dolled Up,* on Phoenix Records out of New York. We recorded the show on September 1, 2000 at Smith's Olde Bar in Atlanta, and the disc came out a few months later, in December. It sold really well by our standards for the first 3 or 4 months, until the record company imploded in a shady haze of legal infighting and greed and bullshit. We were handcuffed from even selling records at shows--that's when we fully and finally decided to avoid "real" record companies as much as possible."

On this live CD they covered a song I turned them onto years before—Eddie Hinton's "Breakfast In Bed"—as well as memorable versions of "Payin What I Owe," "Who Do You Belong To," and "End of the Show." Bill McKay played keyboards on this album. It's an out-of-print gem in the Bloodkin discography. Dark clouds gathered for the new millennium.

"The truth is the truth/ But the law is the law..."
  "Taboo"

Zac's death sent them reeling. Times changed. To me, the band really got back into songwriting at this point. The songcraft during this period retained a little more heart and wisdom. No smoke & mirrors. A new maturity emerged. Danny was getting out there a little bit more now. Chris Barrineau left the band and Paul "Crumpy" Edwards filled in on bass. David Barbe served as a serious anchor for the band during this time. The band was working on *Community Gospel Rehab* songs while Zac was still alive.

I remember Danny gave me a cassette of these songs before they were mastered. The rough piano version of "Limb From Limb" still almost sounds good to me as the final rendition. And Danny changed a line to the original tune, which I still hear when I listen to the album track. These songs were recorded from October of 1999-April 2001. There was a bit of strangeness going on within the band, but by this time I was gone. I didn't see how it was going on a daily basis anymore, but I was no fool. The road began to grind on them a little bit. Years and years of traveling to bars to play until 3 am, load equipment, get paid, stay coherent and then go sleep in a hotel and drive another 300 miles a few hours later to the next gig wears one down year after year. It's not for the weak of heart...or those who are in it for the wrong reasons.

I consider *Community Gospel Rehab* as a formidable album. Most bands can't write songs like this at all their entire careers. William Tonks played a strong musical role in these songs. He's an expert of the highest order regarding any instrument with strings. "Jazz Funeral", "Love's Getting Older" and "Limb From Limb" rank as some of their finest material. A maturity aged with the music. "Kingly" was written for Zac. These were all basically newer songs. Maybe only one or two of these songs linger from the Apartment C6 days. An eerie darkness from festering habits stained all actions. As Bob Dylan sang, you could "Smell the tail of the dragon..."

•• •••

With Zac went the last shot at the brass ring. Now the brass ring had to be redefined on Bloodkin's terms. They had to keep making records even if no one could find them to buy outside of Athens record stores and at the merch table of a Bloodkin show. They began recording *Raving Beauties* at Widespread Panic bassist Dave Schools' home studio in Athens. Onward. I remember standing next to Danny in the vocal booth of a studio setup in Schools' house when he sang "Cheap Speed," which was an older song from what I remember. *Raving Beauties* almost seemed like they were on autopilot. As far as rock bands go—for any other band--this was a solid record; for Bloodkin it sounded like they were sleepwalking to me.

Danny provided a clear glimpse of the band's state of affairs around this era when he revealed in the *One Long Hustle* liner notes:

"During the making of *Raving Beauties* we accepted help from several investors, and by the end of the day we were nearly $75,000 in debt. Before the record was released, Crumpy told us he wouldn't be able to go on tour except regionally on weekends. There were no hard feelings, he just couldn't do it. What really bothered me was that Eric said, 'Well, who cares, we just won't tour," although we were already signed with a booking agency and the tour was halfway booked. We called up the agency, said, "Sorry," and canceled, wrecking our prospects for working with any professional booking agency for years to come."

Trouble brewed in the Bloodkin camp.

After September 11, 2001—as we all know—history shifted. Changed. Everything on a global level felt different. Complicated times. Welcome to the 21st century...

"The preacher at my church told me you better not fuck crazy women / You're pissing away your passion."
"Limb From Limb"

In 2002, Widespread Panic's lead guitarist Michael Houser was diagnosed with pancreatic cancer. A weird melancholy fell on anyone around the Bloodkin, Widespread Panic or the Athens music community. Michael Houser's *Door Harp* resonated during these times. Danny was asked to sing on Houser's album *Sandbox* before his death. These melancholy sessions were recorded at David Barbe's. Danny started living in Atlanta around this time, and his songs took on another expansive quality. Time changes everyone, and knowing them as long as I did...they remained the same, but I could see things affecting them like they affect us all...heartbreak, death, lack of funds, boredom, frustration, demons and betrayal.

Bloodkin knew what it felt like to have other people listen to your music, and act like they weren't...or say they were and weren't. We all knew they were great songwriters...but when you look out there at some of the bands people were just throwing their money at, it was just disheartening. But, there's the way it ought to be, and there's the way it is. Being an artist in the old days meant you don't receive accolades for your trade. Only in the rock & roll era of the Beatles, Stones and Dylan did artists get put on a pedestal and paid. Art, like any other commodity, you have to put it out there. For most artists, death is a great career move. People can choose to like it or not. No one is above criticism. Everyone is a music fan. Or everyone has a journal they write in. Anyone is a music fan with strong opinions regarding what's good and what's not. But that's like watching a football game on TV, and saying you could have completed that pass. Panic's bassist, Dave Schools, once told me regarding being an artist and catching attitude from some drunk, civilian or redneck, "There's always one asshole in the back of the room with his arms crossed, saying 'I could do that.' Well you know what? You ain't doin' it..."

Panic's Michael Houser died in August of 2002. Everything seemed surreal. Distance between everything and everyone seemed to reign. As aforementioned, Danny was living in Atlanta where Bloodkin was playing more gigs in the city. Since I also lived in Atlanta we spent a good bit of time together during this time when we could. Danny was writing songs for what was to become *Lesser* that came out in 2003. This Daniel Hutchens solo record contains several of my favorite songs of his like "Shebang Delang," "Orchard," and "Modigliani Eyes." The entire mood of this collection of songs still resonates. I remember reading Danny the liner notes I wrote to *Lesser* to him at his girlfriend's house while he was laying in the bed. The sun was already down as I read.

Later, Danny made another solo record called *Lovesongs For Losers*. Tension emanated in the Bloodkin camp during this time. Fragmentation. The next couple of years pervaded a reflection, reconstruction, tension and dealing with the way things were at the time. Everyone was strung out. Burned out. I remember Eric becoming reluctant to hit the road around this time. I was glad to be distant from the day to day grind so they were always happy to see me when I'd come to visit because dissent on all sides was in the air between them. The wheel grinded on into the gloomy unknown.

"We kept stripping and singing Hoping the money'd roll in/I guess I'd do it all again."
—*"Another Lost Son of Gypsy Rose Lee"*

By 2004-2005, a new dynamic rotated for everyone involved. David Nickel joined the group on bass. Danny wrote of Bloodkin during this time: "We were like a mobile psychiatric ward, pharmacy and rock n roll band all rolled into one." A new political, personal and artistic vibration filled the air. They returned to David Barbe's studio to record *Last Night Out*. Two of their greatest songs are on this album—"Another Lost Son of Gypsy Rose Lee" and the title track retain a real spook. Patterson Hood had a quote about this album sounding like the ended of the road for Bloodkin, and it took him to "a place he didn't want to spend too much time."

By this time, the Drive By Truckers—now a high profile Athens band—commanded a respect in the industry. They were certainly the darlings of the underground press. The Truckers seemed to fill the void or took the path Bloodkin paved for years to a much more significant destination. Although the Widespread Panic/Bloodkin connection remains important in both bands' histories, their connection comes through songs and songwriting. Bloodkin as a band were never a perfect fit in Panic's jam band audience. Patterson and the Truckers drove straight into the indie world and built a home there for blue-collar southern rock bands that had strong punk leanings.

I had found a new home of my own in 2006 as editor and contributor to Swampland.com. Amongst my music writings for the site, I saw the rise of the Truckers and how their audience differed from Widespread Panic's. I'd watched Luther and Cody

Dickinson form the North Mississippi Allstars, a band that consistently provides a gritty dose of rock and blues, but like Bloodkin, they were slightly out of place in the jam world of Panic. I wrote about all these bands and more, but I saw a purpose in Patterson and the Truckers that could not be denied. It reminded me of Bloodkin, and I could not help be but impressed with their tenacity.

As the Truckers' built their audience, Bloodkin could only watch from the sidelines. Their records and shows seemed to come and go without anyone really paying attention even though the same Athens heavies such as Todd Nance, John Neff, David Barbe, Jon Mills and William Tonks couldn't wait to play on their songs. The next several years brought ruthless change, hard core realizations and neglect an artist feels when he's been doing something a long time, but it doesn't pay off. They hit a wall. Torn & frayed, indeed. In a mysterious turn of events, Danny got married and eventually started a family. The Saturday morning Danny got married—we were in his Memphis hotel, dressed for the wedding at Graceland—I told him I was getting a divorce. Those are not the best circumstances to inform a person of such events unless you were truly brothers. Danny and I switched roles, and Eric continued to drift farther into the sea of full-blown alcoholism. Things were not the way they used to be anymore. Fallout & aftermath was all around. By 2007-2008, you could feel everyone was operating in uncharted territory.

In 2008, the band could no longer remain silent regarding Eric's drinking. He coughed up blood one night in Jacksonville, Florida, and they basically said "you've got to get help cos you're scaring the fuck out of us." With Danny married and doing solo albums and Eric facing rehab, Bloodkin found its rock bottom.

"You got nothing left to show / Cos you're good time is over and done..."
— *"Good Time Over And Done"*

Eric successfully completed rehabilitation program and hasn't touched booze in four years. Like the most hopeful rehab stories, Eric's sobriety created a new focus. He executed un-wrecking courage when handling late night scenes, dealing with drunks and playing music without taking one sip or one snort. He was forced to return to the scene of the crime, so to speak, to carry on his trade. He did it. The Bloodkin duo had new lives—Eric in his sobriety and Danny in the grounding power of his family. They were ready to record new songs.

Much had changed for Bloodkin since *Last Night Out*, and for the first time since the early days the changes were largely positive. Not only did the band have a renewed sense of purpose, the Internet leveled the playing fields for bands that didn't have a big record label in their corner. Bloodkin's music that had previously only been available to a select few could be found in a couple of computer clicks. Also, a new generation of southern-tinged rock bands led by the Drive-by Truckers had assembled a powerful audience ready made for our heroes. When they went to David Barbe's to record "Baby They Told Us We Would Rise Again," there was a finally plan in place.

With a strong push from the Truckers' camp to their formidable fanbase and press following, Bloodkin's *Baby They Told Us We Would Rise Again* earned glowing reviews in mainline magazines like Rolling Stone and important indie music sites like Pitchfork. The Truckers had lent their musical talents on the record and Patterson wrote extensive liner notes about Bloodkin's journey that put the band into context for a new generation of fans and listeners. He penned this for the *Rise Again* album liner notes:

"...I've seen Bloodkin go through many changes. They have endured trials and tribulations that would have ended most bands. I've played with my partner for 23 years but Danny and Eric actually have a couple of years on us. They moved down to Athens, Georgia together from West Virginia with then and now drummer Aaron Phillips) years before I moved here and have remained a fixture through thick and thin. Honestly, mostly thin, as they have never received anywhere near the recognition they deserved. Ever. Sometimes the blame could be placed squarely at their feet, as like most artists they can and have been sometimes their own worst enemy. Some of their trials were thrust upon them but through them all they have persevered.

I have to admit that it was somewhat irritating to someone like me who has spent over twenty plus years in close proximity to the band and their work to now see them begin receiving the credit they long ago deserved. Yet, it made me proud of them to see the hipsters finally acknowledging their talent. David Barbe stands as an integral player in the Bloodkin saga during the later years. In some ways, he kept the band together by overseeing their recordings."

Baby They Told Us We Would Rise Again unleashed newer songs like "The Viper," "Ghost Runner," and "My Name Is Alice," while "Wait Forever" emerged from two decades before. After all the years of playing they finally started to get a little recognition and respect. They now possessed a formidable catalog they could rely on, and keep things interesting. Eric's playing was sharper than ever. In 2010, Danny co-wrote another song with Widespread Panic called "True To My Nature" on the album *Dirty Side Down*. Like old hookers, politicians, and buildings, they were respectable now.

······

Epilogue

"Two years later Lancaster was rolling through Montgomery on a Sunday/He couldn't find no black place to eat/So he made a picnic down by the river/Ran into some Baptists washing each other's feet."
"God's Bar"

The band worked on *One Long Hustle* for about seven years. It's a 5-CD collection of their first 25 years as a group. The box set is a handsome package that was designed by the same lady who designed several of the Atlanta label Dust To Digital's timeless releases. Most of the music on the box set is being heard for the first time, but it also serves as a musical guide for the entire Bloodkin history. I can only hope that the new fans seek this collection out and then follow the trail back to the entire catalog. *The One Long Hustle* box set really puts things in perspective. Bloodkin's work aged like wine. They've lived all the rock & roll craziness and patrolled the edge so long that now they can just play and deliver songs. They are indeed seasoned players. The core band now, Danny, Eric, William Tonks, Jon Mills, Eric Martinez and Aaron Phillips all stand as experienced veterans.

Bloodkin just keeps working. Their story proves, no matter what you do—there's no glory in the work itself but only the results. All the hours when no one was around or cared about what songs they were writing did not deter them. It's not pretty and it's not easy to do what they've done—just from a songwriting perspective—much less all the other things to keep a band together 25 years when the money is not rolling in. Rock & Roll is not proving you're a star, getting up in people's faces in bar and trying to convince everyone you're a badass...it's the music. Just like people who believe getting drunk or high and hang out in bars makes them an artist. It's not an act or an image...especially in these days. The music industry isn't about rock stars anymore...it's about those who see it as a trade. Bloodkin falls in a tradition with musicians like Muddy Waters, Townes Van Zandt, Blind Willie McTell and Hank Williams. Bloodkin prove to be a formidable rock & roll group, and their songs transcend time.

In everything I write I always try to leave myself out of it. In the case of Bloodkin, I cannot tell their story without telling my own. We all know the other's wisdom, triumphs, obstacles and wherewithal, but at the end of the day, I know they appreciate my work and soul no matter what. Likewise. Since Danny got married and I got divorced six years ago, we've entered into a phase where the Hutchens home is a sanctuary to me. The old friendship ties through the years proved life saving to me.

During the time Widespread Panic asked me to write their induction into The Georgia Music Hall of Fame, drummer Todd Nance, a long time friend of Bloodkin, told me how I fit into the scheme of things around Athens. It was humbling for me as he explained his perspective on my writing and the way it emanated from my brotherhood with Bloodkin:

"James, you've been writing about Athens music as long as I've been here. You've got to see a whole generation of Athens bands come up. You've been around long enough where you can see the children of musicians you grew up with playing music. When you read some of these music publications you can tell the writers have about five years of history. Your depth goes way beyond that. Your background is very heavy.... You can't fake your perspective. Or try to write like you."

In December of 2011, sax player Bobby Keys played a show with Bloodkin at the newly rebuilt Georgia Theatre. Keys played with the Rolling Stones, The Beatles, Leon Russell and a long list of others. The evening was titled "Exile On Lumpkin Street," a play upon the Stones' greatest album and the address of the Theatre. It's no accident the Stones longtime horn player gravitated to Bloodkin. Bloodkin know the Stones material as well as anyone and have certainly lived as close to the same edge where the Stones lived during *Exile On Main Street.*

The rehearsal the evening before the show was even more triumphant for me than the actual show. To see Bobby Keys aggressively leading the band through rehearsal in Widespread Panic's practice space was unforgettable. At one point, Danny and I were outside talking and I heard the band playing that jam part of the Stones song "Can't You Hear Me Knockin'"—where Bobby plays that memorable horn part—and I said to Danny (who is playing with the Stones longtime horn player!) like a

•• • •••

kid—who has heard *Sticky Fingers* thousands of times—"Man, I gotta go hear this," and I ran back inside to stand eight feet away from Bobby Keys playing one of his trademark licks. I was quite proud of them...

In liner notes for *One Long Hustle,* Danny wrote about his songwriting after all these years:

"All the heartbreak and horseplay in the Bloodkin songs—the erotically supernatural crazy women, the drugs n booze—these are all just details in the larger story. They're characters in the play. They're vehicles of temptation—and I rode those vehicles hard. It was all experimentation, testing the envelope, fishing for glimpses of truth. The songs were really just gospel songs, documenting the search, the pitfalls, seductions, distractions and detours, the questions that always led to more and more questions."

This all brings things back to the present, December 2012. All the folks begin to drift into the Georgia Theatre now for the *One Long Hustle* and 25th Anniversary show. Everyone came to pay his respects. A documentary about the band is currently underway. More recordings and gigs linger on the horizon. It all revolves around Eric's guitar sound, and I can say that Danny Hutchens stands as this generation's best barroom rock & roll poet even when there are almost 20 people on the stage. It was a glorious night and an enduring sound that swirled around that building.

Many changes transpire in 25 years. As writers, musicians, roommates and soul brothers we've seen bad business deals, death, marriage, divorce, near deaths, addictions, depressions, shallow loyalty, jailings, behind-the-curtain secrets, heroic fun, unfiltered hilarity, professional & personal peaks & valleys, betrayals, unforgettable influences and glorious work in various forms. In the end, we're all still here forging onward. As friends, we're more like family now; Danny and his wife Kristy provide a home for me when I visit Athens. As artists, Bloodkin's survival shines more than a glimmer of hope for me—or anyone—to pursue art without compromise.

Walking out of the Georgia Theatre that December night with my ears ringing, I felt like I'd been baptized with redemption...

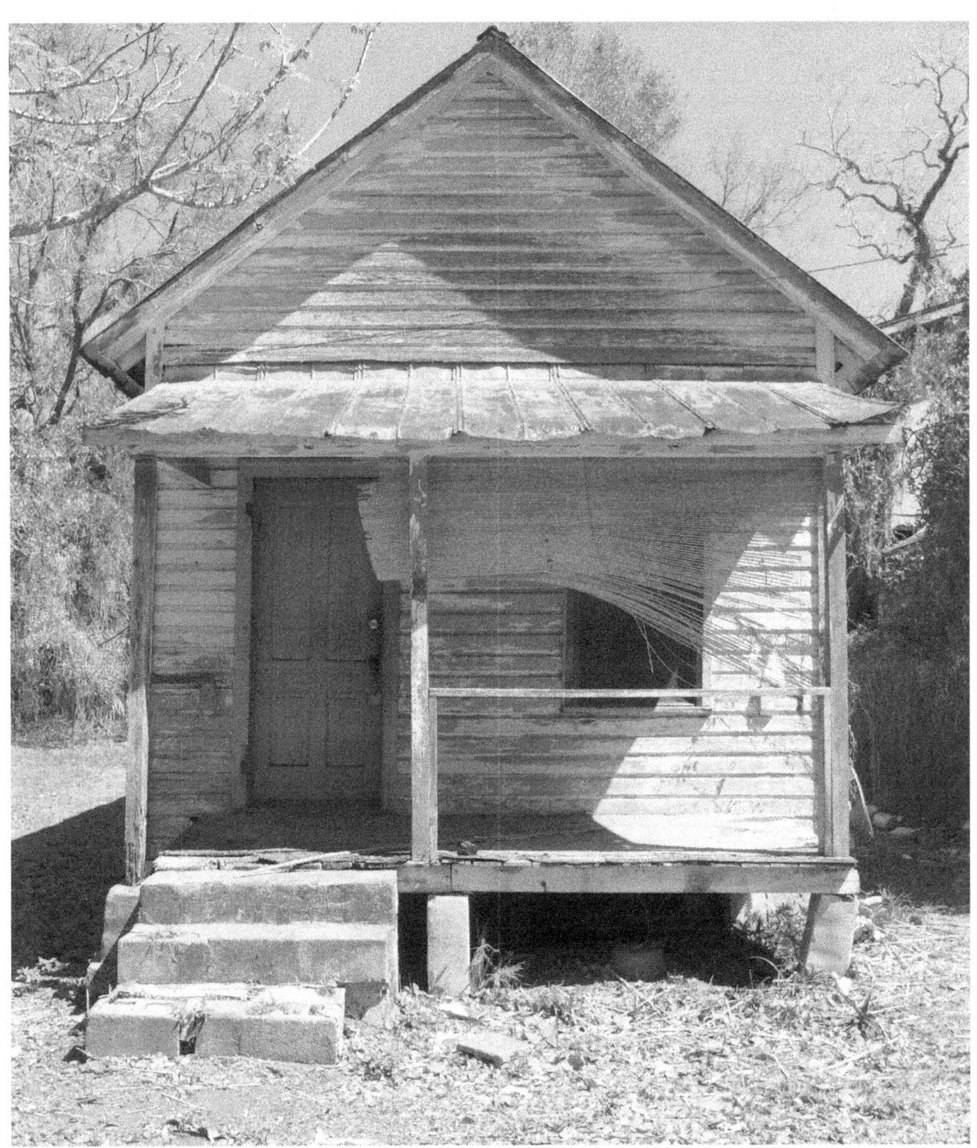

"Georgia Shotgun Shack"

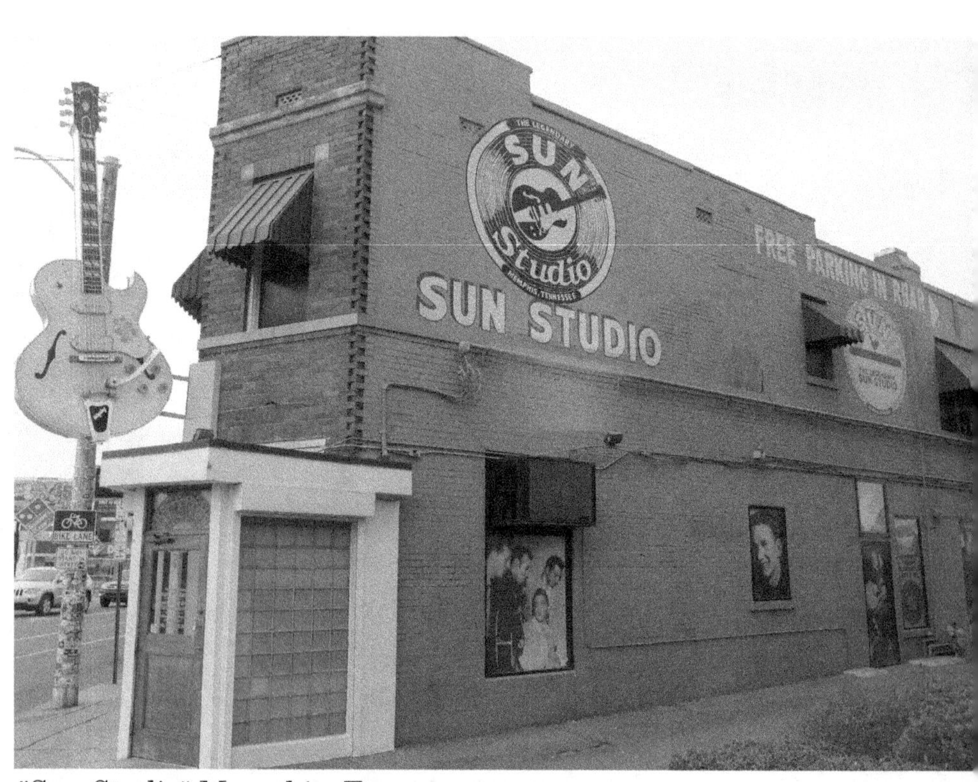

"Sun Studio" Memphis, Tennessee

••••••

Clarence Fountain Interview: Higher Ground

In 2002, I crossed paths with the Blind Boys of Alabama's Clarence Fountain. The group just released Higher Ground as they enjoyed a new wave of music fans after singing for years in obscurity like many artists in this collection. The Blind Boys retain their own blend of blues, gospel and soul music in their style. Mr. Fountain proved soulful during this interview, and his words still make sense thirteen years later. This interview preserves why the Blind Boys of Alabama exist as an American music treasure.

On September 3, 2002, Real World Records released the new Blind Boys of Alabama album titled *Higher Ground,* featuring Robert Randolph & the Family Band as the backing musicians. This gospel collection covers traditional and original songs, as well as compositions by Jimmy Cliff, Aretha Franklin, Stevie Wonder, Funkadelic, Curtis Mayfield, Prince and Ben Harper, who sings on three of the album's songs.

This soulful CD may land the Blind Boys another Grammy award, but if nothing else, *Higher Ground* elevates modern gospel and spiritual music to another level. This summer I spoke to Clarence Foundation of the Blind Boys about *Higher Ground.*

You grew up in Alabama, right?

CF: Yes, old Alabama.

What were some of your musical influences growing up?

CF: Well, we always listened to music that was out at the time, whatever it was—a hit in gospel or rhythm and blues at the time. B.B. King had out "3 O'clock In the Morning," and that was a big record of the day. It was a big hit for him. That record was out in, oh let me think, 1952 or 1953. He had out one of those blues hits, and that's really one of the ones that put him on the top. Everything we could hear we listened to because it made us better to know how to get out and sing to the public. We were able to concentrate on what was going on in that day or year. Rock and roll was just beginning to get big and it made us aware of what was going on, so we went out and wrote a couple of tunes because we were on Specialty Records out in California—a very good label. They were big time in gospel, but they also had Little Richard and later Sam Cooke, the Blind Boys, Soul Stirrers, the Gospel Harmonators, and all those good gospel groups. They made a pile of hits for Little Richard. Art Rupe was a smart man.

I'm sure you lived a very religious upbringing. Talk about how it influenced your music and life.

CF: My mother and father were in the Methodist church. My daddy played a big role in the church. They had a pretty good choir so I used to chime in with them; even when I was too little to sing I was getting my music thing down. In 1944 we started to hit the road. I was eleven then, and I was tired of school. The Talladega School for the Blind had twelve grades, but the school had been standing since the 1880s.

The Talladega School for the Blind was where you met the rest of the group?

CF: That's right. 1939. Me, Jimmy Carter, George Scott, a guy named Johnny Fields, Tommy Gilmore—all these guys were the guys who would go to sing. We used to listen to gospel music every day. The Golden Gate Quartet was a big thing in that day. They were already in society singing to the masses of people.

Charles Driebe, the Blind Boys manager, told me last week in Europe someone asked you to inform them of the first album you ever bought, and you told them only 78s existed in those days, because there were no albums. That goes back a ways.

CF: Right. Well, you know back in those days it was only 78s because albums hadn't been discovered yet.

It appears the Blind Boys' message has always remained the same—to spread the gospel. You guys never sold out for big money, which seems to be even more difficult in

those days. Y'all remained true to the spirituality of the music, even with hits like "Oh Lord Stand By Me" and "I Can See Everybody's Mother, But I Can't See Mine."

CF: Yes, our intention has always been the same. It's interesting for you to be aware of that because, you see, we wanted to sing gospel and they wanted us to sing the blues. We were there when Sam Cooke made his big rock and roll debut. We were there when the man gave him his contract because he gave us one too, if we wanted it, but we didn't want to do it because we weren't a rock and roll product. When Ray Charles came along and started the ball rolling then in the early 60s we went to California and we had a chance to really go places because they wanted a contrast between Ray and I. they thought that contrast would be a good thing so there would be competition. I didn't want that, so I didn't do it.

Competition between you and Ray Charles shouldn't have been necessary.

CF: Well, see, they figured they could take some money and say, 'Here boy, take this money.' That's what they wanted us to do, but they figured out I wasn't that kind of guy. It was much harder then. They knew you didn't want to turn money down.

They figured you'd take the bait, forcing you to feel as if you were just lucky to get offered a deal.

CF: James, you got that exactly right. Our turnaround happened when I met this guy that wrote a play and took it overseas, and it was not successful, so what he did was he came and wanted to talk to our guitar player who was playing with the Blind Boys. He introduced us to this guy. So we sat down—me, Morgan Freeman, and a couple guys—and we put music to this play called *The Gospel at Colonus.* What they did was take it to Broadway, and then from that we were able to launch our career. We didn't really know how big we were overseas. Between 1983 and 1988 when *Colonus* went to Broadway, we did a lot of plays in Atlanta, Texas, Chicago, and all these places. We were singing in the play. I did a little acting with Morgan—but when this play came out it was an instant hit and we got a chance to sing to the masses of people. That enabled us to get an agency out in California and then we started going all over the world.

You guys won an Obie Award for *The Gospel at Colonus*.

CF: Yeah, that's pretty good. I think it would have been much better, but the producer of the play offended some guys on Broadway and they decided to let us go. Even in spite of that we came out smelling like a rose.

To what degree do you believe money and fame dilute an artist's talent or faith?

CF: Here's what I think about that. See, God has the last word on everything. Of course, quite naturally, there are a lot of people who don't believe that. God has a way that is not known to us. We don't understand God's way. The Bible says, "His ways are above ours as high as the heaven is from the earth." So, I'm saying that to you because I remained faithful in everything I did, and the Lord has blessed us now more than he ever has. But you have to wait on God. You can't say this was supposed to happen and all that. It's God's plan. When you walk the straight and narrow and do the things god wants you to do, he'll bless you in your age. He'll bless you more than ever—and that's what he's done for us now. Things are jumping these days.

Over a period of sixty odd years, the Blind Boys have played tent shows, revivals, folk, and blues festivals. You've appeared in the TV show Beverly Hills 90210, and received the NEA National Heritage Fellowship in 1994. You opened for Tom Petty in 1999, and recorded with artists such as Robert Plant, Peter Gabriel, Lou Reed, and Ry Cooder. Now an HBO show called *The Wire* uses the Blind Boys version of the Tom Waits song "Way Down In the Hole."

CF: All of that is God working. People must be able to see that.

It's refreshing to know music so authentic and alive still delivers a message to wayward pilgrims in huge festival

crowds, because for some people the Blind Boys' music gets them as close as they'll ever come to church.

CF: It thrills me, you know. Once again, that's God working—not me. You can't do anything on your own without God. With him we can do all things. People just don't realize this. When the tragic 9-11 happened in New York last year that was God waking us up. He's still in control.

Talk a little bit about the two Blind Boy albums, *Holdin' On* and *I Brought Him with Me.*

CF: Okay, well, these are good records on the House of Blues label, but the House of Blues made a mistake. They were with BMG, one of the biggest distributors in the world, and somebody made somebody mad messing everything up and they cancelled the House of Blues contract. You may be able to find these records, but what the House of Blues did, they discontinued working with BMG. When the record companies make a deal with the distributors and a breakdown comes, well, we don't have anything to say because they made the deal, not us. House of Blues can't handle records—that's one of their weaknesses.

Your relationship with John Hammond led to the Blind Boys gathering Charlie Musselwhite, David Lindley, Danny Thompson, and recording the Grammy winning for best traditional soul gospel album, *Spirit of the Century,* a very song-oriented compilation with songwriters including the Rolling Stones, Tom Waits, and Ben Harper, as well as old traditional songs. The Blind Boys possess a great ability to alter the balance between dark and light within songs. When I heard the Rolling Stones version of "I Just Want to See his Face," I always interpreted it as having cynical, "doubting Thomas" lyrics: "I DON'T want to walk and talk about Jesus, I just want to see his face." But you guys turn it around. The Blind Boys render "Amazing Grace" lyrics to "House of the Rising Son" music. Also, on *Higher Ground,* the example shines in reading the 23rd Psalm over Funkadelic's sinister "Me & My Folks."

CF: You know I met that ol' George Clinton the other day. He's a nice cat. But, yes. You know the Stones covered an old song of ours called "The Last Time"

That's right. Didn't they change it a little and made it into a boy/girl thing?

CF: Right. I didn't envy them for doing this, but down the road, we came along and did one of their tunes and I could really relate to that song, because originally I always wanted to see God's face. My faith has always been upbeat. I've always believed that God can do anything except fail. God cannot fail.

So, on September 3, 2002, Real World records will release *Higher Ground*, a choice collection of traditional gospel compositions along with cover songs by talented songwriters featuring the Blind Boys of Alabama backed by Robert Randolph and his Family Band. Talk about this new project.

CF: Robert Randolph better be careful. He's gonna go rock and roll, if he ain't already gone. That's what I think because money to young people is not what it was in my day. All we really wanted to do was make a living. We weren't worried about how much money we were gonna make in the future. He should be careful because they are going to try and switch him over to rock and roll.

***Higher Ground* is a very strong album. It's much more gospel than the bluesy *Spirit of the Century*. *Higher Ground* blends the blood of old gospel singers with the blood of new gospel players, and it creates a strong effect.**

CF: Well that's what they wanted to do. I went along with them because they had a good idea and they wanted to appeal to the young folk. When you can appeal to the masses of people, you got it made. What we try to do to these songs is put the gospel flavor into them. We take out the words that don't mean anything. For instance on the Stevie Wonder song "Higher Ground" the lyric goes: "lovers keep on loving"—we take that out: "prayers keep on praying"—we put that in. We don't want to say things that make

•••••••

us look like rock and rollers. I just wanted to sing and serve God—that was my most important thing. When you can sing all faces of gospel you got it under control. We can sing contemporary, we can sing traditional, four part harmonies, five part harmonies—you ring it, we can sing it. I'd like to get one more Grammy. I'd be real happy with that. I think this next record, *Higher Ground*, is a real good record. We can pick up some good information in doing the things we do and doing them well. The Lord will take care of the rest.

Calls To Harry Crews

From late 2006 until April 2013, I operated as the paid editor/ writer for Swampland. We suffered a couple of serious setbacks, which paved the way for a couple of other imitating publications with financial backing to progress with Swampland's ethos. Money talks, eh? But, a lot of good work came out of that considering all the forces one must reconcile. I read over this Swampland dispatch, and I realize—outside of Hunter S. Thompson—Harry Crews counts as the only other interview I was so close, but never got to conduct. Crews died in Gainesville, Florida, on March 28, 2012. At the time, I passed messages between Harry Crews and Paul Hemphill. They're both gone now. I thought sooner or later I'd get the opportunity to ask the writer questions I pondered for years. But, so many plates were spinning on both sides that it never happened. I regret it. These two conversations do capture the essence of Harry, especially if you're familiar with his work.

Call One: July 27, 2007

One of my heroes remains the Georgia writer Harry Crews. Some of Crews' books such as *Feast of Snakes, Florida Frenzy, The Gospel Singer, Scar Lover, Body, The Gypsy's Curse, Blood and Grits,* and *Childhood: Biography of a Place* rank as timeless literature.

I've been trying to contact Crews for over a year concerning an interview. This morning I decided to call him at home—lo and behold, he picked up the phone. I must say that 25-minute call was one of the most interesting conversations I've ever had over the phone. When he asked my name and I told him he said, "That's a good name. I'll remember that name." High praise from the man who wrote this hardboiled story called "Poaching Gators for Fun and Profit."

"Being raised alongside the Okefenokee Swamp, I had early on developed a healthy respect for gators. When I was a boy I saw Willard Stucky and Leonard Miller—both of them in their early twenties and about half drunk at the time—go in a little pond with the intention of catching a gator that wasn't even five feet long. God knows why they wanted to take him alive, but they did, so they backed their truck right up to the bank and went in the water. They finally did get him alive in the bed of the pickup, but not before he beat the clothes off both of them with his tail and he chewed one of Willard's hands until it was crooked forever..."

He's an expert. Harry informed me of several projects he's working on. He told me my Alma Mater, The University of Georgia, bought a lot of his work for display. We discussed fitting an interview into his schedule. He expressed interviews over the phone were out of the question. "I'm 73 years old, and at this point my time is very valuable. Maybe you can come down and see me in a couple of months." We agreed on his plan. So, a Swampland interview with Harry Crews looks like a reality.

I informed him writer Paul Hemphill was recovering from throat cancer and I plan on completing our interview when he regains his strength. "That's terrible," said Crews, "we're all gettin' old and dying off."

Call Two: February 19, 2008

"In the time I was with Bronson, I came to believe that while he would not back off from trouble, he would go to considerable trouble to avoid bullshit. To fight over a fat lady you don't know and have no interest in is bullshit and Bronson knew it, so he let the guy back him down the floor. There is so little bullshit in the man that he will do almost anything to keep from having to deal with the bullshit in somebody else. But after he's backed as far as he can go, if pressed, he will break your arms for you. He is, in fact, the straight-on, tear your balls off kind of guy that he so often portrays with such power on the screen."

Harry Crews on Charles Bronson
The Knuckles of Saint Bronson

So, yesterday...during a break...I flipped through the channels and caught a brief scene of Charles Bronson's Death Wish 3. It made me think of a story Harry Crews wrote called "The Knuckles of Saint Bronson." I decided it was time to attempt another try at interviewing Harry Crews. My friend—the great writer Paul Hemphill—warned me about visiting Crews: "Just watch out for his fucking dogs."

•••●••

When I mentioned interviewing Crews to the ultimate professional John Sayles, he said: "That should be a fun date." I'd left Crews two messages since our conversation last summer, and I planned on leaving another message this evening. Then, on the third ring, Crews' female friend picked up the phone and handed it over to Harry.

Mr. Crews told me he gets up and writes every day "until I'm broken." He's suffering from a physical ailment which requires medication he's not crazy about taking. I'm well-aware he hates phone interviews and I suggested I make the trek to Florida to go on the record with him. No doubt, at 73 he's quite busy. One doesn't write 38 books in a lifetime and remain unfamiliar with the term busy. I told him the last thing I would do is pressure him, and the classic Crews spark flashed:

"You ain't gonna pressure me man. Nobody fucking pressures me. I don't allow it—it doesn't happen. Anyway, yeah we can do it." Harry told me some movie people are going to visit him, so we must coordinate a schedule. I'd like to go down in two weeks..

"I'll be in touch in a week or so," I said.

"Yeah, well, hurry up because I'm dying. Yes, be in touch. Come down and we'll do it."

••••••

The James Ponsoldt Interview: From North Georgia Red Clay To the Hills of Hollywood

James Ponsoldt counts as another Athens, Georgia, artist I interviewed during a turning point in his career. At the time, Ponsoldt finished filming his third movie, The Spectacular Now. His debut film—Into The Black (2006—-starred Nick Nolte. Ponsoldt now commands his fair share of respect in Hollywood. His latest film, End of the Tour, earned acclaim in the film world. He's also worked in television. As I write this intro, Ponsoldt's next film, The Circle, starring Emma Watson and Tom Hanks hit theaters April 28, 2017. The sky's the limit for James Ponsoldt...

Athens, Georgia filmmaker James Ponsoldt was born in 1978. His father worked as a college professor and his mother was a writer. His grandfather created book covers for Agatha Christie novels. At an early age, Ponsoldt developed an affinity for storytelling, photography and theater. It's rare such a young filmmaker makes an impact on the indie film community, but the work of James Ponsoldt commands respect. A soulful resonance drifts through his films. The fertile bohemian grounds of Athens, Georgia, served as James Ponsoldt's storytelling garden that spread to Hollywood like kudzu covers north Georgia's roadsides.

Ponsoldt's latest film, *Smashed,* hits theaters on October 12. The movie tells the story of a couple who try to salvage their relationship once one of them becomes sober. Smashed stars Mary Elizabeth Winstead *(Death Proof, Grindhouse* and *Abraham Lincoln: Vampire Hunter)* and Aaron Paul *(Breaking Bad).* Vetiver's Andy Cabic and the Fruit Bats' Eric D. Johnson scored the soundtrack for *Smashed.* Ponsoldt's first feature film—*Off The Black*—starred Nick Nolte. The film earned critical acclaim. Other Ponsoldt films include *Rush Tickets, Comin' Down the Mountain, Junebug and Hurricane* and *We Saw Such Things.*

In August, Ponsoldt finished filming his latest movie *The Spectacular Now* (starring Jennifer Jason Leigh and Mary Elizabeth Winstead) in his hometown of Athens, Georgia. His production office operated out of the old R.E.M. office in Athens. Ponsoldt's work is gaining wider acclaim, and on the heels of the release of *Smashed* he may find himself on the way to the Red Carpet. In this interview we discuss growing up in the South, his early works, influences, southern perspectives in Los Angeles, Nick Nolte, *Smashed* and *The Spectacular Now*. I encourage everyone to go see *Smashed*. For this writer, it's good to see a fellow scribe from Georgia expose his work to a wide audience. Ponsoldt is a first rate storyteller...

James Calemine: Talk about growing up in Athens, Georgia, and how you eventually got into filmmaking through early influences...

JP: Athens is a great place to live and to grow up. I was born and raised there. My parents moved there in the late 70s because my dad took a job at the University of Georgia law school. I was born the same year they moved there. I spent the entirety of my childhood until I graduated from high school in Athens except a very brief period when my father taught at Tulane. Athens was a great place to grow up. It's a very cultural town and a town that's very friendly towards the arts and creative folks. Maybe because it's the deep south you certainly feel the tension....it's a red state with a couple of blue towns if you want to put it that way and be political. You feel the tension.

It's not like growing up in San Francisco or New York where you grow up thinking everyone is progressive, creative and open minded and it's not necessarily like that everywhere in the deep south. It's a great town—a mecca—for southern creative weirdos. Growing up in Athens you definitely grow up with a great appreciation for college football and really good music. I didn't chose to live there. I was born there and that's different than choosing to move there when you're 18. My parents were always very supportive of my creative endeavors. I was always taking photographs, doing theater and drawing comic strips which was a segue into my film making.

My mom wrote short stories. Her father, my grandfather, painted book covers—including a lot of the Agatha Christie covers as well as movie posters. So, when I was really little I was already writing stories and drawing and doing cartoons as well as theater. My parents have a dark room in their house so theater, fiction, film and photos were always floating around. It all came together. I started writing for *Flagpole* (Athens art newspaper) when I was 15 because I really loved music. I was doing album reviews and going to concerts....that was the only way I could get into the 40 Watt Club (laughs). At the end of high school I knew that I wanted to make movies. It all culminated from music, acting and storytelling. Certainly by the time I got to college the goal was to make movies.

You attended Yale and Columbia...

JP: Yeah, I went to Yale for undergraduate and then to Columbia for film school.

This is the era of your early short films like *Rush Tickets* and *Coming' Down The Mountain*...

JP: A friend of mine from Arlington, Kentucky, Colin Spoelman (he runs a whiskey/moonshine company called King's County Distillery), he and I wrote a feature screenplay about a family dealing with Oxycontin addiction while we were in college. His father was a preacher and he would send articles from Harlan, Kentucky, about all the Oxycontin stuff that was going on in the late 90s before it was actually a big nationwide story. It was all about getting addicted, selling drugs and going to jail and we wrote a feature screenplay called *Coming Down The Mountain*. After my first year in film school we made a short version of that feature film script that was about 25 minutes that was shot in Kentucky. That wound up going to a premiere in France and a lot of festivals. That was the first real experience for me going to film festivals, meeting other filmmakers, presenting films internationally and it set up my next short film...

Which was *Junebug and Hurricane*, right?

JP: Exactly. I tried to hit as many festivals around America and other countries as I could and I met a lot of folks that way whether it was filmmakers, producers or lawyers at festivals.

When did you move to Los Angeles?

JP: I moved to L.A. full time in 2006, but I moved there earlier in 2005 when I was still pursuing acting and coming out to L.A. with my manager for acting during pilot season. I was also in graduate school at the same time and I was kind of split on where I was going to put my focus. I wanted to make a feature film and I had just written *Off The Black*. I didn't know how long I was going to stay in L.A. so I went back to New York City. Maybe it was March of 2005 and then I started putting *Off the Black* together and shot it later that year. I had my fill of winters in the northeast. That was my main reason to get to L.A. because I couldn't handle the winter weather in New York anymore. It made me just want to stay in bed. So in the spring of 2006 I moved to L.A. I've been out here ever since except one year when I moved to Virginia to be with my then girlfriend now wife.

Talk about how Nick Nolte got involved with *Off The Black*. He's an old Hollywood actor we all admire. That must have been very gratifying for you to have an actor of that stature in your first feature film...

JP: Yeah, it was great. It was a combination of circumstances. Scott Macaulay played an instrumental role. He did films like *Raising Victor Vargas, Julien Donkey Boy, Gummo, Saving Face* and *Idlewild*. Nick Nolte was suggested to me and they asked me how I felt about him. I really love him as an actor--he's one of my favorite actors. He's funny, scary, weird...I was kind of afraid of him (laughs). I've seen the awful mug shot that everyone saw. I thought he might be a really scary alcoholic, but they assured me he was a lovely guy and that he was wonderful to work with. They told me I should get him the script and if he liked it we should try and get him. They got him the script and as it turned out he liked the script and we met out here in L.A. and he wanted to do the movie, which was very cool.

Nick really is a sweet guy. He's kind of like a playful hippie. He's very much like a kid at heart. He's very fun to collaborate with. What I know of Nick, I've never seen any films that have approximated who he really is. He never seems like he's acting. It's like his acting is invisible. He's very disciplined. He's fun to work with. I was proud of the acclaim we earned for a first feature film with *Off The Black*. There were a lot of people who really helped make that happen. I'm always thankful for those who supported me.

••••••

Talk about your short film you made after *Off The Black* titled *We Saw Such Things*. It retains an 'old Florida' vibe.

JP: It's a short documentary film I made that took in place in Weeki Wachee on the Gulf Coast of Florida. It's an amusement park that's been there for over 60 years. It's a place where they have a live spring where women dress up like mermaids and perform underwater by doing these sort of synchronized swimming movements people can watch from these underwater tanks. They have this elaborate set up where the swimmers can stay underwater for about an hour. It's cool. It has this weird old-time Florida vibe to it for sure. They were down there before Disney World. In 2007, they were having an anniversary performance where they had all their old 'Aqua Belles' put on a show. Basically, it was a bunch of elderly mermaids putting on a performance—and that was the documentary. It was this gang of elderly women coming together after all these years to put on their big show. It was a short documentary about the Weird Old South. It played at various festivals in Florida—especially the one in Sarasota, which was appropriate.

Your latest film, *Smashed,* comes out on October 12. It stars Mary Elizabeth Winstead (*Death Proof*), Aaron Paul (*Breaking Bad*) and Vetiver's Andy Cabic along with the fruit Bats Eric D. Johnson wrote the soundtrack. It's the story about a couple struggling with alcoholism. What were the seeds for the story? One gets sober...one doesn't...

JP: Well, as far as the seeds of the story—a lot of the people I grew up with all knew something about alcoholism or drug addiction, but nothing too abstract. I've seen addiction affect a lot of people I care about. Many people know about this on one level or another. I met my co-writer—Susan Burke—about a year earlier in L.A. She went through her own struggles with alcoholism and she's been through it all. It started by us telling stories about the dumbest things we done when we were drunk. Then we began to focus on the story of alcoholism and how two people start out partying and then later realize they have to have a relationship. We've seen tons of addiction stories before of all kinds. I wasn't interested in telling another one unless I could put my own stamp on it. I wanted real humor and warmth there as well.

Where was *Smashed* shot?

JP: Mostly in an L.A. neighborhood called Highland Park and a few surrounding others. Some of them were L.A.'s oldest neighborhoods. The houses were built back in the 10s, 20s and 30s. Primarily for the last half century or so they have been Latino neighborhoods. So you feel a tension of old Latino, Mexican-American owned taco places, auto shops or whatever and then young hipsters on bicycles opening record stores and coffee shops. Highland Park is a neighborhood that could be pretty insular where people walk a lot and ride bikes. It reminds me of Athens, Georgia. That's what attracted me to it. *Smashed* is not a movie about hipsters, but there's a lot of people I would label as hipsters in Highland Park. You see a lot of houses getting flipped. Old families moving out of the neighborhood and new families moving in.

The film has a stellar cast including another UGA graduate Kyle Chandler (*Friday Night Lights*) and Mary Elizabeth Winstead, a North Carolina girl. *Smashed* appeared at some prestigious film festivals.

JP: Yeah, *Smashed* showed at the Sundance and Toronto film festivals. There are others ones in France, Zurich, Moscow, Mumbai, Stockholm and Rio De Janeiro. The film opens in New York and Los Angeles on October 12. We have a couple of screenings here in L.A. for the next couple of days, and then I fly to New York. We're trying to get as many people to see it as possible. I'll be in a movie theater on October 12.

What creative qualities you learned in the south did you bring to L.A and New York?

JP: I think growing up in the South and attending public schools and being raised by academics gave me a certain comfort level with people growing up. I spent a lot of time with people of different backgrounds and different income levels both black and white. I grew up with kids who were raised by their grandparents because the mother was in jail and the father was a junkie. I also grew up with kids like me who had parents like mine. I guess the South I grew up in there was no sense of snobbery.

•••••••

Where I grew up anyway—I went to Cedar Shoals High School in Athens. It had a pretty high drop out rate. As a college professor's kid I was probably one of the wealthier kids there. In some ways, I had a guilt complex because I got to leave town—I had opportunities they didn't.

I guess I brought that to Yale. There was a lot of wealthy people there, but they were very driven. It was different to meet people from all over the world. Most of the kids I grew up with never left the South...much less hanging out with kids from Hong Kong and Denmark. I love Athens. It's probably my favorite place on the planet. This summer I made a film there. It's my home. It's where my parents live. My sister lives in Decatur. I carry it with me everywhere I go. Los Angeles feels remarkably similar in a lot of ways. It's rare that you meet someone in L.A. who is really from there. There are definitely people who have been here for generations, but there are a lot of transients here and a lot of them are from the south. Atlanta is like a smaller Los Angeles—it's a sprawling metropolis with a lot of communities and neighborhoods. Both towns are car-cultured. There's a downtown, but there are also suburbs and sprawls. L.A. is very laid back—it's not a real snobby culture like people might think. Everyone is pretty friendly. I love New York, but I think it's a much more proper city—like Chicago or some city in Europe. Everything goes upwards, while in L.A. and Atlanta things move outward.

It's great you have Mary Elizabeth Winstead (*Death Proof, Grindhouse, Abraham Lincoln: The Vampire Hunter*), in *The Spectacular Now* as well as *Smashed*. She's from North Carolina...

JP: Yeah, she has roots and family in North Carolina. She's not Mormon, but when she was young she moved to Utah. But yeah, she's a southern girl.

Jennifer Jason Leigh (*Rush, Fast Times at Ridgemont High, Road To Perdition*) stars in this film. You also have another University of Georgia graduate–Kyle Chandler (*Friday Night Lights*)–in *The Spectacular Now*, which you just finished filming in Athens this summer...
JP: Yeah, Kyle went to high school not far from Athens as well.

He lives in Texas now. It was a dream come true to film in my hometown. Our production office was the old R.E.M. office. We got it when they broke up. It was really hot (laughs). I almost forgot how humid it gets in the summer. We shot in the dead of August—the whole month. It was great to work with some people that I worked with before like Mary. Her part in *The Spectacular Now* is very different than her role in *Smashed*—it's sort of a 180.

What is the story behind *The Spectacular Now?*

JP: It's based on a novel that came out a few years ago written by a writer from Oklahoma. That's where the book took place. I did not write this one. It was adapted by a writing team who co-wrote films like *500 Days of Summer*. They did a beautiful job of adapting it. It's a great portrayal of adolescence. It's a cross between *Ferris Bueller's Day off* and a fairy-tale type thing, but the story is about how a person doing what they want affects those around them. The screenplay and the book actually remind me of my own circumstances in high school. I've read very few things that actually reminded me of what it was like to be in high school. This project happened at the right place and the right time. The fact that there were producers who were okay with filming in Athens really helped. It all just kind of happened and it went really well.

You've run the gauntlet of an independent filmmaker in L.A., New York and beyond. Now that your work is gaining recognition and you're getting more projects under your belt. What has been the hardest thing for you to learn?

JP: Well, probably time management (laughs). What to focus your energy on. I discovered you don't want to put all your eggs in one basket and I've tried to keep different things going on. I've gotten better at that—even with my free time. That goes for everything—as far as projects I'm trying to get made whether or not they get made is out of my control in some cases. In other cases, it's a matter if money is going to come in or not. Or it's just being productive in my free time and writing. Or, even time spent on the set and squeezing every second out.

•• • •••

How long did it take to film _The Spectacular Now?_ I'm sure there's always a deadline...

JP: We shot _The Spectacular Now_ in 25 days. I filmed _Smashed_ in 19 days. It was really fast (chuckles). It's a sprint. These low budget films have to be made fast. You have to plan because once the clock is ticking on the set you can't screw around. You're burning money quite literally. If there's a thunderstorm where actors are carrying dialogue on outside—you've got to make up for it and add a day at the end. It takes a lot to keep it all going--when one problem is solved another one presents itself. You have to be good at collaborating with people and making people want to work hard. Everyone wants to work hard and do a good job if they believe in what they are doing. I try to foster a good working environment. I'm very grateful for the people who are willing to work with me.

Smashed opens on October 12. What's left to finish on _The Spectacular Now?_ I suppose next summer or fall it'll be out?

JP: We have to edit the movie. All kinds of work needs to be done like special effects, visual aspects and sound design. We're working on that into January. The hope would be a release next summer. A lot of things have to happen before that, but yes, a summer release would be nice.

Well, congratulations. I hope _Smashed_ really takes off. Proud of ya man. Good luck out there. See you on the Red Carpet and I'll talk to you soon...

JP: Thank you very much James. Same to you man...

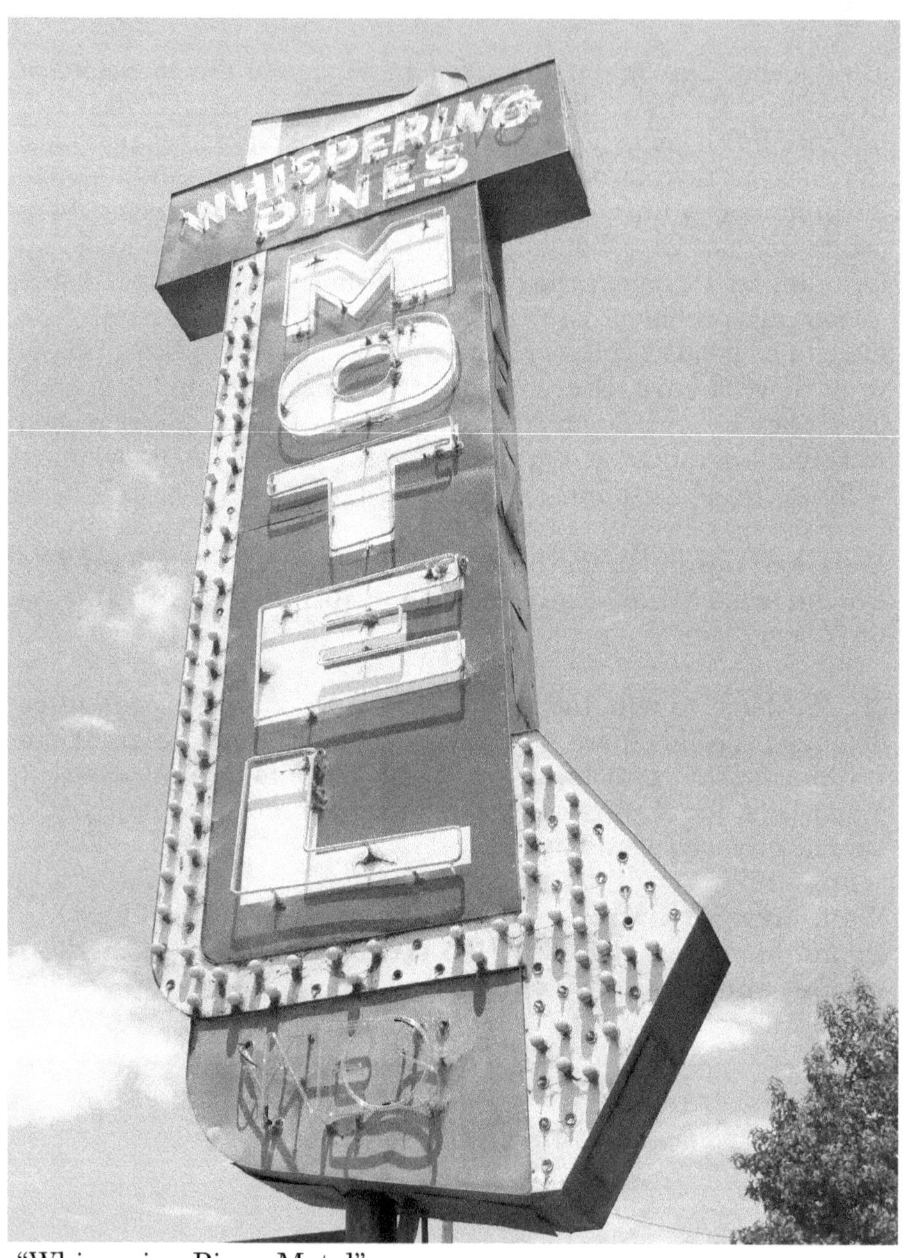

"Whispering Pines Motel"
Asheville, North Carolina

●●●●●●

The Gonzo Tapes:
The Life And Work Of
Dr. Hunter S. Thompson

In March 2005, I was scheduled to interview Hunter S. Thompson after three requests over a year's period. I considered giving up after my third request until Thompson's agent called me to say the interview was set for March 1. Unfortunately, nine days before the interview, on February 20, 2005, Thompson shot himself in his Woody Creek, Colorado, kitchen. I later wrote a couple of articles for the Woody Creeker a magazine run by Thompson's wife Anita. It still stings the interview was set, but never happened...

"People who count on luck don't last long in the business of defusing bombs and disarming landmines, and that is what my business seems to be. It helps to know these things. Muhammad Ali was not lucky. He was fast, very fast..."

-Hunter S. Thompson

These are the original work tapes of Hunter S. Thompson. His personal audio cassettes and reel-to-reel tapes were transferred to digital by Don Fleming. Fleming was given access to Thompson's tapes—stored in the "war room" of his Woody Creek, Colorado, home—by Thompson's widow Anita.

Thompson, an inveterate audiophile, carried his tape recorders everywhere. He'd record his surroundings, interviews, conversations and monologues. These recordings, spanning the years of 1964-1975, find Thompson riding with Hell's Angels, violating various laws in Las Vegas with a drug-addled attorney, breaking down in Africa before the Foreman-Ali fight and burnt-out in Saigon during the end of the Vietnam War.

The tape recorder was Thompson's most significant tool. Some of these monologues would be transferred verbatim into his books. Producer Don Fleming wrote this in the box set book regarding this particular collection: "This collection represents a select but essential, portion of the remarkable audio tape archive Thompson created. Hearing these recordings helps us to better understand the unique Thompson craft and technique, but ultimately what makes them so riveting is Thompson's personality. His monologues and conversations often sound like his writing. The original cassettes were recorded in the field, usually under less-than-ideal circumstances. The sound quality, as a result, varies widely. I've cleaned them up to some extent, but intended to leave enough grit to keep it authentic."

Disc 1: Hell's Angels

These recordings served as the backbone of Thompson's first book, Hell's Angels, regarding the motorcycle gang. This disc contains interviews with Hell's Angels, a Fourth of July bust, the first meeting between Ken Kesey's Merry Pranksters and Hell's Angels at Kesey's La Honda property during a time when the Grateful Dead played many gigs at these motley gatherings. The disc also preserves Thompson and Beat poet Allen Ginsberg getting pulled over by the cops after leaving a Hell's Angels party.

Actual photos of the cassettes, original manuscript pages, photos and napkin notes are included in the box set book. Thompson's first book ends with him being beaten by the Hell's Angels. This closed the era of Thompson's early career and this disc verifies a changing of the guard.

Disc 2: Fear And Loathing In Las Vegas

This disc includes the actual dialogue between Thompson and Oscar Acosta while they ran amok in Las Vegas, which emerged as Thompson's literary sapphire of the same title. To actually hear Acosta's voice is interesting because he does not sound crazed at all during the notorious "One Toke Over The Line" interlude. Once again, the recordings served as the fulcrum to Thompson's 1971 classic. By the time of these 1971 recordings, Acosta was a high-profile attorney and activist for the Chicano movement in East Los Angeles. The actual conversation between Acosta and Thompson regarding getting whacked out on drugs while attending the D.A. Conference on Narcotics And Dangerous Drugs proves nervy and brilliant in hindsight.

This stellar collection proves Thompson clearly was never so stoned that he could not document his experiences onto tape. A 21-minute segment at "Terry's Taco Stand" verifies Thompson and Acosta's high jinx were in fine form...especially when Acosta asks where "The American Dream" is, and the girls working at the Taco Stand think they are talking about a bar. Just like in the book, one waitress responds: "Wasn't that the old Psychiatrist's Club out on Paradise?"

Disc 3: More Fear And Loathing In Las Vegas

"As usual, you're afraid of Mexicans, aren't you? Goddamn you're weird Thompson. Well, that's what I'm here for," Acosta says to the Good Doctor in the first part of the third disc. It's amazing all of this material was preserved. I knew Thompson constantly used tape recorders, but I had no idea to what extent. Thompson reveals in a monologue he's not sure what kind of story he has on his hands during the "Oscar Fled In Terror...Drug Up...Weird Road" segment. Thompson, cornered in the desert, while in a rented and thoroughly trashed white Cadillac by the police, is recorded on tape as Thompson narrates everything as it unfolds around him. This CD contains classic Thompson in a Neal Cassady-type streamlined narration that never loses its edge. Thompson's description of the wrecked hotel room after Acosta's wake of destruction in "Vegas D.A. Final Notes...The Whole Room Is Total Chaos" sums up the eternal strange and savage odyssey Thompson and Acosta spearheaded.

Disc 4: Gonzo Gridlock

In 1972 Thompson covered the Presidential campaign. The book, *Fear and Loathing: On the Campaign Trail 72'* was published in 1973. During that year, Thompson prepared for his next project. These recordings contain "Guts Ball," "Cozumel," 'Fear And Loathing in Acapulco," "Freud's Cocaine Papers," and "Fear And Loathing In Kinshasa." Acosta disappeared during this time, inspiring various theories on his whereabouts. Thompson believed he was killed on a boat during a drug smuggling operation.

Thompson began analyzing Sigmund Freud's *Cocaine Papers*. He explored the drug on tape. One of the entries begins: "I've done what most people would consider an excessive amount of coke." Thompson tested Freud's findings as well as social conceptions and misconceptions concerning the drug. Thompson's one real failed story was the Ali-Foreman fight in Zaire. The tape shows Ralph Steadman tried to coax a story out of Thompson. Thompson gave away their ringside tickets. His voice sounds unhinged during this segment. He even lets out various unsettling squeals and sounds. He says, "Fiendish. The thing is so bad there's no way to write a story about it." Or "There's no way you can conceive what's going to happen to us tonight." Thompson never avoided even the most bizarre environments. He even managed to smuggle two elephant tusks back to the States after this African trip even though he never wrote the story.

Disc 5: Fear And Loathing In Saigon

Disc five begins with a woman named Gloria Emerson—a *New York Times* reporter who spent several years in Vietnam--assuring Thompson Saigon was the place to be for his next story. Thompson wavered, but eventually he left for the war zone. He recorded everything from local radio stations and music as well as machine gun fire to bickering journalists, arguing with a desk clerk and final wisdom from a vicious American war. At one point during his stay in Saigon, Jann Wenner suspended Thompson's *Rolling Stone* salary, which made his life insurance policy void, which enraged Thompson and may have contributed to his failure to deliver the story Wenner originally had in mind.

The final track, "The Last Dispatch From Saigon" Thompson commentates American evacuation from Saigon like a cold-blooded newsman leaving the perilous grounds where he lived. Thompson flew out on Vietnam Flight 783—the last commercial flight out of Vietnam—to Hong Kong. "I have a suspicion I will not be back to Vietnam," are Thompson's last words on this collection.

Each disc contains sleeve photos of various items in Thompson's home. Disc one is a photo of his front door (Gonzo symbol engraving on wooden door) steps; disc two a bookshelf; three, a note on his typewriter; four, a mantle photo; five a shelf of his record collection all of which gives this box set a personal feel. The listener can be alone in the room with just Thompson's voice... for hilarious moments...or eerie ones. Like a ghost from the past, Hunter S. Thompson shall never die as long as his work is read and his voice heard. I look forward to the 1975-1986 tapes. Take heed, *The Gonzo Tapes* take you straight to the heart of darkness...

······

Walking with Zambi:
The Colonel Bruce Hampton Interview

I first met Colonel Bruce at the Georgia Bar in Athens, Georgia, during 1993. The Colonel sat with Widespread Panic's guitarist Michael Houser. I walked in with Bloodkin's Daniel Hutchens. The Colonel was busy in the early 90s. I caught up with him again in 1996 right after his role in Billy Bob Thornton's Sling Blade. We crossed paths over the years. Musicians such as Derek Trucks, Widespread Panic, Tinsley Ellis and any other musicians that cross his path will say the Colonel's influence transcends years. The Colonel is a southern gentleman of the highest order. He's a blues poet from outer space. This Swampland interview transpired in 2011. At the time, the long awaited documentary about the Colonel, Basically Frightened, hit the street. In 2016, the Colonel starred in the Tyler Russell film, Here Comes Rusty.

On May 1, 2017, "Hampton 70: A Celebration of Col. Bruce Hampton transpired at the Fox Theatre in Atlanta." Some of the guests included Peter Buck, Derek Trucks, Chuck Leavell, Billy Bob Thornton, Warren Haynes, Kevn Kinney, Jimmy Herring, Dave Schools and John Fishman. Hampton collapsed and died onstage that night. That's a hard act to follow...

"I do not come to you as a reality. I come to you as a myth."
-Sun Ra

"I never had much control
Until I got to Arkansas..."
-Colonel Bruce Hampton
"Arkansas"

Colonel Bruce Hampton was born Gustav Valentine Bergland III in Oak Ridge, Tennessee, on April 30, 1947, and grew up in Atlanta, Georgia. His music transcends mundane boundaries. Bruce always walked to the beat of a different drummer.

His music has been compared to the work of Sun Ra, Captain Beefheart, George Clinton and Frank Zappa. After nearly 50 years of making music, Colonel Bruce retains a rare degree of sharp insight, worldly wisdom and musical wonder.

Behind the Colonel's avant-garde music, exists a soulful, smart and zen-like artist. Colonel Bruce was the first male child on his mother's side in generations not to attend West Point. As a toddler, Colonel Bruce was cared for by a family nanny--Liza Mae Williams--who was born into slavery and exposed the young boy to gospel music. His grandfather, W.A. Cunningham, coached the University of Georgia's football team from 1910-1919.

In Atlanta, as a teenager in the early 60s, young Bruce often snuck into The Royal Peacock Lounge where he watched Otis Redding, James Brown, B.B. King and Albert King perform on many occasions. Colonel Bruce started his first band in 1963. He formed the Hampton Grease Band around 1968. This group often opened for the Allman Brothers Band in Atlanta's Piedmont Park. The Hampton Grease Band released *Music To Eat*, which was the second worst selling album in the history of Columbia Records; the first being an instructional yoga album.

Bruce recorded on Capricorn and Terminus Records for years. In liner notes for the 1978 album *One Ruined Life of A Bronze Tourist,* Stanley Booth wrote: "He is, I can't help thinking, one of the bravest musicians I've ever encountered." The Colonel always refused to compromise his music for mass consumption. Years later, he formed the Aquarium Rescue Unit and the Fiji Mariners. All the musicians to ever play with Colonel Bruce Hampton admire him.

Through the years the Colonel has played and collaborated with Widespread Panic, Tinsley Ellis, Warren Haynes, Allen Woody, Jeff Sipe, Rev. Jeff Mosier, Paul Barrere, Oteil Burbridge, Matt Mundy, Jimmy Herring, T. Lavitz, Stanton Moore, Chuck Leavell, Cedell Davis, Kevn Kinney, Susan Tedeschi, Derek Trucks, Ike Stubblefield, Grant Green, Medeski, Martin & Wood, Mike Gordon, Blueground Undergrass and many others. The Colonel played an integral role in starting the H.O.R.D.E. tour during the 90s.

Colonel Bruce Hampton has recorded over 18 albums in his career. He also played a role in Billy Bob Thornton's masterpiece *Sling Blade.* Other related projects include providing a voice-over in the TV show *Space Ghost* as well as the leading role in a film Mike Gordon directed titled *Outside Out.* Widespread Panic's John Bell wrote this about the Colonel in the liner notes for the *Arkansas* album: "Pretending is easy, but in Bruce's company, you're so aware of your own flavor of B.S., it just becomes more comfortable to surrender to his presence...I'm spewing my own brand new flavor right now--but after having been kindly dismantled by Bruce so many times since birth, maybe that observation comes close to being genuine."

Lately, the Colonel has been playing with his groups, The Quark Alliance, and Pharaoh Gummitt. The Colonel prepares to hit the road in February and March. The Colonel's sense of humor is often overlooked because of the gonzo nature of his music. I don't want to demystify the Colonel's image, but every time I talk to him I find him to be a distinguished—and very humorous--southern gentleman. Three days after we conducted this interview, the Colonel appeared on the first night of Widespread Panic's Wood Tour in Atlanta. The group rendered an old Bukka White song the Colonel adopted called "Fixin' To Die."

In this interview, we discuss the Colonel's early musical influences, his Atlanta roots, the Hampton Grease Band, the H.O.R.D.E tours, musical instinct, Billy Bob Thornton, spring tour dates, future plans, Widespread Panic, literature, wisdom, his insight to the end of the Mayan calendar on December 21, 2012 and the upcoming Colonel Bruce documentary titled *Basically Frightened: The Musical Madness of Colonel Bruce Hampton* due out in March of 2012.

James Calemine: Let's start at the beginning...you were born in Tennessee, but your family roots are really in Atlanta.

Colonel Bruce Hampton: Right. Yeah, I only stayed in Tennessee about two weeks. My family has been in Atlanta since about 1830. I've got definite Atlanta roots.

Is it true your grandfather W.A. Cunningham served as the University of Georgia's football coach from 1910-1919.

CBH: Right, then he took them to war. After the football game--he got them all dressed up and they went to World War I. Isn't that terrifying? He took the whole team. He was a captain then. We just found a picture of him about a year ago with all these football players. Bob McWhorter was an All-American then on the team. What's amazing to me, Bill Kurtzman and I have known each other for 40 years. His grandfather was with

George Halas who started the Chicago Bears and played against my Grandfather in 1919. I believe it was on November 15—they played to a 7-7 tie in Augusta, Georgia. Georgia played Tulane. When we both found that out we said it was impossible. Just impossible...

Were you ever a big football fan Colonel?

CBH: I have been. I don't follow it like I used to. I've seen so many games over the years. I watch it occasionally here and there. Music takes time, and I'm doing a lot of projects so it's time consuming.

What was your first musical memory?

CBH: Well, when I grew up in the early 50s I heard a lot of stuff and then Little Richard and Chuck Berry came along. Then I knew I found something I truly loved. That was 1955 or 56. I was a very young kid, but I remember being ecstatic because it brought so much joy, chaos and rebellion. I grew up in the Eisenhower 50s, and all of a sudden Little Richard comes along and I went 'My Gosh.' For my money, there's still no better singer in rock & roll than Little Richard.

I've read when you were a baby—Liza Mae Williams—took care of you. She sang spiritual songs. I'm sure that was a musical memory long before Little Richard.

CBH: Oh, there's no question. Listening to her when I was 2, 3, 4 years old and what she would play or sing. It was unbelievable. I don't want to sound ridiculous about it, but I remember the feeling of the music to say the least. She'd play Mahalia Jackson, Rosetta Tharpe and all the greatest gospel music that's ever been played. I remember that music very vividly when I was growing up. You've done your homework James. Have you seen the movie yet (laughing)?

No, I haven't seen the documentary yet. I've done my research—heh heh. I know you bought your first guitar from John Huey who later became the president of Time magazine...

•• • • ••

CBH: Yeah, I bought my first guitar for $60 from John Huey the chairman of *Time* magazine.

What kind of guitar was it?

CBH: He'd remember better than me, but I think it was a Fender Stratocaster without a case. I wish I had it now, and we could all retire (laughs). I think it was a 1959—probably worth 15-30 grand now.

How old were you then?

CBH: Oh, I was 16 or 17. I've never been a serious guitar player like so many of the greats. I enjoy playing guitar. It's a freedom of expression for me—there's a million guitar players that are better, but I just love to do it. I don't want to play in the symphony with it or anything of that nature. It's just a wonderful instrument to express yourself on.

You grew up in Atlanta. Talk about how you used to sneak into the Royal Peacock Lounge and see Otis Redding, James Brown, B.B. King...you caught a glimpse of that every night between 1964-1966 from what I understand, right?

CBH: I used to hide under the stage. To show you how things have changed, I'd sneak out and ride a moped 8 miles away with no helmet at 15 in the middle of the night. I'd put my moped at the front door and walk in. They would hide me under the stage. Eventually they let me stand on the side of the stage and I got to see the best music that's ever been done.

Around that time you began to get your first band together.

CBH: Yeah, my good friend Harold put me in a band called The Four of Nine. I started playing tunes and paying dues. I started to learn what it's all about because I had no idea. I feel like I'm just starting to learn now. After 50 years, I feel like I'm just beginning to learn. And I'm 165 years old! (collective laughter)

175

•• • • ••

Even your most far out music never really strays too far from blues, country or jazz music. You studied and played all that old music before you started your own thing. You learned the ropes way before you put out your first record *Music To Eat*...

CBH: That's true. Yeah, that album was in 1969. In 68 and 69 we cut it, and I think it came out in 1970.

The Hampton Grease Band opened for the Allman Brothers Band in Atlanta's Piedmont Park. You were friends with those guys before they had an album out.

CBH: Oh yeah, we opened for the Allmans a good 15 or 20 times in Piedmont Park. I got to know all of those guys.

Were you discouraged by the reception of *Music To Eat?* You don't strike me as being discouraged by anything...

CBH: No, I've never been discouraged. I'm honored to play music. No, you're right, I've never been discouraged—ever. Sometimes I've slept in the Nebraska woods. If stuff goes the way it's supposed to go everything collapses into place. On my planet there's a different kind of gravity. So, I can't be discouraged on this planet. There's a set of rules and the only constant thing is change. And stuff changes. I've never really wanted to appeal to a whole lot of people. I do what I do and I follow my instincts. I do what I like. In order to survive in this business you develop an image or project one and pound it until people dig it.

I like to do different things everyday in the studio. I may want to dribble a basketball all night if the session requires that. Or bring an iron and do some ironing if I have to. A lot of people wouldn't like me ironing, but I'm a damn good iron-ner...(laughter)...I'm not sure if iron-ner is a word, but I wonder how many there are? I'm really good with irons.

A good man with an iron is hard to find.

CBH: That's what I say.

•• •••

Let's switch gears. You played an integral role in starting the H.O.R.D.E tours back in the 90s. Talk about that a little. I always loved the concept...

CBH: Well, we'd been playing with Phish, Blues Traveler and Widespread Panic—everybody was there at the same time and nobody was doing much business. So John Popper asked me 'What would you guys do in the old days?' We toured with four or five bands to keep the ticket price down and do 30-40-minute sets. That's how it was done. Especially in the R & B world with 6 acts on one ticket...Aretha, B.B., Joe Tex, Solomon Burke and Albert King for $2.50 (laughs). That's how it worked back then. So, JB, me, John and Trey met in Bill Graham's office and we wanted to keep the ticket prices down. We had 6 or 7 groups on the bill--that's almost been 21 years ago. It was a phenomenal success.

It lasted 7 or 8 years. At the first of it we let all musicians run it and we didn't want to talk to ASCAP or floor drillers or whatever. Nobody wanted to deal with it or was capable dealing with those small details. So it got turned over to people who could actually run the thing. It was a lot of fun. We had everybody in every town sit in with us.

I really picked up on your music during the Aquarium Rescue Unit and Fiji Mariner years. You eventually met Billy Bob Thornton through Phil Walden at Capricorn Records, which of course led to your role in *Sling Blade*. You also appeared in Thornton's directorial debut about Widespread Panic—*Live From The Georgia Theatre*.

CBH: Yeah, Phil Walden was managing Billy Bob at the time. I think Phil had us and Jim Varney at the time. I knew Billy Bob started working on an Otis Redding film so I already knew of him. He was already writing the screenplay for *Sling Blade*. I knew Phil before then. We got together in 1990. Billy said he was working on this movie. He was doing a TV show with John Ritter. I guess it was April of 95 when he shot *Sling Blade*. He shot the whole movie in a matter of a couple weeks. I don't think there was a third take in it unless there was a lighting or a technical issue.

But he just breezed through it. I've never seen anything like that. The most amazing thing about Billy Bob is his life was on the line with every bit of money he had in this film. Every day he'd go to the janitors and the cooks and he'd check on everybody. 'Is everything okay?' I saw him do that. I just thought, 'What a guy.' He life was on the line and he just knew this thing had to work. I'd see the daily screenings and I was thinking this is one of the best movies I've ever seen. Billy Bob is an amazing guy with amazing talent. You don't see people who write, direct and act anymore—they are few and far between. There are really five or six who can do it all. I remember a couple of us had to fly back to do a scene or two, and then he edited it, and put it out pretty quick. It's a perfect film. I haven't seen it in ten years, but people tell me they see it all the time. One day I'm going to watch it again. It's a masterpiece. I've only seen it four or five times. I really need to watch it again. That guy is unbelievable. He's got a new film coming out called *Jayne Mansfield's Car*. The guys I play with are in it. I can't wait to see it. It's coming out this summer I hope.

You've got some dates with your band Pharaoh Gummitt coming up. I like the R & B feel to that music.

CBH: Yeah--we try to play everything--jazz, blues, country, R&B, bluegrass, but yeah fifty percent of it is R & B. It's the stuff we all love and we do five or six of my tunes. The guys in my band are very young and they've never had an opportunity to play it. The music is amazing and that's what I grew up on. To me, music has to come from the church, folk music or outer space. You can be a sophisticated folk singer, but it's got to come from those places or I can't listen to it. Or it doesn't make sense to me. It's gotta have a story and some soul. I want to hear from the people who have nothing to say instead of those who want to say something.

I have 3,000 questions, but last night Todd Nance (Widespread Panic drummer) encouraged me to ask you about playing with Three Dog Night.

CBH: (Chuckles) Well there's a great deal of mythology with that story. We did cause a full-scale riot in front of 8,000 people

••• • ••

in 1968. We were opening for Three Dog Night, and we considered covering all of their tunes before they came out. We were booed off the stage in five minutes! Doing "Joy To The World" for about 20 minutes with another 20 minute guitar solo was not what they had in mind (laughs). Yet, I've talked to 30 or 40 people who were there that night, and they said it was the greatest concert they've ever been to. My guitar player acted like a wrestler and challenged 8,000 people to a wrestling match! We were not courting the rock ballad crowd in 1968 (collective laughter). We were way too weird for them.

What's coming up that we need to keep an eye out for as far as your music goes? I know you've been recording some...

CBH: I never know what's going to collapse into place. I'm in a band with Dennis Palmer and David Williams--that's really avant-garde stuff we do four or five times a year called The Egyptian Windmill Operators. It's really gone stuff. I mean, really gone. I've got the Pharaoh gigs coming. I'm also going to be doing some quieter stuff with a piano player and a drummer. I'm down to about 3 days a week on the road. I was on the road for 30 years. I just do 2 or 3 days a week now. I'm going to Canada in the summer to do the Jazz Fest. I'll be out in California also. I just don't work hard as I once worked. I'm 65 and it starts to hurt when you stay up until 3 in the morning.

I want to ask you about Widespread Panic. Since they are winding down on their 25th Anniversary...what's the most important thing you remember about them?

CBH: They are probably the nicest band I ever met at the time. Always have been. They were so young when they started. They used to work and play at the Uptown Lounge in Athens. Dave was the doorman, Todd tended bar and I think JB was hanging around playing the pinball machines. I remember thinking about Dave Schools at the time, 'Wow this young guy really knows a lot about music. More than anyone I've ever heard. He was discussing Miles, Trane and Monk. I was just blown away by his musicality. Panic was a breath of fresh air. In the 80s everyone had bad hair and stupid shoes. They were good cats.

They were at the right place at the right time and it worked. You just didn't find people like them. There weren't people like that back then. It was really positive and uplifting to see people with such good intentions.

Can you explain the Energy Room up at JB's place in the mountains? I know he told me you experienced it. I'm curious. I'd like to visit...

CBH: I can't explain it. Nope (collective laughter). It's on the other side of the moon you might say. Just wear a long sleeve shirt (chuckles).

What's the word on this documentary coming out on you, *Basically Frightened?*

CBH: It will be out March 23-31 at the Atlanta Film Festival. Hey James, how old are you?

I'll be 44 in February.

CBH: Do you still live in Atlanta?

I moved back to south Georgia a couple of years ago. Before I lived in Atlanta for many years, I lived with Danny and Eric from Bloodkin for about four years in Athens after I graduated from UGA.

CBH: Oh, wow.

I've got another question for you...

CBH: Ask me anything James. You are a man and a writer with the best intentions. You only find one out of a thousand like you. It's always a joy to talk to you. So I thank you.

That's high praise coming from you. I'm humbled and flattered. Hey, what are you reading these days?

CBH: Well, I don't read much anymore these days. But I've been reading Jiddu Krishnamurti's *The Intelligence of Thought*. I've

••••••

been reading Vladimir Nabokov. Of course, I'm a big Hunter S. Thompson fan. I love him. I think he's very funny.

After all these years, what's been the hardest thing to learn? Musically, or personally?

CBH: Wow, interesting question. The number one thing to learn in life is to get rid of Ego, which stands for Edging God Out. When you think you're doing something you're in bad trouble. There's a thing called faith and there's a thing called confidence and then there's a nasty thing called Ego. That's a tricky thing. You can't let Ego cripple you. I've seen it ruin people more than drugs, booze or relationships. That's what usually kills a band or a football team or whatever—Ego. For others, it's drinking, drugs and relationships. Clarity is also a danger to me (laughs).

You got that in before I could say money...

CBH: Yeah, money. I'm not sure what that is yet. I've never had to wake up and say, 'Well, I have too much money.' It's amazing how serious people take it. People change for money and I find that ludicrous. They think it's a serious thing. You gotta pay the bills and be responsible and all of that, but I've seen people sell their soul for $1.50 and it disgusts me personally. I try to treat janitors and presidents the same. Power is a silly thing. I've never understood it. What does power do?

So, Colonel...what do you think about the Mayan calendar ending on December 21, 2012, when some say the end of the world is coming?

CBH: Well, to me--it's after the end of the world. To me, the world ended a long time ago...

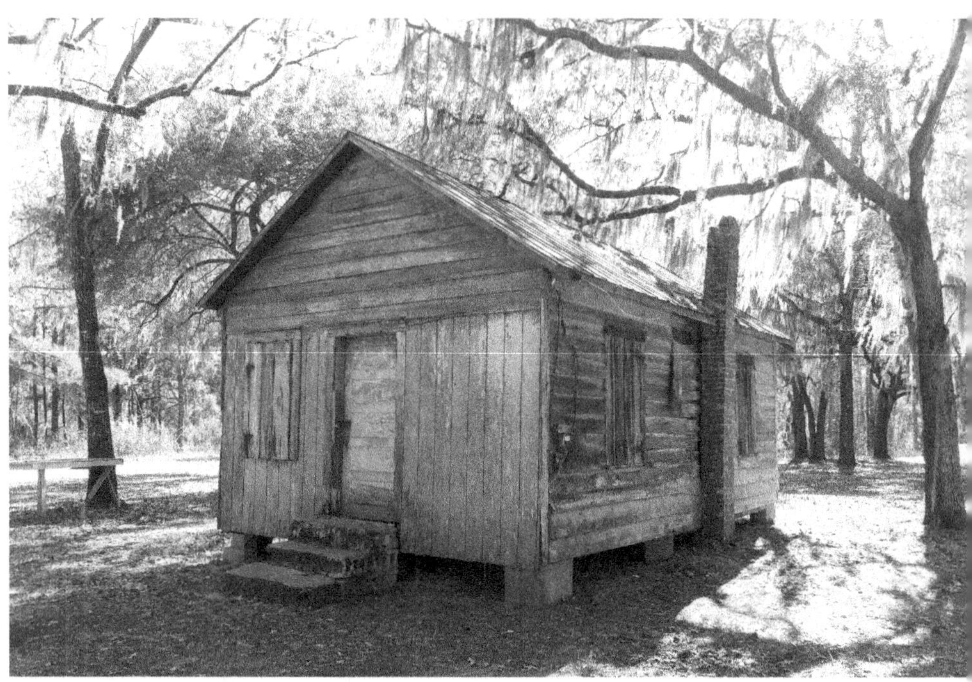

"Crescent, Georgia"

Lance Ledbetter Interview
Dust To Digital's Divine Grace

I discovered Lance Ledbetter's amazing label—Dust To Digital—around 2005. I'd read somewhere that Bob Dylan gifted Neil Young a box set called Goodbye, Babylon for Christmas. I felt curious as to what Dylan would give Neil for Christmas. I tracked the label down in Atlanta, GA., where I lived at the time. Lance invited me down to to the D2D headquarters—his house—and he told me his story. He gave me a copy of Goodbye, Babylon along with five or six other box sets on that December day. After I wrote various articles and reviews pertaining to the label, Lance and I sat down and conducted this touchstone interview years after we met.

In 2016, Ledbetter's label earned another Grammy nomination for Music of Morocco: Recorded by Paul Bowles, 1959.

The story of Dust To Digital is a divine one. In the late 1990s, Lance Ledbetter set out to discover rare recordings of gospel music. His journey led him to issuing landmark box sets that rank as some of the most memorable recordings in American music. Dust To Digital transfers rare 78 rpm records to digital form. In 2003, Ledbetter began the Atlanta, Georgia, label. The same year, Dust To Digital released a remarkable 6 CD box set—*Goodbye, Babylon*—that was lauded and praised by critics and music fans alike. Bob Dylan later gave a copy of *Goodbye, Babylon* to Neil Young as a gift.

The music of Dust To Digital is not mainstream, but it never goes out of style. Of course, most music fans aim for the more accessible discoveries based on taste. However, any music fan that discovers Dust To Digital will not forget the experience. It's old American music from mostly the 1920s, 30s 40s and 50s. The songs, literature and artists on this label represent the most authentic and enduring of all spiritual music. Most of the music from Dust To Digital's catalogue can only be heard through the label's 13 releases. Each box set represents a different genre and style of music. The packaging itself remains unforgettable, complete with top-shelf books and every *Goodbye, Babylon* box set was packed with Alabama raw cotton. In the Preface of the *Art of Field Recording Volume 1* book, Ledbetter wrote of his redemptive intention:

"In February 1999 I set out on a search to find early 20th century recordings of gospel music—the rawer and the more unbridled passion, the better. The music was for a weekly radio show I was producing in Atlanta, and the reason I was focused on this specific genre was because of the difficulty I had encountered locating reissues of religious music to broadcast. My initial findings led me to Joe Bussard, a record collector in Maryland who had amassed 25,000 commercially recorded 78 rpm records. We talked on the telephone, and he started sending me cassettes of his gospel collection. Listening to them, I was in disbelief that so much of this incredible and historic material was unavailable on CD. I began to see this research as a reissue project rather than a radio playlist because I knew the music could reach more listeners on CD than over the airwaves.

"Once I decided to reissue the music on CD, I started to look beyond Bussard's collection and to seek out more recordings. This led me to the Library of Congress, an institution that had been sending out fieldworkers since 1928 to gather American folksongs. Using battery-operated recording devices, the LOC's field collectors could record musicians in their natural environment, which is a stark contrast to the studio recordings on 78s. For gospel music this was significant because an engineer could go to a church or a festival and capture much longer performances than previous technologies allowed. Not only did the equipment allow for portability, but wider diameter discs were used in the 1930s and 1940s, and magnetic tape, which came into general use in the 1950s, also had advantages. No longer was a little more than three minutes the maximum length of what could be recorded..."

Among other accolades, appreciators and critical recognition--the prestigious Grammy Awards pursue Dust To Digital's soulful products with dedication. In 2004, *Goodbye, Babylon* was nominated for Best Historical album and Boxed Set. In 2006, the *Fonotone Records* release was nominated for the same category. Last year, Dust To Digital won a Grammy for the *Art of Field Recording Volume 1*. This weekend (January 31), Ledbetter travels to Los Angeles for the Grammys again since *Take Me To the Water* is up for another Best Historical Album nomination. In this definitive interview, Ledbetter discusses the provenance of the Dust to Digital, each release in detail, the art of recording, musical intent, historic significance and what is on the horizon for this inimitable label. In my humble opinion, Lance Ledbetter is an American hero of the highest order...

James Calemine: We've got a long journey ahead of us... so let's begin. Where did you grow up?

Lance Ledbetter: I grew up in LaFayette, Georgia. It's about 30 minutes south of Chattanooga, Tennessee.

Did you have a musical family?

LL: Not too much. My mom played piano, but far as our family goes...her side of the family that we would see every so often had several musicians in it.

You were born on an Easter Sunday. Did you have a real spiritual family?

LL: Oh yeah. Very religious Christian upbringing...

Did you hear a lot of music growing up?

LL: Yeah, I did. When you compare it to *Goodbye, Babylon* it was some of the same songs but probably not as ecstatically captured like it was in the 20s and 30s. I learned a lot of songs back then.

Where did you go to school?

LL: LaFayette High School and then Young Harris College and then Georgia State. Young Harris was just a two-year school in northeast Georgia.

In college you had a good appetite for old music. Then you started working in a radio station, right?

LL: Yeah, when I was transferring from Young Harris College I really enjoyed music and two of the things I wanted to do no matter where I went to school was work at a radio station and to intern for a record company. Two main objectives that were probably more important than school—it was just what I was going to be doing because those were the two things I was interested in. I moved to Atlanta and probably within two weeks I was doing both. I got hired on at WRAS and started interning with a company called Table of the Elements.

You've told me this story before, but for the sake of the readers I want you to tell it again. What was the impetus for Dust To Digital and what became *Goodbye, Babylon?* You wanted to be able to preserve all this soulful spiritual music...

LL: What turned me onto it was when I went to Young Harris ... well, growing up in high school I had a close-knit circle of friends who were really into different types of music, mostly rock music...

By the way, can you play any instruments?

LL: Yeah (laughs), I was in some rock bands back in high school. When I went to Young Harris—that was my first exposure to a lot of kids from the Atlanta suburbs that were into the hippie-folk world. So, that was new territory for me because we didn't really have that where I grew up. So, I made friends with some of those people. The music they were into was not really to my taste, but where we always found common ground was at a place in North Carolina that we would go—John C. Campbell's Folk School—that was a place that carried on traditional music—folklore-type activities and that was my first exposure. Then when I moved to Atlanta, I was staying up on all types of music publications.

What year did you move to Atlanta?

LL: 1996. It was right after the Olympics. I was always reading a lot of music publications and the Internet. It was around this time, a buzz started about *The Anthology of American Folk Music* was reissued and how it was such a groundbreaking LP box set when it came out in the 50s. I read about it over and over in different magazines and then in 1997 when it finally came out I got a copy from a friend who worked at WREK. I was really curious to hear what all the music magazines were talking up so much. I got it and took it back to my apartment and listened to it—not knowing what to expect—and I fell in love with it. It was one of those moments where your life changes. Nothing was the same after that.

So, I was still working at WRAS and then there was a show called "20th Century Archives" that came on Sunday mornings. The DJ who did that show was Brian Montero. Our common ground was we were big John Fahey fans. We sort of co-hosted a Friday free-form show. He played a lot of Yazoo LPs and different things from that era. When he was going to leave the station because he was graduating and didn't think anyone wanted to take the show over. At that point in time, all I had was *The Anthology of American Folk Music.* I said I was willing to give it a shot. I started doing the show "Raw Musics." I started going around town looking at different used LPs and re-issues from the 20s and 30s.

That's when I realized I could find country, blues and jazz but with a show time at 9AM, I wanted some really good gospel music. That's when I started looking into who were the record collectors that actually owned the records that Yazoo and such put out and that's when I came across an article online about Joe Bussard. I got in touch with him and that's when I told him what I was looking for. I think it was $20 a cassette he started sending. One gospel tape a week. It took me a year and a half just to go through what he sent me. It would blow my mind. I was playing a lot of it on the radio. It started really eating me how so much of that stuff he was sending you couldn't find it in a record shop. It was nowhere to be found. That's when I started thinking, 'OK, I've always loved record labels and how they have this curatorial existence.' I wanted to find out how you re-issue some of this gospel music. Originally, I thought it was going to be a single CD. Over time—a year and a half—listening to those cassettes it dawned on me.

So, I'm sure it gets into copyrights. How did all that work?

LL: Well, what I did with several of the re-issue labels that I followed I talked to their owners and I found out from them what you'd have to do. What rights are necessary for you to put this out. Is this label still around? Who do you talk to at the label? Just a lot of footwork. Also, trying to find out who these artists were. There are so many of them—you'd look them up on the Internet and nothing would come up. After a while and a lot of searches I started noticing how some of these artists were showing on this playlist of a radio station out of Washington D.C. The name of the show was "The Dick Spottswood Radio Show." I emailed him, and at that point in time, I'd been working on it for about a year or so I had a substantial amount of research that I'd been putting together from what I could find.

His response was sort of like, 'Wow, we've been waiting for something like 78 collectors and DJs that focused on this.' I guess everyone sort of noticed there was this black hole for gospel music. Fortunately, when I came knocking researchers and musicologists just opened the door. When I showed them what I was putting together I'd say 95% of them were eager to help however they could. They were very receptive. They knew it was an untold story—one of the big ones. So many focus on blues that was one of the driving forces that led me to gospel music because there was so much great music. I wanted there to be an access point people could approach this music. The stuff that was out there was so scattered...

At this point did you have any particular landmark artists you wanted to expose?

LL: It wasn't even the particular artists. What I wanted to do when I was compiling *Goodbye, Babylon* was I wanted to highlight sub-genres of gospel music...this gospel Christian genre umbrella.

Like Sacred Harp...

LL: Exactly. You got blues guys masquerading as Deacons of their church for the recording companies, jug bands from Memphis that were going in a cutting spiritual records. There were so many different types of music. What I wanted to do was represent as many—if not all—of the sub-genres I came across and I wanted them to be the very best example of what was repre-

•• • •••

sented. I just kept digging deeper and deeper. I was talking to a lot of musicologists—a lot of them were helpful too. They'd point me in another direction, 'You need this guy from Kentucky.' It just kept growing.

So, were you still at the radio station by this point?

LL: What happened, in February of 1999—ten years ago this past February—I decided this was bigger than the radio station, and in my mind the radio station was kind of a hindrance to research, so I left the radio station. When I started going on it at a 40 hour a week basis in February of 1999. I started pouring over cassette tapes a record collector was sending me—about two per week. I was living in an apartment in Decatur and I had my tape deck set up, my headphones and I was just making notes on tracks I liked, artists I kept hearing more stuff that I liked and certain artists I didn't care for just trying to research all of this out and that part of the project took a year and a half.

It wasn't until about a year into it when I had extensive lists that I put on my computer, that's when I started felt like I was ready to find out the musicology side of things. To seek out people who really knew more than I could find. That's when I started to realize with Joe Bussard on the phone up in Fredericksburg, Maryland. He has about 30,000 records.

He's the Fonotone Records guy...

LL: That's right. He's one of the premiere 78 collectors of American vernacular music in the world. I'd ask him questions and Joe knows a lot, but when it came down to the minute details Joe just didn't know a lot about them. Then I started to wonder who knows about this stuff. Then I went around to musicologists. I got in touch with Dick Spottswood and he knows a tremendous amount about every kind of music from that era. What he knew about the gospel artists and songs was spectacular. The other thing he knew was, 'Oh, I see you've got some Sacred Harp on here—you'll want to talk to Buell Cobb in Alabama.' He heard the African-American secular quartets and he told me I'd want to speak with Doug Seroff in Murfreesboro, Tennessee. He knew the network of the extreme specialists.

189

•• • •••

So, that was the first year and a half was a huge band of songs. The next year and a half was doing all the research. Musicologists from all over the country—even several in England, one in Italy and one in the Netherlands—I was going around asking about particular articles written about particular person. Or a song I was interested in. did they found out information about this song—or a specific recording session. Who was playing tambourine on this track? We were getting down to the brass tacks. That took another year and a half.

It can almost be broken into three chapters: collecting the audio, figuring out how you re-issue it. The next year and a half was gathering the research. The third year and a half was putting it all together. At that point, I had over 300 tracks and I whittled it down to 160. It's 135 songs and 25 sermons. I organized The *Goodbye, Babylon* tracks by theme. Then we started laying out the book. There's a woman here in Atlanta, Susan Archie, who is most well known for the Charlie Patton *Screamin' And Hollerin' The Blues* box set, which is gorgeous—everything you could say about it. It took a year and a half to lay the book out. I found the box company up in Canada. Technically, they make boxes for corporate giveaways, and I asked them if they could do this box set. They told me to send them the specs and they could do it.

Then I talked to my uncle's brother in Alabama and we lined him up to get cotton for the boxes. The cotton came from when I was talking to Susan about the book; she kept saying there should be a motif. I designed the wood box in my head then had it drawn up and we got a prototype. I was looking at where the CDs fit in the center of the box and there were these two areas on the left and the right and I told Susan I was thinking about using raw cotton to make it more organic and natural. I always wanted it to look like something that you'd find in the General Store in 1928. As soon as I told Susan I was going to use raw cotton—she was like, 'That's it! That's your motif.' So, she sort of ran with that on the CD sleeves and the book.

What's the significance of the book cover?

LL: It's based on a Sacred Harp hymnbook. It's an oblong book and the Sacred Harp hymnbooks are oblong. The size was already based the text on a 1911 Sacred Harp hymnal.

•• • •••

Finally, the first copies of the timeless, *Goodbye, Babylon,* appear on your doorstep...

LL: That was a story too. At that point and time living in Midtown and the wood boxes show up. We were going to do 1,000. In my mind, it was all just going to logistically happen as it happened. I should point out also, when we were designing the book, the thing I wanted to do was I wanted each page to represent the artist and the song—from Mahalia Jackson to Roosevelt Graves to Hank Williams to Ola Mae Terrell. Each person would be equally represented. To me, I felt the way this set was put together it was just the sum was going to be greater than all the parts. In my mind, sister Ola Mae Terrell was just as great as Hank Williams.

So, anyway, when the boxes showed up in Midtown, they weighed 2 pounds apiece, and there were 1,000 of them. This 18-wheeler pulls up to my apartment. It was crazy. We dealt with it as it came. Then the books showed up. The CDs showed up. My girlfriend April—who is my wife now—her sister had a condo that she was selling. It was vacant and she moved out and we ended up renting that from her, which was in Midtown also where we started doing a lot of our assembly. It was a surreal thing because we didn't think...I thought we'd just sell 50 to 100 copies. I didn't think it would take off. It all showed up in October of 2003, and I would say by February of 2004 we sold out of the 1,000.

Tell the story of Bob Dylan giving Neil Young a copy of *Goodbye, Babylon* as a gift. That story served as the seed of how I actually tracked you down a few months later...

LL: Yeah. That was 2005. It was an article that was used on September 17, 2005. That was surreal as it gets. In January or February of 05 is when we went out to Los Angeles because it got nominated for two Grammy awards. I thought that was surreal as it could get. I remember it was like a Saturday morning and I got an email from my friend, a blues researcher up in Canada and he asked me if I just heard Weekend Edition, and he said Neil Young is on there talking about *Goodbye, Babylon* and I should listen. When they posted the audio it was surreal. Neil Young just talking about *Goodbye, Babylon*...

••• •••

How did Dylan get a copy of it?

LL: I guess he bought it from us. When he came through on his tour I got invited over to The Tabernacle by their sound guy Jules. Dylan's guitarist at the time—Larry Campbell and his sound guy Jules—were big fans. They said Dylan was too. I went to dinner with them. I even got to watch Bob's show from the side-stage, which was incredible. They just said Bob was a big fan. I didn't get to meet Bob, but they gave me his badge and one of his harmonicas, which was a crazy experience. His badge looked like a sheriff's badge that said 'Dylan.' The harmonica has a piece of grip tape on it with the letter B. It came right off the side-stage right after the show. I got to hang out on the bus with the band and talked to them. I couldn't believe they were such big fans. It was intense...

Neil Young and Bob Dylan have a lot of fans, so I'm sure that stirred some curiosity. Everyone wants to know what Dylan is giving Neil. You know, Larry Campbell played on the new Black Crowes record—recorded at Levon Helm's—and I gave the Crowes' guitarist, Luther Dickinson copies of *Goodbye, Babylon, Fonotone Records* and the *Anthology of the String Bass*...he loves that stuff.

LL: I remember you telling me that. You always spread the word. That whole year was crazy. We're putting together *Goodbye, Babylon*—hand-assembling, working our fingers to the bone. One thing in the back of my mind while working on *Goodbye, Babylon*—I went from 300 tracks to 160. I earmarked the 140 tracks that got left off. There were 15-18 tracks I thought would be a killer Christmas CD. Christmas CDs get a bad rap, but I thought some of the songs were so killer.

That turned into the Dust To Digital release, *Where Will You Be On Christmas Day?*

LL: That's it, *Where Will You Be On Christmas Day?* which came out in 2004—just in time for Christmas and that was pretty much driving around in Atlanta in between assembling *Goodbye, Babylon* listening, just hand-picking stuff. And those 15-18 tracks left over from Goodbye, Babylon besides talking to several musicologists we were able to fill out the CD at 24 tracks.

It's amazing no one ever really found any of this stuff. Fortunately, you came along.

LL: I know. I don't know why. I think a lot of it has to do with now—even though *Goodbye,* Babylon took five years to compile—an awful long time—but I think if you had tried to do it in the 60s or 70s—it would've taken a lot longer; maybe ten or twenty years. Now, information can be sent rapidly. The research is much more available even now since I've put out *Goodbye, Babylon.* I just did the liner notes for our Baptism CD that is about to come out. There are huge newspaper archives online—it's really changing. So, I think why people in the past haven't done it is because I think it would have been virtually impossible.

That's true of this information age. What about actually transferring the 78s to digital? The technical aspect of sound quality...

LL: Absolutely, I've talked to people from the 60s when the 78 re-issue world-companies came up. It was done for a completely different purpose. Back then it was done just so collectors could hear other people's records. They might have every Mississippi John Hurt record except two records and somebody could do a re-issue of all of them so the hardcore collectors could hear the ones that are missing. I've talked to several of the people who did the mastering and now pretty much mastering is going to be done on the computer. Splicing is done easily—it's a mouse-click away. Taking pops and hiss out of 78s in those days was done with razor blades. You can't imagine. If they have a pop now, it takes a second. Back then they'd splice it together again and listen to it all over just for one pop. So, that's one example of how things have changed.

It's all a serious history lesson. So, after the *Where Will You Be On Christmas Day?* CD came out how did things progress from there?

LL: Well, when *Goodbye, Babylon* came out and it had the level of success that it did we were pretty overwhelmed by going right in and running a record company full force. That's when we had to decide if we'd go away for another four and a half years and come back with an epic box set like *Goodbye, Babylon,* or would it be better to put something out that year to keep our name on people's minds and send the message to our audience and music fans that we would be putting out things besides epic box sets. That's when the idea came to me that we should do a Christmas CD and get it out in time for Christmas.

Did you know *Goodbye, Babylon* was nominated for a Grammy at this point?

LL: It was weird timing because *Goodbye, Babylon* came out in October of 2003 and missed the deadline for 2004. The cut-off days are always weird. I had these songs left over from *Goodbye, Babylon* that would be great for a Christmas compilation. Once again, Dick Spottswood really came through on the Christmas stuff. I reached out to him and told him my idea about the Christmas album. We had those 15 tracks, and he contributed his ideas based on his radio show because he was doing thematic programs. He'd done a Christmas show for 40 years and it came together with just he and I working on it.

When we were talking earlier, you mentioned Joe Bussard was sending you cassette tapes. Were those tapes just for *Goodbye, Babylon* or did they turn up on what came to be the next Dust To Digital release, Fonotone Records?

LL: No, that was stuff that ended up on *Goodbye, Babylon.* What we would do, whatever we would decide would be for the box set he would drive down to Washington D.C. and have a fellow by the name of Jack Bowers—he's still alive—he's in his 90s to do the digital transfers. He recorded Duke Ellington back in the day.

You engineered an alliance with Joe Bussard, and that was the next Dust to Digital release...

LL: Joe and his family came to us and saw us as a potential vehicle for Joe's Fonotone Records label that he ran out of his parent's basement from 1956 to 1970.

•• • •••

Is the *Fonotone Records* box set still out of print?

LL: It is. We did several thousand copies and the demand—there are still people that want it, but for us to press up one thousand copies it would be expensive. There needs to be more of a demand. It's not a good financial idea yet.

It's another beautiful box set...with a church key, photographs, a killer book and some of the best Appalachian music you've ever heard. There are deft pickers on that compilation...

LL: Yeah, on Fonotone it was three different types of performances that Joe recorded. One was when Joe would go out on these record trips looking for 78s he'd bring his tape recorder and record musicians for them to make a record. The second was Joe and his friends who would listen to the old 78s and then do their own renditions of the songs. The third was for record researchers like Mike Seeger's or Steven Grossman—different people who wanted copies of records so they could learn from them and Joe would always say, 'I'll make you a copy of everything if you make a record for me. To me, the one thing that came across working with Joe on that Fonotone Records—it was all about fun. He was running a company as a kid out of his parents' basement. He was just having a good time. The Fonotone Records box set came out at the end of 2005.

For the next release—*How Low Can You Go? Anthology of the String Bass*—did you plan it to be the next release or was it a decision that came up quickly? You already covered, blues, gospel, country, Appalachia and now it was jazz.

LL: That was the idea of Dick Spottswood too. He had done a few things for Rounder Records. He'd focus in on different instruments and he suggested to us that we should examine the string bass. There was material he put together for it. I thought it was a great idea that had never been done before. I thought it was a historical box set.

It was a real New Orleans-based project. You were continually covering new ground…no one geographic area. *How Low Can You Go? Anthology of the String Bass* also contains an indelible book…

LL: That's what we always try to do is create an overwhelming experience for the listener. To let them travel back in time and re-create an experience.

The next Dust To Digital release is a CD and DVD of *Desperate Man Blues,* which preserves the story of Joe Bussard who started Fonotone Records. He'd ride up to the most rural country home and buy records from them…

LL: That's right. They shot that film (on DVD) right after Joe did all the digital transfers from *Goodbye, Babylon.* My friend Todd and I went up to visit Joe for the first time. I'd talked to him on the phone before, but I went up this time to visit him. The film crew from Australia just left. They were there for three weeks and he told us about it. Then I finally saw the film about a year and a half later. I love that film. I tried for a long time to convince the filmmaker from Australia to let us re-issue it. He wasn't so sure about going with such a young company, but finally he decided to let us put it out and I'm happy we did. That was probably the most releases we had come out at one time towards the end of 2006. Within a month's span we put out *How Low Can You Go?, Desperate Man Blues* and the *I Belong to This Band.*

***The Sacred Harp* records are fascinating. Had you ever heard that genre before you began researching it?**

LL: No, I didn't. The first time I heard Sacred Harp singing was on the tapes Joe was sending me. There was not a lot of information on it, and I was blown away when I heard it. It got my attention and ear pretty quick. I started to do some research, and I'd probably say a month or two after I heard the 78 I got in touch with a guy named Buell Cobb from the Sacred Harp Institute in Alabama and he invited me over to a Sacred Harp convention. There were about 150 people singing and it sounded just like the 78s. It was incredible. When I started looking on my own after hearing the music off the tapes and got in touch with Buell Cobb I didn't know if it was still being performed or anything. We put some of the Sacred Harp 78s on *Goodbye, Babylon.* For us, we just wanted to show our appreciation for that musical form.

Now, I want you to talk about the released *The Art of Field Recording Volume 1* and *2*, and how you met Art Rosenbaum.

LL: That was through George Mitchell. As you know he's done incredible work over the years with so many great musicians. I'd come across his work in the research for *Goodbye, Babylon.* When the *Goodbye, Babylon* box set came out, I wanted to give him a copy. He invited me over to his house and we had lunch and talked for a long time, and that's when Art's name came up. That was another name I came across while working on *Good-bye, Babylon.* I'd never really thought about getting in touch with him because I didn't know him. George said I should. So, I sent Art a copy of *Goodbye, Babylon,* and then I drove over to Athens and we had lunch and talked about The University of Georgia library archive. We went down in the basement to the archive and it was unbelievable how much tape and DATs that Art had down there. We listened to some of it and it was just unbelievable. I couldn't believe there was so much great material that was only accessible if you went to the UGA media room at the library. Art and I talked about how to go about issuing this material. We did the sample CD and then the following two years we released *Volume 1* and *Volume 2* of *The Art of Field Recording.*

I think Art brings a very unique approach to this music. To me, the strongest parts of what he done is that he didn't limit himself. A lot of people if they really get into music and records and field recording they tend to gravitate to a certain genre. Like they will just collect blues or country or jazz. What's amazing to me Art was collecting gospel, blues, bluegrass, country—he has an adventurous spirit as far as what he enjoyed musically. To me, that was an incredible part of the story. Another part was his wife Margo accompanied him on these field trips. She would photograph the musicians. You would actually get to see a picture of the actual song being recorded as you were hearing it. That's amazing. The final thing that was great about the story was he'd paint from memory these musicians. From a box set standpoint, all the elements were there to have a really strong presentation of Art Rosenbaum's incredible contribution to music.

Another thing was he's a great musician...

LL: That's right. He more than downplayed that on the box set. He's on a couple of the tracks playing backing music, but absolutely, he's a very great banjo player—he's written a couple of books on instructional guides on how to play banjo. It's pretty amazing because a lot of the material that he recorded...the reason he started recording people back in the 50s was because he wanted to learn their music. He'd ask Pete Seeger how to play his songs. Pete told Art, 'Don't learn from me. Learn from the guy who taught me.' Art took that to heart and started to go out on his own and explore and try to find musicians to learn from. It's the source. Art has some really strong criteria he believes an artist should have for him to record them. One is, he wants either a family member or friend that handed the music down. He doesn't want to record something someone learned from a record or CD. I think that's pretty unique to have such a strong and definite criteria for recording people.

Volume 1 came out in 2007. That was really a big year for us because at that point in time we got an email from a writer from The New Yorker whose wife bought him *How Low Can You Go?* a year or so earlier. Somehow he subscribed to our email list and he wrote me an email about a release party at The Melting Point in Athens for the *Art of Field Recording Volume 1*. The writer talked to his editor and got enough money to come down and survey and see if there was enough material for a story. He came down and spent the night hanging out with Art. I saw him the next morning and I asked him if he thought there was enough material for a story, and he said there was enough for ten stories! He was blown away, which was special all this was with Art and his connections to these musicians and how interesting the musicians were. The set came out in 2007, and the New Yorker article came out in April of 2008 and that was the biggest thing that came along since the *Goodbye, Babylon* set came out. That was the most attention we'd ever had.

*****

***The Art of Field Recording Volume 1* won a Grammy.**

LL: It did. It came out in 2007 and was nominated for Art's liner notes and Best Historical album. We ended up flying out to Los Angeles in November 2009. I really did not expect it to win. I think we were up against Miles Davis and Nina Simone. I just thought there was no way. They did the announcement where they did the liner notes before they did the Historical category. Terry Gross' husband from NPR won the liner notes. I thought we'd seen this before—we'll take the loss, but in the next category they announced our names. It was one of the top five feelings of your life. You just can't believe it. We went up onstage and gave our speeches. They took us on a little media junket and talked to different radio and television people. It was incredible. To me, it was so special to see Art getting to experience all of this because he'd been working on all of this for 50 years. And at this point to get recognized up onstage was great. We go out there at the end of this month to see if *Take Me To The Water* will win. I'm not so sure. We're going up against the Woodstock box set and the Woody Guthrie box set.

There's a real spook to the Dust To Digital release of *Melodii Tuvi: Throat Songs and Folk Tunes From Tuva* as well as *The Black Mirror* recordings. Those are the label's dark horse recordings because they aren't American...

LL: Oh yeah. It's music outside of the English language. They are more challenging releases, but we were really excited to do both of these. Those two CDs came out at the same time as *Art of Field Recording Volume 1*. We were very happy just to be able to get a box set and those two CDs out.

Say something about the *Victrola Favorites* release...

LL: That ended up missing the Christmas push. We usually try to get them in stores before Christmas time. That came out in January of 2008.

Did you and Art plan to break up *The Art of Field Recordings into two Volumes?*

LL: Yeah, we did. We set out from the get-go to do Volumes 1 and 2. Really I think Volume 2 is in a lot of ways better than Volume 1 based on what we learned as far as some of the audio and where we could go to get better source material. I think it came out even better. The fact that Volume 1 won the Grammy it's always going to be the one that gets recognized the most. Volume 2 was not nominated. I thought maybe—I wondered why it wouldn't be—but maybe it's anticlimactic to have won it last year and then be nominated for something so similar for the next year. I think that was the case.

When I attended the Grammy Award party last April at the Highland Inn that's when I saw the book *Take Me To The Water*. Now, at the end of the month you're flying to Los Angeles because it's up for a Grammy. Talk about the book...

LL: That's right. That party was a great night. What happened with that book was there's a collector named Jim Linderman. He collects folk art and different furniture from different periods—he's just a collector. One thing he was interested in collecting for about 20 years is baptism photos. After *Goodbye, Babylon* came out sometime in 2006, I started receiving emails from Jim Linderman saying, 'I got these photographs,' and then he started sending these photographs and JPEGS to see if I'd be interested in doing anything with these photos. It was a little like the Christmas CD because I knew in doing *Goodbye, Babylon* there were some strong baptism songs and there were ones we'd considered and didn't put on there. I thought the photographs were so powerful that I wanted to work something out with Linderman. So he came down to Atlanta and came to the house. We sat and talked. He brought two large archival books with him. After we talked he told me he trusted and liked me enough to leave these photographs with me. He got on a plane and flew back to New York. We scanned all the photographs. Then I wondered how I was going to do it. The whole book took about a year and a half to really get it right.

Outside of *Goodbye, Babylon*, what Dust To Digital project has taken the longest to get out?

••••••

LL: Well, that one took a lot of time, but the one that took the longest was the *Art of Field Recording Volume 1*. Art Rosenbaum, myself and my wife April worked on Volume 1 pretty much on a daily basis for 13 months. Everyday we were going through material, photographs, Art was writing and we were editing. It was a massive amount of work for Volume 1.

Let's talk about a new release by Reverend Johnny L. Jones...

LL: He's a special guy. Tremendous musician. The way we learned about him was through Cole Alexander who is the guitar player for the Black Lips. He had a cassette copy of one of Johnny's records that came out in the 60s and 70s on Jewel. There was another local musician—Bradford Cox from Deerhunter—who I spoke with about him. Cole thought it was just the greatest gospel music he'd ever heard. So, he tracked down one of Johnny's records. There's a radio station in Grant Park here in Atlanta—WYZE—that's a gospel music radio station. He decided to stop and go in. Johnny was from Atlanta and he ran a church called Second Mount Olive Baptist Church. Cole was curious to find out if he was still around. He went to the radio station and asked them if they'd ever heard of him or knew anything about him, and they said he did a radio show there every Saturday.

Cole ended up meeting him, and hanging out with him for a while. Then he contacted me and told me the story and that it might be something I'd be interested in pursuing. I said I'd talk to Johnny. When I talked to Johnny I thought he'd say, 'Yeah, I've got those first seven records I did for Jewel back in the 60s and 70s and that's all I got.' Well, we start talking and he told me he had reel to reels of tapes from his recorded congregations that wouldn't all fit in the back of my truck. He'd been recording his service every Sunday for broadcast on the radio station since 1957. He's still preaching at The Second Mount Olive Baptist Church. He's 73 years old. He's one of a kind. He's someone to talk to, a very special guy. We ended up transferring about 90 hours of his performances on digital. We've got the first record that came out last month. We're working on the second one, and we want to see how the response is on that in the record stores and the music world. There's so much material.

•••••••

At the height of his surge, the church suffered several tragic incidents like fires, but at the zenith of his congregation in Atlanta the number of people coming to his church every Sunday was about 1,700. There are some powerful recordings. He had an organ player, electric guitar, electric bass and drums backing him up; pretty much a rock band behind him. They let people sing along...

These type stories cheer me up...

LL: Oh, I know. To know that there is somebody out there like Johnny Jones making music. We've been to his service several times and it's two and a half hours long. Two hours of it is music. He has a very musical mind. He started playing piano when he was 12 and he just kept going. He's always upbeat, always positive.

JC: Talk about the *Au Clair de la Lune* project.

LL: That was something I read about in the *New York Times*. The back-story is a fellow by the name of David Giovannoni from Maryland—he and I met at an audio conference in Seattle several years ago. I read this article saying the Academy of Arts and Sciences in France had found these sheets of paper that had this wavy edging to it and soon they announced this David hopped the next plane to Paris because they knew exactly what it was— what they were. An invention back in the 1850s and 1860s discovered a way to capture sound on paper. When David heard about that he went and did these scans on these pieces of paper called Phonautograms.

They brought them back to America and had an audio laboratory in Berkeley, California, to figure out an algorithm to get the sound off the paper. Sure enough, they got one to play back. I got in touch with David and said this was too important to have the first recording of the human voice that's ever been played back. We wanted that voice as a physical object. It would be a tragedy if we didn't put it on a CD. He agreed. He let us cut a 7-inch. The inventor Edwin Leon Scott, he's reciting the lyrics to "Au Clair de la Lune". It's pretty chilling. It's not something you want to listen to if you're feeling upbeat or something to pat your foot to, but as a music historian or librarian you want this in your collection because you want to be able to refer back to the first recording of the human voice.

So, *Utne Reader* magazine named you one of the 50 Visionaries changing the world...

LL: This magazine called *The Utne Reader* got in touch with us and said I made this list as one of the people changing the world, that's all it says...

Well, I agree with them...

LL: Thanks James. I appreciate that. By the way, I wanted to congratulate you for your name being mentioned in *The New York Times* for the Jim Dickinson interview...

Thank you kindly. So, what's on the horizon for Dust to Digital? Any upcoming releases you can talk about?

LL: One we're really excited about is—we've been talking about it for a couple of years and it's finally going to happen. There's one track on *Goodbye, Babylon* called "It Ain't No Grave" by Brother Claude Ely. It's the first song on CD 2. His nephew was over in a London record shop and he heard his uncle coming through the speakers. He asked what it was and they told him it was a box set called *Goodbye, Babylon*. Macel learned there was this ongoing interest in his music. He decided he was going on a search and talk to as many people as he could—family members, people in his church all around Kentucky, Virginia and Tennessee trying to find people that could tell him about his uncle. He wrote a biography on Brother Claude. He interviewed me for the book with the connection on *Goodbye, Babylon* and part of his story. I told him I knew he was probably going to shop it around to University Presses, but I told him if he ever wanted us to work on it with him that I'd love to do it.

Time goes by, different presses changed hands, various delays, editors and finally he contacted us. We agreed on terms to put it out. The agreement was drawn up and not a month into it we find out Rick Rubin produced Johnny Cash record coming out at the end of February called *Ain't No Grave*. The title song is by brother Claude Ely. I was excited about the book no matter what, but for us something like this to happen is big. I think we have a certain amount of people that are like you and me that are really interested in old music. I think for something like this where you have the Johnny Cash record coming out with that song on there I think a lot of people who really love that song and record we've got a whole book about the man who wrote the song, the history of the song, his history and a CD of all unreleased material by brother Claude. For us, it creates an audience that we normally don't get. Hopefully, they'll work well together.

When will that be out?

LL: Right now we're set for July 1, but we're hoping—especially with the buzz around this new Johnny Cash album, we're trying to get it done just as quickly as we can.

Anything coming out before then?

LL: Yeah, there will be. We're sending off next week a record—we signed a 78 collector who is doing his first project with us. We're going to put that out on vinyl. It's World String Music that's coming out as an LP. It's a great compilation he put together. Other things are, the same person is also compiling and we're finishing up a box set of 4 CDs of African music from the 20s, 30s and 40s. We're also getting the first John Fahey recording out this year—that's been a long time coming. I'm ready for that to be out. We've been working on it for the past couple of years, but we're finally moving forward on it. It will be out this year as well.

Well Lance, congratulations man. You're one of my heroes. I'll be pulling for you at the Grammys. Keep up the good work....

LL: James, thanks so much. Thanks for all the exposure. I'll get something out to you in the mail next week...

Godspeed...

Kirk West's Photographic Memories

Kirk West's first photography book, Les Brers, captures his work during his years working with the Allman Brothers Band. West's new book Blues In Black and White revolves around Chicago bluesman. His work will be featured at the National Blues Museum in November 2017. This interview was conducted in 2007.

Kirk West plays an integral part in The Allman Brothers Band organization. West began taking photographs in the '70s which included hundreds of musicians such as Merle Haggard, Bob Marley, Jerry Garcia and The Allman Brothers Band. In time, his photographic skills led him to the Allmans' camp.

The Allman Brothers trusted West enough to compile and oversee their landmark *Dreams* box set. In 1989, West became a full-time employee of the band. West created artwork for the 1990 *Seven Turns* CD as well as various other promotions for the group. Several years ago The Georgia Music Hall of Fame showcased West's remarkable photography. His work embodies a personification of art in the sense that his photos suspend and preserve moments in time that capture a specific action in the past that will never happen again.

Kirk and his wife, Kirsten, moved to Macon in 1993 and began cultivating The Big House Foundation—an organization dedicated to preserving a home and history for the Allman Brothers. The vast contents of West's collection contain multitudes of priceless memorabilia. The Allman Brothers lived in the Big House from 1970-1973 where many tragic and glorious events happened.

Duane Allman was leaving the Big House when he was killed in a motorcycle accident. Bassist Berry Oakley was taken to the Big House before dying at the hospital after his fatal motorcycle wreck. Gregg Allman wrote "Midnight Rider," "Ain't Wastin' Time No More," and "Hotlanta" at the Big House. Dickey Betts penned "Blue Sky" and "Ramblin' Man" in the same house, located on historic Vineville Avenue.

In this extensive interview Kirk talks about his photography, the Allmans, the origins of *Hittin' the Note* magazine, The Big House Foundation and other interesting topics.

••••••

So, what's goin' on?

KW: Well, it's scramble time. Y'know we're loading in and heading to New York.

Well, let's get to it. You grew up in Chicago, right?

KW: Well, actually I grew up in Nevada, Iowa, spelled like the state. I moved to Chicago when I was 17.

When did you get your first camera?

KW: My grandmother gave me my first camera when I was about 8 years old. I still have it—a little green, plastic—it had 620 film. It was a little square Brownie box type camera. I started shooting pictures when I was 8 of all kinds of weird little things. My Dad had been an amateur photographer when he was growing up. He was the school photographer—yearbook, and all that kind of shit. My Dad wasn't around much. My Mom was divorced when I was 3. I just came by it kind of naturally. My grandmother gave it to me and I just started snapping. When I was 13 I got myself a part-time job after school working for a Chrysler dealership. I was a little gearhead. This town had like 3,500 people in it—it was a real small farm town in the middle of Iowa. For anybody that was a car nut there were four good jobs in town: The Standard Station, the Chevy dealer, the Ford dealer and the Chrysler dealer. I got a job as the car wash kid and learned how to change oil and stuff when I was 13-14. They had a drag racing team, this Chrysler dealership.

I didn't realize your race fever went so far back...

KW: Yeah, this was drag racing. They had a race team; they were successful. I'd go out on the weekends and be the gopher and I'd shoot pictures and sold some to the local paper because they were a winning team and it was a big deal. It got like that — I shot mostly cars and drag racing until I moved to Chicago and I started shooting music.

How old were you when you moved to Chicago?

••••••

KW: I was 17, right out of high school.

I guess by then you owned a pretty good record collection.

KW: I wouldn't call it that, y'know. We were pretty poor. When I got out of high school, I probably had a couple hundred albums. It was all about vinyl because 8 tracks didn't sound that good. They were only for cars. They were a horrible format. So, it was all about vinyl. I moved to Chicago and jumped into photography with both feet. I was going to concerts every weekend—shooting pictures, doing drugs…hanging out in blues joints.

That's really when you started shooting a lot of blues guys, right?

KW: Yeah, it was totally alien to me. I grew up in a town with 3,500 hundred people. There were no black people in that town. They knew nothing about black people. They weren't racist, but there were no black people there.

What year was it when you were 17?

KW: '68.

Trouble was about to hit the fan…

KW: Yeah, it was—I went to Chicago for the first time in the summer of 1968 which is why I moved there in the fall. I turned 18 just as I got into Chicago. I graduated high school in June of '68—turned 18 in October and went to the Democratic convention in the summer of '68. It was a helluva summer. So, I turn around and made another feeble attempt at Iowa State and lasted six weeks and then packed up my car and drove to Chicago. That's when it started—where a lot of shit kicked off. I had been exposed to the blues through some of my friends' older brothers. It was San Francisco psychedelia and Chicago blues…that was my combination.

A lot of your pictures at The Georgia Music Hall of Fame-a couple years back—proved a formidable collection. By

around 1970 you probably started catching up with The Allman Brothers Band.

KW: Well, I saw them before I heard about them. They were playing this joint in the entertainment neighborhood on the north side of Chicago. The hippie section was along Well Street all through the later Sixties. It started to get fairly dangerous —there was a lot of turmoil going on in Chicago, a lot of shit kicking off. Three or four blues clubs around Rush street, but mostly they were these 1970's equivalent to singles bars. Pick up joints. They'd have a lot of music, but they weren't serious listening rooms. At this time we were 19 and there's this one place—none of us were old enough to drink yet, so we all had fake IDs and were floating in and out of the joints and I came to a place called "Beavers" that's where I first saw The Allman Brothers. They were loud. They looked like us—we were hippies with tie dies and mutton chops and shit like that, but they were really fucking loud and they were okay—they were good, but we weren't there to watch music, we were there to get close to chicks. We hung around about an hour and it wasn't the kind of sound you you could talk over, so we split. A short time later I was at a friend's house and I saw that first album and I recognized the guys as the guys we saw that night, and so I put it on and listened to it at a moderate volume and fucking fell in love with it. I went out the next morning and bought two copies of it. I left one at home and took the other one wherever I went. I saw them again down here in Atlanta — '69 and '70 were a couple of good years for hitting rock festivals.

Right around the time of the Byron Pop Festival...

KW: That was the second time I ever saw the Allmans was July of 1970.

You stayed in Chicago a while, right?

KW: I didn't live in Georgia until 1993. I stayed in Chicago, well I left Chicago in the fall of '70 and high-tailed it to California. I was dodging bullets and policemen. I got out there and spent about a year in northern California. Then I came back to Chicago to face the music. I was in and out of Chicago from '68 to '77.

I'd spend a year or two in Chicago and then I'd get restless and go to Colorado. I kept coming back to Chicago. I was in Florida —facing some serious criminal charges and got my act together and quit being a deadbeat, cleaned-up and after about a year and a half or two years of sobriety I moved back to Chicago.

Did you ever have to worry about the draft?

KW: I got a 1Y Deferment which was a health classification. I had epilepsy when I was in junior high school when I was 13 years old. I took a mild dose of Dilantin for about five or six years. It was a childhood epilepsy—petit mal, didn't really have seizures, I just lost consciousness. It was enough to keep me out of the draft.

Kept you from having a foot shootin' party (Duane threw Gregg a "foot-shootin' party when Gregg shot himself in the foot to avoid the draft)...

KW: (laughs) That's exactly right. I don't like cold weather so I wouldn't have been much of a Canadian either...so that kept me out and gave me freedom to protest the war without feeling like I was gonna get yanked.

But you're taking pictures the whole time...

KW: I had a nice 35mm with three or four lenses. You shoot your environment—that's what I did. All those years I was a dope fiend I shot my environment. I got really chilling pictures of young people that ended up dead. Living in vans and traveling. I shot nothing but black & white. During my professional career I only shot color if somebody was paying me to shoot color. I shot black & white every day of my life. Once I snagged on to it. Back when you're doing the little box cameras—shooting things at the drugstore—it's mostly color film but in the very early days it was bad color—black & white stayed truer. When I was in high school I didn't shoot for the yearbook or the school paper, but I was really good friends with the guy who did, and I'd go over and use his dark room. He'd print stuff for me. Black & white was the way I saw the world.

**What photographers, if any, did you try to model yourself
after?**

KW: There was a guy named Larry Clarke—he put out a book
called *Tulsa, Oklahoma,* that impacted the whole thing for me.
William Penn was a portrait photographer that I really admired. A Canadian by the name of Joseph Karsch was a very
famous portrait photographer. I didn't shoot a lot of stuff outside. I wasn't a landscape guy. I wanted to do brutal stuff like
Tulsa. As years progressed, you see the stuff Jim Marshall shot
as far as music photographers Annie Leibowitz and the Rolling Stone photographers…those were the guys that always had
the access. In the early Seventies they weren't creating studio
environments outside or in houses, they were using 35mm and
most generally it was shot with a wide-angle lens which puts the
subject in its environment, which is different from what Karsch
did or William Penn because they created formal studio settings.
The music photographers were always putting the subject in the
context of their environment. So, I've done both—I do both.

**You've taken a lot of up-close photos of artists and ordi-
nary folk…**

KW: Throughout the Seventies and into the Eighties once I got
back to Chicago and got settled, I got real serious about it. I got
real serious in '77. I'd been clean for a couple of years—I wasn't
shootin' up dope no more and I had the ability to buy a nice set of
cameras. I decided that's what I wanted to do. I really got down
to business in '77. I became obsessed—I shot every day, all day.
I'd shoot the world around me—two or three concepts a night. I
had a couple if partners and we formed a little co-op. See, we had
different notions… you had the KISS, Genesis guys and a lot of
punks at that time. I was a country boy—I was shootin' lots of
blues. There were other guys that shot nothing but blues. I shot
all the country in town, and nobody wanted to touch that…

You meet the Allmans in the late '70s, right?

KW: I started shootin' pictures of 'em as a freelance guy in '73.
It wasn't until '79 that I started making any kind of serious in-
roads with them. I'd gotten to know them on a very casual—

here's some reefer kind of basis. Musicians are always happy to see a smiling face and then hands them something—so we got to be friends like that...

By then The Allman Brothers Band was in shambles...

KW: Yeah, see that's the thing. I had been introduced to them and gotten to know them throughout their heyday—their heights, but by the time I got serious about photography they had fragmented. Dickey was out with Great Southern—Gregg playing with the Nighthawks. He had a little band. Sea Level was happening. Butch has a band. So, everybody had their little fragmented pieces and they were little extremely gracious and accepting.

It was a little easier to get to them.

KW: Well yeah, y'know when you're playing joints instead of stadiums all the glad handers turn away from you. The people that didn't—it was a valuable relationship during these periods. In '79 when they got back together, I go out as the shooter. I did a lot of freelance with them—all I was doing was photography. I shot the stuff for their '81 and '82 video releases. I did all kinds of publicity stuff. Then when they were fragmented—it was '88—I got to workin' on the boxset. The Clapton *Crossroads* thing was out. Polygram was proposing to do a Brothers package and the guy that was the head of that department started scouting around. There was no Allman Brothers organization at that time because everybody had their thing. Everybody kept saying talk to Kirk—he knows where all the tape is—he knows the deal. All through the '80s I had started working on this book project. In the course of gathering data, memorabilia and documents—I also gathered tape. So, when the record company got serious about it, I got involved in it and they made me associate producer of the whole package. I rounded up all the photographs and that was my forte, but I knew all the tape also. I knew the lineage, and I knew the story. So, they hired somebody else to write the notes, the essay, but I was deeply involved in the rest of it. Then they got back together in '89 and went out as the photographer for the first leg and then they lured me as assistant tour manager because they had somebody that didn't know how to talk to them. I officially started drawing a weekly paycheck in the summer of '89.

Right around 1992 or '93 you moved to Macon...

KW: In '93 we bought the Big House. We came down—I came down in the fall of '92; I'd been working, playing around down here in Macon. I'd been down here a lot through the '80s digging' and looking for stuff for this book and taking up boxes of tapes. This was a ton of old tape in the studio basement. I came down and started doing that, and Chank Middleton turned me on to the people who own the Big House. Cedrick Lesley was the guy.

He didn't own it when the Brothers lived there did he?

KW: No, he bought it from back taxes in 1987. The house was crumbling pretty quick. It hadn't been tended to for a number of years. It changed hands several times throughout the '70s and '80s—nobody kept it up. They didn't have any money to keep it up. So when we bought it in '93 we overpaid for it and threw every dime we had into it. It needed new everything—it had no heating or air. We spent as much renovating it as we did buying it and we still ran out of money. We never got it to the point where we really wanted to have it, but it's fine, very stable. Two or three rooms we really would've liked to do different, but we never did.

The Mule came in not long after that and made their first record...

KW: They were just an idea when they came in. They moved in here in late May of '94. We moved everything out of those two archive rooms and they set up where the band used to rehearse and they had a name and a landfall of songs that they were trying to make their own. They were here for about two weeks. Haynes was living in Duane's room. It was the three of them and Eric Hanson. For 10-12 days they sat down here and worked. We wouldn't let 'em play electric after midnight.

(Laughs) They had to get all their work done before the midnight hour.

KW: And those motherfuckers don't like to get up early. But we let 'em play acoustic after midnight so we got every bit of their

••• •••

music on acoustic versions. Woody playing an acoustic bass, and Haynes playing acoustic or dobro and Matt playing a cardboard box. We taped all that shit. It's pretty cool stuff. They did that and went downtown and played their first gig.

When did the idea come to turn the Big House into a Bed & Breakfast?

KW: We came down here with that idea. However, the city—with building codes and zoning don't really make it economical to have a Bed & Breakfast in the city of Macon. So, we were gonna have four guest rooms and live here with two museum rooms. That was our invention. Be here five or six years, do a Bed & Breakfast, we just let people stay here. Gregg came a few times. Butch stayed here, the Mule, Jaimoe was always coming through. It was wild. It became what it had been. They'd say man it's fucking amazing to be able to come back here and sleep in your old bedroom after all these years. So many wonderful and tragic things took place in this house. We had a couple of funerals here for the roadies that passed. It was good that it was a home. It brought the family back together on a number of occasions. It was a real blessing that we were able to do this.

When did you and Ron Currens get *Hittin' the Note* together?

KW: Well, I met Ron in '85 or '86, '86 I think. We were doing a little thing a gal and I were doing up in Chicago called Les Brers. It was mimeographed—quarterly newsletter. She quit doing that; her and I split up when I went to work for the band. I quit having anything to do with Les Brers and she did it for another couple of years. She quit doing it in '91, I believe. So then in '92 this gal that I know came to me with this idea that her and her husband were gonna start a little home publishing company. The first project she wanted to do was the Allman Brothers fan club. But she didn't know jackshit about the Allman Brothers and Les Bres had been discontinued. I didn't have time, but I rounded up Ron Currens, Joe Bell, and Bill Ector...

By the way, how is old Bill (Ector—*Hittin' the Note's* publisher)?

KW: Bill's fine. He had a large tumor removed. He's doing a little bit of radiation just to make sure. It's made him a little foggy, but he's fine. He was always a little foggy (laughter).

John (Lynskey) told me the day he got out of the hospital, he went to the Waffle House. From brain surgery to the Waffle House is a great sign.

KW: It was incredible. It was a benign tumor on, not in, his brain, so they were able to cut him open and take it off. If you can get a lucky brain tumor—Bill got it.

Once you got those guys *Hittin' the Note* started coming together?

KW: Yeah, once I got them rounded up. They were gonna provide content. We were gonna have it published in Chicago and these guys from Atlanta were gonna provide content. She lasted about an issue and a half—she never put out her second issue. Kirsten and I took it over from the publishing standpoint. We would administer the newsletter and the fan club. The boys down here would do the writing. Ron was the editor, Kirsten was the publisher beginning with issue two and I was they wrangler. That lasted until Pete moved to town in '97.

That's around the time I began writing for *Hittin' the Note*. Maybe eight months later.

KW: I remember the ceremony when Currens turned everything over to John Lynskey. Lynskey took over as editor. Pete took over from Kirsten as publisher. That was all about the same time Pete moved down here. We were still operating out of the Big House. We bought the house next door in '97. So, all that took place in that timeframe.

So, let's talk about these upcoming Beacon shows... what's going on with the Brothers?

KW: We're gonna work this year—not a lot. Last year we worked a lot more than we had in a number of years and this year we're going into exact opposite direction and we're gonna do a couple of festivals. We're doing Jazz Fest, Memphis in May, and Wanee Fest. Then we'll work in August and that's it.

Any plans for recording?

KW: It's hard to say. I think they want to. I don't think there's any real pressure to record. It doesn't make any sense to get in there and force it. I think Gregg's got a notion he might want to do a record on his own. It's hard to say. I didn't think the band would stay together this long. When I met my wife, Kirsten in '91, I told her, we'll only be at this for a couple of years. Who knows what the fuck's gonna happen.

You're a main staple of that organization.

KW: I'm not gonna let these bastards run me off! (laughs)

You've got quite a lot of Allman's memorabilia...

KW: Well the museum thing is interesting. Kirsten and I've had nearly 25,000 people walk in the front door of our house when we bought it in '93. That's a lot of interruptions. We don't charge admission. I'm obsessed but Kirsten isn't. We're down here because she wanted her husband to be happy. Now, it's time to make sure her husband keeps her happy. I started hearing her about five years ago. She wanted to get the hell out of Macon. She wanted to go out west. She wanted to be in New Mexico. We used to vacation in New Mexico. We love it down there. From a business and a land standpoint, it's a long ways away. It's the other side of the world when you're talking about rock tours. We found a beautiful house and we were going to go to New Mexico. We still owned the house next door, and I was trying to sell both houses who wanted to do what we did. I didn't want to have everything auctioned off—this tells an important story here. A lot of people wanted the collection, but they didn't want the house. A lot of people were poking around. I found a couple different guys that both had the right combination of heart and intention and money. A lot of folks had some combination. Some had money but not the right intentions. Both of these guys were ready but neither one of their wives wanted to live in Macon. But they came up with the interesting notion of a charitable foundation. One guy came up with the idea and helped us establish it —while this other guy wrote the first big check. They were both on the board of trustees for a good bit and then they both kinda passed into the history of this thing. We started three years ago seriously pursuing this concept and we built it with a board of directors and a board of trustees from around the country and started raising money with the intention of the foundation buying the collection and the house and appreciating it as a traditional house museum. We tapped our first million. We paid for a documentary film we will release.

Wasn't a bit of that shown at the outing in January in Macon?

KW: Yeah, we showed the trailer. So, you know we got a lot of irons in the fire. Kirsten and I will move out of here in May. We're moving out of here in May.

Where 'ya moving to?

KW: Shirley Hills—the other side of town. We found a nice house that Kirsten fell in love with—we're not going to New Mexico. It became apparent in this process that I had to be in the midst of it for a good while—at least a couple of years after it appears. I'm gonna have to stay involved. I'm a real fundraiser. I'm the heart—we got a great team. We're starting renovations in June. Soon as we're out of here. We've had serious support here, in middle Georgia. Most of the money has been raised in New York and Chicago. We started with a couple events in Atlanta. We didn't want the town of Macon to think we came up with this idea that we wanted them to fund this for us. We wanted to do this for the community, not by the community. But you know, the way communities are once it looks like it's gonna be the real fucking deal, they want their name attached to it. There are a couple of organizations here in town who will really contribute to the Big House Foundation once this change happens. I'd like to put at little pitch out there. We're looking for anybody that's got a good heart and some old-house renovation talents. Carpenters, drywallers, window men, we're looking for someone who can do floors. We've got a lot of volunteer labor-people from San Diego, North Georgia, and a guy in Savannah I'm trying to track down.

·· ·· ··

So when you get home from the Beacon run this will be all on top of you...

KW: Oh, I know. Balls to the wall. We come back, I got two days here and then we go to the Wanee Fest. I get home on the 16th but we've been in the moving and cleaning process since September. We've moved—this house was absolutely packed to the rafters with memorabilia that was not on display. We had a guy who donated to us about 4,000 square feet of office space downtown in a brand new building. This particular space is a big loft space that hasn't been finished yet. It's the best building in Macon. Down on Mulberry right across the street from the rock and roll hall of fame. Beautiful building. We're on the second floor, with the U.S. Marshall Service (laughs).

Ah, the irony...

KW: Oh yeah, the DA is above us. Saxby Chambliss' office is up there.

Well, at least you're safe. We'll get a future update from you later—maybe display more of your photos...

KW: We're as safe as milk. I'll tell ya, those marshals didn't know what to make of us when we started hauling' shit in there. We carry our laptops in backpacks, right? You got these long haired guys with weird looking outfits on—they're just looking. Yeah, I'm really glad we got a chance to do this. If you wouldn't mind, link the Big House Foundation Website where you can bid on tickets, and instruments at auction fundraisers. I enjoyed this...thanks for asking me...

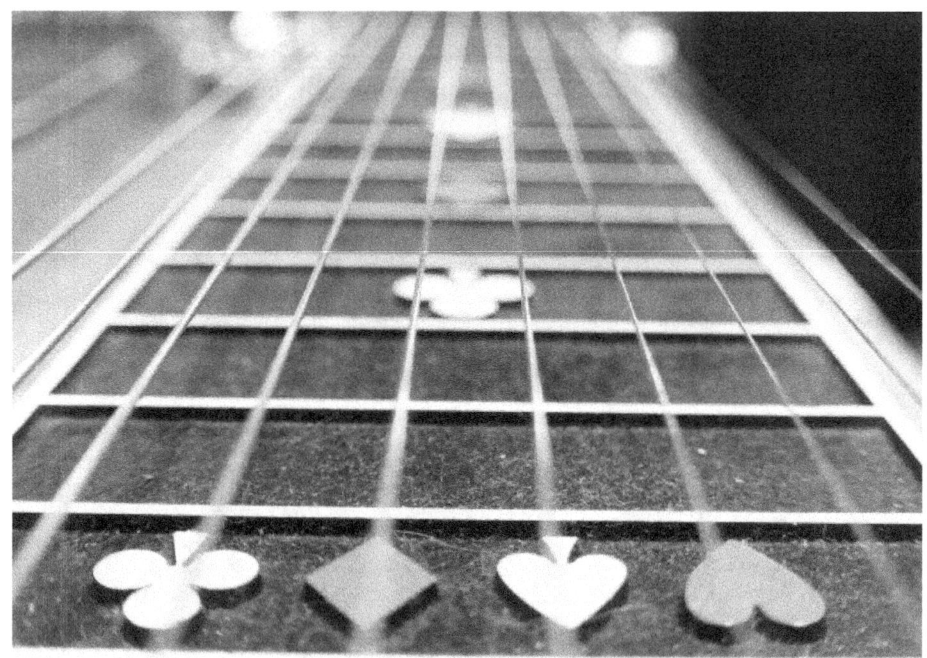

"Pedal Steel Guitar"

Tim Duffy Interview: Music Maker Relief Foundation

I met Tim Duffy in 1997. I was one of the first journalists to discover Duffy's singular foundation, Music Maker. Tim sent me each new album upon release, and I wrote reviews and stories of some of their earliest collections. Up to that point, I'd never discovered this treasure trove of American blues musicians. Years later, I finally looped back around and interviewed Tim. Music Maker Relief Foundation is going stronger as ever...

Music Maker Relief foundation, a non-profit organization, assists neglected southern musicians with daily expenses, instrument acquisition, recording, tour support and medical needs. Tim Duffy started Music Maker in 1994. Duffy, a trained folklorist, exists as—arguably—the most distinguished field recorder in the last four or five decades.

Taj Mahal, the Rolling Stones, Eric Clapton, Bonnie Raitt, Pete Townshend and Pink Floyd are some of Music Maker's past contributors. No other musical organization like Music Maker exists. Duffy has recorded over 200 artists, and released over 70 Music Maker CDs. The Music Maker archive exists as a treasure trove for timeless American music.

In this extensive interview, the Music Maker president tells of his musical background that most never achieve in a lifetime, before he even originated Music Maker. Duffy elaborates on the organization's early days up through Music Maker's most recent developments, and a glimpse into the future for this singular American musical cause.

So, let's go back a ways...talk about how you first got into music.

TD: Well I grew up around New Haven, Connecticut. Woodbridge.

What year were you born?

TD: 63.

••••••

You have a couple of brothers, right?

TD: Yeah, three brothers—two older, one younger.

What was your first instrument?

TD: Saxophone. I got that around five. But I picked up the guitar when I was 15. I grew up listening to Robert Johnson. When I was a kid I knew 10 Robert Johnson songs—but Robert Johnson, Leadbelly, Woody Guthrie, Ramblin Jack Elliott, Louis Armstrong, the Beatles, Bob Dylan, Brahms, Vivaldi, Merle Travis, and the Grateful Dead were early influences.

When did you move south?

TD: Did you see that movie *Fame*? One of those art schools? I went to one of those places for art and played guitar and then I went to a college in North Carolina where you could take banjo lessons and study. I got a job. I got invited by a fellow named David Holt—who plays a lot of Doc Watson. He was an entertainer, and he was running the program. You had to work 15 hours a week. They hired me to be on the Appalachian music crew. So I went around for a year and a half recording all those old mountain musicians that made records in the 20s and 30s—Doc Boggs kind of guys. I became aware of the elderly great southern artists. I started learning to really play from them. Then they wanted me to take Biology or something in school so I quit. Then we moved up into the hills—into the mountains above Asheville with this old hillbilly family called the Stewarts. Their people had been there for 200 years. I hung out with them. I was digging fence post holes, learning how to play music from them. Old Granny was a ballad singer. Then I got a chance to go to Indonesia to study Balinese music. I ended up going to Kenya and stayed there for close to five years from 83-87 studying Swahili music. From when I was 19 to 23 years old. I'm still in touch with those guys. Now Taj (Mahal) recorded with some of those musicians and now the music is gaining some popularity, but back then no one knew anything about it.

So, you covered some ground before you returned to the south...

220

•• • •••

TD: I came back because my father was sick and then he died. Then my wife and I moved—we didn't know where to go and we moved back to Asheville to another musician's house—Samuel Turner Stevens, an old mountain man, and we were dead broke and had nowhere to go. So we lived with him in an unheated cabin up in the mountains—that was rough. We stayed there for a while and then Denise (Duffy) got a job in Winston—in her field at the time—in the apparel industry and I got invited by Dan Patterson to go to the UNC Chapel Hill Folklore program. I worked there at the southern Folklife collection. Glenn Hinson—one of the great blues collectors introduced me to a guy named Guitar Slim Stephens. I spent a year working with him. At that time in the late 80s and early 90s—I guess Paul Oliver wrote in 1967 that the blues were dead. That it was an extinct tradition. Not much field work had been done in the 70s and 80s, or the 90s—very little. I soon found out from this guy that there were a dozen guys in Greensboro that can play the hell out of the country blues. On Guitar Slim's deathbed he told me I needed to find a guy named guitar Gabriel. I couldn't find anyone to take me to that section of town...you know this story...I met Guitar Gabriel and that's how it started. I was helping him and then we'd play gigs. Then he introduced me to his old Carney friends like Willa Mae Buckner, Mr. Q, Captain Luke, Macavine Hayes, Guitar Red, Preston Fulp, and all these different people. From 1991 to say 1994, I made a living as a working blues guy traveling around with these guys. I learned quickly the record companies had no use for these kinds of people—or dealing with them in a correct manner. So we started Music Maker Relief Foundation with our programs. For example, Musician's Sustenance—you know people who live at an average income of $18,000 a year can't afford heat, electric, food, medical, or whatever and the last thing on their mind is music. So we try to help with that situation—monthly grants to help a lot of musicians who can't play anymore and you don't even hear about because they're crippled or living in nursing homes. A lot of people like that we help on a monthly basis. Others ones that move into our next program—Professional Development—where, say someone like Cootie Stark or Adolphus Bell as a recent case who spent 35 years traveling around in his van the last 15 years, homeless, and help him make a record—help them get passports. Last year he traveled ten times overseas. Now he owns his own car and his van, he has a nice apartment, and a career in front of him. We've produced over 70 CDs. The CDs were grant free to the artists. We put them out there to help them make money. We have Cultural Accesses where we do programs like our congressional Blues Festival where we lobby our nation's legislators and tie in big corporate people to let folks know about the importance of our American musical traditions or we set up these touring programs over in France, South America, Australia, and some in the States where we introduce people or do things like talk to the press—to people like you—about it. Then we have Emergency Relief—like the New Orleans musicians fund. After Katrina we set up a fund to help 3,000 displaced musicians from the storm.

Music Maker's New Orleans musicians like Slewfoot...

TD: ...Yeah...Slewfoot, Carey B, and the great guy Alabama Slim, I sent you that, right?

The one with Little Freddie King—*The Mighty Flood?* Yeah, I got that one...

TD: That's a great record. He just toured France and did 18 shows. He's going back in March and he's got a career going. We helped him move out of New Orleans and back into New Orleans.

I'm a big fan of Dave McGrew's *Tramp Ballads*...

TD: Yeah, that's a great one. Phil Minger is another guy we did like that. Larry Short is another one.

You've had some very influential musicians lend a hand to the Music Maker cause. Talk about how you were able to reach musicians like B.B. King, Eric Clapton, and the Rolling Stones.

TD: Well, B.B. King and Taj Mahal were really the first one's to step up and help us out. I went out to L.A. to meet B.B King and he was recording Deuces Wild and I became friends with his producer. Taj Mahal was there and he heard about me because I was with a record company called N2K—they were trying to get his help. N2K was what Larry Rosen did after GRP Records. It was short lived, but it was a cool label. They gave me a budget. Rosen just loved the mission of the foundation and they had money and they gave me a budget and a deposit for a new van. I drove around for a year just recording everybody while they were figuring something out, but it was fun. At the end of that I got bought by another record company called Cello Recordings. They gave me a budget. I flew out to L.A. and met B.B. and he just loved the mission. He had a recording session going on. I went to Los Angeles, New York, and London and he introduced me to everybody—the Rolling Stones, Dionne Warwick, Tracy Chapman, Pink Floyd, Eric Clapton, Pete Townsend, Lou Reed, Elton John, Bonnie Raitt, Heavy D, D'Angelo, the Roots, and Taj Mahal. That's where I met all those folks.

Talk about Taj Mahal, he's played a vital role in the organization.

TD: Taj is the biggest one…everyone like Clapton and Bonnie, they always reach across, lend their name and write a check to help us—they are wonderful people, but Taj has taken things to another level. He's been hands on—staying on the phone with me on a weekly basis since 1996 when I met him. He's helped me figure things out. He's recorded with dozens of these musicians—like Cool John Ferguson, Pure Fe, Etta Baker, John D. Holeman, Beverly 'Guitar' Watkins, Cootie Stark, Mudcat, John Lee Zeigler, the Carolina Chocolate Drops owe Taj a huge thank you. He's like our press agent. He'll fall in love with an artist and people come to talk about his career, and all he'll talk about is Music Maker artists.

Taj played with Dave McGrew…

TD: Yeah, this is a fruit tramp who sleeps under railroad bridges—who I think is one of the great Woody Guthrie type figures around. Taj thought so too when he met him, and he produced the first two songs on Dave's record in one day. Taj also hosts the Fishin' Blues tournament that helps us raise money.

You just got back from Costa Rica for that tournament, right?

TD: Yeah, it turned out great. Little Freddie King came down. Adolphus Bell, Mudcat, and Taj's trio played. I forget the fellow who won the tournament, but we all had a great time. We caught a lot of fish and raised a lot of money. We plan to do it again next year.

Was Mr. Bill Lucado there?

TD: Lucado was there. He showed up at the concert and we hung out with him. He's doing fine. We had a good time with him. It's a great event. Y'know Taj put out that record with Etta Baker that did really well. We met Etta when she was 80 years old and no one would give her a record deal. We ended up putting out four records for her. We've made her golden years not a time of struggle—the finances were taken care of and she earned it. We chased down money that was owed to her. We did a lot for Etta and Taj surely did a lot too.

Another favorite Music Maker artist of mine was Atlanta's own Frank Edwards...

TD: That's a great one...

His *Chicken Raid* CD stands as a fine recording. And I find it amazing that just as he finished recording the last song on his record at your place, he got into a car to go home and he died in the backseat...

TD: What a guy. Yeah, I mean we're the only one who are really taking care and dealing with these musicians in a correct manner. The only other guys that did it in a big way—a lot bigger than me—was Fat Possum folks with R.L. Burnside.

Maybe, but the Music Maker roster is quite formidable.

TD: Well, Matthew wasn't trained as a folklorist or field collector. He didn't find anybody—those people were already around. We go out...I spent five years in Africa with a top Columbia PHD Linguistic Field Researcher. Glenn Hinson and Bill Farris trained me. At this point I don't think there's anyone—it's amazing the work was done to find all these artists in the 90s. It just goes to show white people were wrong in the 60s. They thought when the people died, the music died, but the music lives on. Younger generations pick it up. Tradition changes but it's still tradition—guys like Pink Anderson's son, Little Pink, he's one of the most bad-assed country blues guys around. People like Cootie Stark...

Well, blues great Curly Weaver's daughter is another Music Maker artists. She used to watch her dad and Blind Willie McTell play parties and fish fries...

TD: Yeah, Curly Weaver's daughter, Cora Mae Bryant. Hey, I just found another guy—Boo Hanks—whose father played with Blind Boy Fuller, and he plays just like Blind Boy Fuller. Met him towards the end of last year—he's great. The music's out there. See, everyone wants to say that it's over, but culture doesn't let things die that quickly and there's so many great artists out there. I just happened to meet some wonderful people on the way. Y'know I have state of the art acoustic recording equipment made. Some of the finest stuff ever made to record these guys with...

The quality is always great on Music Maker recordings...

TD: There's only three companies in the world...see, they're audio file recordings most of 'em, like Waterlily is a special microphone and preamp built by Marc Levinson.

He was involved with Cello Recordings, right?

TD: Yeah, he helped get that going. He's designed sound for Lexus cars. He's an inside the industry guy. So, this stuff we have sounds great. Most old blues recordings sound muffled or harsh—these are beautiful recordings. I have so much music now—in December I put 30 records together with a friend. I probably have hundreds of these recordings. The unreleased vault is huge with thousands of hours.

How many artists have you recorded?

TD: I don't know, over three hundred.

•••••••

That's quite a bit.

TD: Yeah, and it's in depth. Not just in passing—it's their whole repertoire.

There's nothing out there like Music Maker. That's why I've been writing about and trying to expose people to it for nine years…it's a musical reservoir…it's the only place…

TD: …Where you can find it…now, everyone's tapped into all the old great guys. Everyone knows what's been recorded in the past. All the reissues…I love Big Bill Broonzy…every time another CD comes out I love it…and it's great, but how many times can you re-package a Robert Johnson record? But these Music Maker musicians no one knows about. I listen to Cootie Stark, and to me he's just as powerful as a Son House character. I love Son House, but I love Cootie Stark just as much. Frank Edwards is another one.

Since I went to the University of Georgia, the musician I loved to see around town--that is now a music Maker artist-- was Neal Pattman. I got to see him 18-20 years ago around Athens.

TD: Yeah! Look at Neal Pattman—those records are kicking! If you see the new Kenny Wayne Shepherd DVD, Cootie Stark and Neal Pattman steal the show. They absolutely steal the show.

Beverly "Guitar" Watkins is another fine example for me since she's from Atlanta.

TD: She's killing it. Who else does that? Nobody?

She played with Piano Red and if people don't the significance of these people's musical lineage and associations, then they should know.

TD: Beverly Watkins had a record produced by Chet Atkins in 1959 on RCA, The RCA Sessions. She's the real fucking deal. John Lennon was listening to those recordings. "Mr. Moonlight" is taken from that in a Beatles song. She's a heavy cat.

There's over one hundred musicians on the roster at Music Maker that you've helped, right?

TD: About two hundred. We've issued over 70 records.

You've generated several millions of dollars for a significant American cause.

TD: Millions, yeah, but it's not as much, it's pitiful how little because I'm not a real business guy. I wish I had a real business CEO—we'd be hundreds of millions of dollars say if I had a real business guy running this thing. Still in America no one knows who I am. Music Maker is more of a world brand because we're known more in Europe, South America, and Australia than in the States.

What are some of the upcoming MMRF-related events or developments?

TD: The Congressional Blues Festival on May 16. We're gonna have Derek Trucks headlining. Mudcat, Sweet Betty, Adolphus Bell, Captain Luke, and Macavine Haynes will be there. It's right at the Capitol at the Mellon Auditorium right across from the Monument on the plaza. You do a lottery. It's sponsored by Volkswagen, and it's gonna be a killer event.

Any new releases?

TD: Well, you know about the Carolina Chocolate Drops. We have this great John D. Holeman with this Australian folk-rock group. They've toured with Bob Dylan and they sell lots of records. I'm friends with the band and they came to my studio a couple years ago to rehearse for their next tour, and on the last day I brought in John D. Holeman and they cut a record with him. They gave their rights to the foundation. It's a beautiful record.

That hits the streets in June?

TD: Yeah, those are our two releases for June. I'll have to get you the new artwork in a digital pack. But, I'm still a sucker in the music business, but we got picked up by this label called Dixie Frog. They're selling Pure Fe and Drink House. They sell quite well and they pay very well. They sell thousands of these things and I couldn't believe anyone was selling this stuff. They're selling 7,000 pieces in France. Here that's not much, but in France it is. It made me think, because I've never sold any records yet per se, except for Etta and Taj. So, I'm gonna try and big push, and sell some more.

You certainly have a treasure trove of thousands of songs and hundreds of recordings. Sooner or later you'll have the world at your door.

TD: We need some business help. We're a small Ma and Pa shop trying to grow. But still, a Ma and Pa shop in the blues world… we're probably the most successful, non-profit organization that's around-period. The jazz foundation is wonderful, Wendy Oxenhorn is great.

Hey, when's that Mo Roots & Blues Barbecue show? I'd like to include that in my Swampland Soul Food Tour.

TD: In Columbia, Missouri. That's gonna be great. It's in August.

Soon I'm coming up to review a couple food places around in your area.

TD: I got one two miles from here. It's great place. Cool John Ferguson plays there.

Cool John still lives in your area doesn't he? He's also a great piano player…

TD: Yeah. We did a great show with Cool John, Captain Luke, John D. Holeman, and Macavine Hayes Friday night. It was just incredible. Y'know, Essie Mae Brooks has a new record coming out; the second one Cool John's done with her. We have a new release by James Davis which is like hypnotic trance music—fife and drum music with a slide guitar. He's from Macon, Georgia. He's an awesome guy. Then we're trying to help another guy that's from Georgia—Eddie Kirkland—he's 83 years old, and his career parallels B.B. King's. He's played with John Lee Hooker for years in the late 50s-early 60s. He's living in Macon and still trying to get by. He's one of the last, great innovators of the blues and never had a huge success.

I'm sure you feel a real sense of urgency with helping and recording these elderly musicians.

TD: Real urgency. When they record and die leaving your studio like Frank Edwards it gets pretty real. You have to get it now because you just don't know what's gonna happen. Yeah, so to capture it is of the essence. If I find somebody real, no matter how busy I am, I'm always ready to roll tape. I'll drop anything to roll tape. I always have been like that. I never stop. I roll tape every month somewhere. Meeting all these old tobacco farmers in their 70s around my area here, and I found an old guy that plays bottleneck slide, and I just recorded him. Anyone that's important and of interest, I'll do it. I never charge them. I don't play any of that artist's recording costs, or the music industry game to put these guys in debt. It's all debt free and it's just about music. The main thing now is to find more resources to get the music out there so it's just not sitting in some archive. We have all of our stuff up on itunes, and CDBaby. We try to make it accessible. The pressure of being famous is ridiculous—it's not about that. Doing the work and having people you know you're doing the work is heavy enough.

But the real people always recognize the real people whether you're famous or not. If you're a great guitar player and haven't sold a million records, the real guitar who has sold a million records knows there's a very fine line between fame and poverty.

TD: Yeah, Cool John Ferguson is one of those guys. He's gotta be one of the world's greatest guitar players.

Mudcat just sent me his new record. I've known him for years. We both grew up in the same area. Talk about him a little bit because he's been around from the beginning of Music Maker.

•• • • ••

TD: Mud is one of the great underground heroes. He's a total re-gionalist. He's famous in Atlanta. He's made a living in Atlanta. He's toured America with Music Maker throughout the States. He's done shows with Taj throughout the States. He has a great following in Europe. He's a great traditionalist. He reaches back. I think he's one of the world's great slide wizards. He's my favor-ite slide guitarist. He has a unique, raw sound. He's developed his own style and sound. He's such a personable guy that when he performs people just relate to him. I knew him when he was 19, and I've always thought of him as a young guy. He's a won-derful player with a wonderful band. He's been a full supporter of Music Maker since day one. He's an incredible guy that makes great records—it's good time party music. That Northside Tav-ern in Atlanta is a great place...

It used to be really dangerous down there. It's not so bad now, but it has become a classic blues dive.

TD: We just got a grant from the Experience Project. And we just put out those *Drink House To Church House* CDs and DVDs.

Yeah, the Volume 1 & 2 sounds great.

TD: This grant will allow us to finish our documentary. We're also trying to do that. There's always something going on. I'm here until the end of March. The last week of March I go out until the end of April. Then May 31st to June 18th I'm on the road. Then the month of July and the first week of August I'm on the road. I'm developing our tour base. We're doing really well in South America, Colombia, Argentina, Chile, and places like that. We're doing well in France, so Captain Luke and Macavine Hayes are getting on these package tours. I'm going out with them to have some fun and make sure they're treated properly to solidify this worldwide tour. I need to figure out how to tour the United States. I figured how to do Europe, South America, and Australia, but I gotta figure out the States.

It'd be nice to see a 40 city Music Maker tour.

TD: Yeah, I need some sponsors to help me because it's hard and there's a lot of competition.

230

•••••••

We'll check in on you towards the end of the summer. Thanks for going on the record.

TD: If you need anything call me.

I'll see you soon for the Soul Food tour...

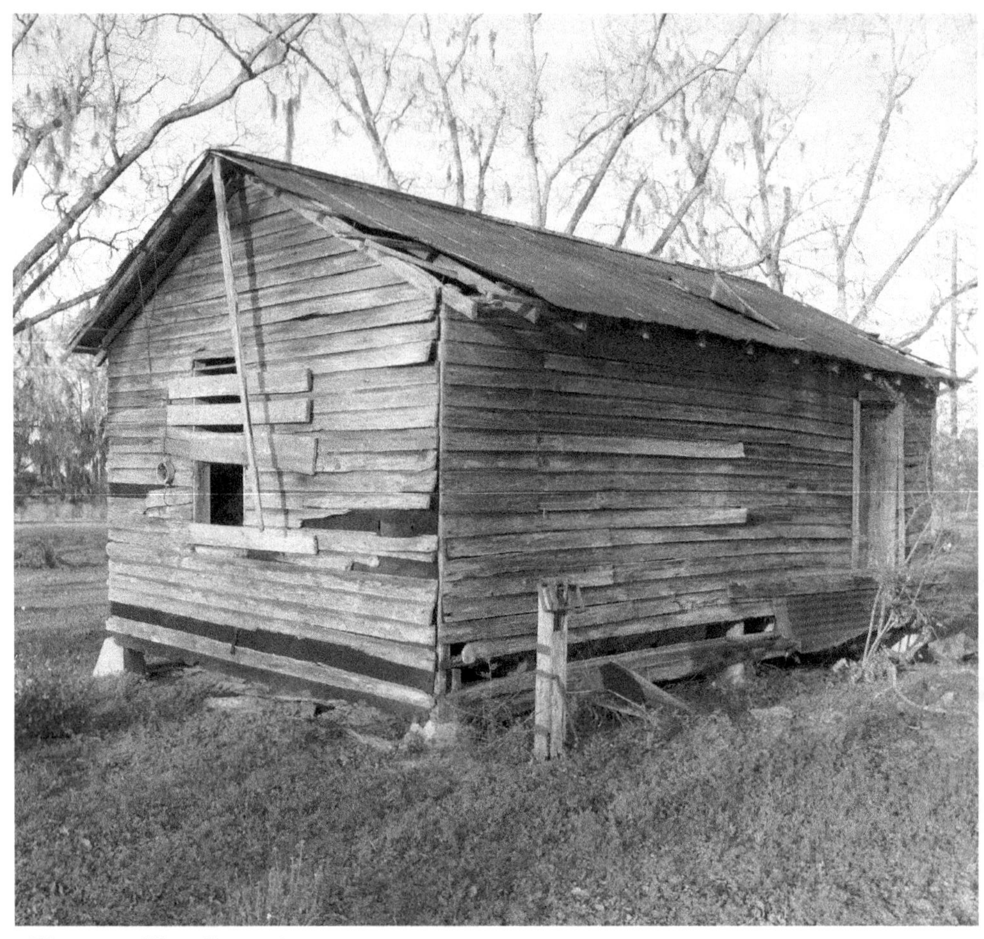

"Homerville, Georgia"

••••••

Charlie Louvin:
Insured Beyond The Grave

Charlie Louvin passed away on January 26, 2011. This interview transpired during his reemergence on the music scene, and experienced well-deserved accolades for a lifetime of music. This interview proves Charlie Louvin knew how to tell a story. What a soulful gentleman, and a true American music legend.

The Louvin Brothers legendary songs transcend time. Born Ira (April 21, 1924) and Charlie (July 7, 1927) Loudermilk, the brothers were raised poor in Henagar, Alabama, and began singing gospel music early in their lives. A few years later they played mostly in Tennessee and Alabama. They changed their last name, and Charlie and Ira began recording in 1949. They cut records for Decca, MGM, and Capitol Records. Their music never strayed from a pure gospel-country path. Once heard, their harmonizing remains hard to forget. Their music dealt with grave matters of the soul...the perilous tightrope between light and dark.

In time, musicians such as Merle Haggard, Gram Parsons, Emmylou Harris, Johnny Cash and Dolly Parton recorded Louvin Brothers songs. After a prodigious career, the brothers went their separate ways, and in 1965 Ira Louvin was killed in a car accident. Brother Charlie forged on, and dedicates a song on his latest CD to Ira.

Charlie Louvin's last CD appeared a decade ago. His latest, self-titled, release due to hit streets on February 20, culls traditional tunes, cover songs, Louvin Brothers compositions, and new material. Special guests on the album include George Jones, Bobby Bare, Tom T.Hall, Jeff Tweedy, Marty Stuart, and Will Oldham.

This interview verifies Charlie Louvin's immense kindness, grace, talent, and soul. He elucidates on his early musical inclinations, the Louvin Brothers career, Elvis Presley, Gram Parsons, Emmylou Harris, and his latest CD.

••• •••

What was your first instrument?

CL: I was up in years. I was like 16 before I ever touched an instrument. My brother Ira played the guitar and he could play Papa's banjo a little bit, and we had a neighbor-boy, his name was Lonnie Justice, he's gone now, but he played guitar. Everywhere we went we had Ira playing and Lonnie playing. I didn't have to...

But you were singing then...

CL: That's right...but it cut down on the luggage I had to carry. So, finally Lonnie got married and his wife didn't like the music part of his life so Ira said to me one day, 'You're gonna have to play something. I'm gonna buy me a mandolin'. That's the way the Blue Sky Boys (played)—the Delmore Brothers had a lead instrument and a flat top, and the Monroe Brothers were the same. He (Ira) said 'I'm gonna buy me a mandolin and I'm gonna learn to play it. I'll show you what chords I know on the guitar.' That's how I started. I was 16—I never did become what they call a "picker," but I could stay with the best of them. If they did the picking—they call that seconding-—I'll second you'. I learned to appreciate the guitar. Ira and I did hundreds, probably thousands of shows—just with mandolin and guitar.

That's a credit to your brother's talent because mandolins aren't so easy to learn or to play.

CL: Yes, and it's a terrible instrument to keep in tune. You've got those double strings. When your strings get about a week old they won't match up. And you can't tune the thing. Ira was a talented boy. When we were going to record the *Tribute to the Delmore Brothers*—we truly admired the Delmore Brothers—we worked a couple of shows with them. Alton had a problem in the fact his brother Rabon was drinker. So, Rabon passed away. We went to Alton's house in Huntsville, Alabama, to show him 12 songs we had chosen to do the tribute. We wanted him to be satisfied with those 12 songs. Did we leave out one of his favorites? We showed him what songs we were gonna do, and he was thrilled beyond words. He was thrilled beyond words. He said excuse me, and got up and walked in the other room and pulled out Rabon's tenor guitar and brought it in there and handed it to Ira. He said, 'I think you ought to play this on the tribute album.' It still had the same strings on it that Rabon had put on it. So Ira removed the strings when we got home. He curled them up and didn't kink them and submerged them in kerosene. He let them sit overnight. He took em out and cleaned em real good and then put them back on the guitar, and they sounded like a new set of strings. He didn't tune it as a tenor guitar, as it should be tuned. We didn't know what that was so Ira tuned it like the bottom four strings on a guitar. Like E, B, G, and D. He did—with very little rehearsal—he played the lead instrument you hear on the Tribute To the Delmore Brothers.

I've never heard of cleaning strings with kerosene.

CL: It's a very good cleaning agent. Good for a lot of things. My Mom used it. She'd take a spoonful of sugar and 6 or 8 drops of kerosene and you eat that real slow and you get rid of the croup. They'd use it when you stick a nail through your foot— Mom would pour a little kerosene on it and you'd go back out and play. I think there's something in kerosene now that poisons you. Can't use it like that now. You do a lot of things when you're raised poor. You don't run to the doctor every time you sneeze or get a cough.

How did you and your brother start writing songs?

CL: The first song that we wrote was about a little girl I knew when I was seven years old. We were lucky. We didn't know we were lucky then but my Daddy owned this little farm or at least he was buying it and everybody around us was sharecroppers. They would come in a mile or two from our house and they'd have some children and they'd rent the land for one year, and about the time you got to know them good they'd move away. So, the first song we wrote was "A Tiny Broken Heart." Pretty close after that we wrote "Nellie Moved To Town." Ira wrote a few lyrics and sent them off to get somebody to put a tune to it, and they'd always come back with an unacceptable tune. We learned we had to do our own melody…there would have been no other way for it to have gone. Ira was a gifted songwriter—or I dream it, and all you have to do is get up and put it on paper. When one comes that way I'm thankful for it.

••••••

One of my favorite Louvin Brothers CDs I bought, although I had a friend who let me record a lot of his Louvin Brothers collection on vinyl, but *Songs That Tell A Story*. That was recorded around 52. You guys already made a few records by then. Talk about how y'all hooked up with Hank Williams' songwriting partner, Fred Rose.

CL: Well, Fred was our publisher. We met him through a man named Eddie Hill. We were working with Eddie Hill in Memphis—worked with him for five years—starting in 1947 and we didn't know any publishers, but we were writing songs pretty often. Eddie said I know a publisher so Ira and I got us a reel-to-reel recorder and recorded about 20 songs on that. Eddie brought it to Nashville and took it to Acuff-Rose and they accepted all 20 songs. Only thing was Eddie put his name on them also as one-third writer. That wasn't right for him to do that but he did it anyway. We were afraid we'd lose a job if we griped about it.

Through that introduction when we met Mr. Rose he was one that got our Decca record deal set up, and that didn't pan out because Decca wanted us to record songs that they sent us. We had plenty of songs of our own so Fred seen that wasn't going to work so we signed a one year contract to cut two songs. Every time a session would come up, we'd get sick and couldn't make it. We did that until the contract ran out at the end of the year. Then Mr. Rose got us a deal with MGM. We cut 12 songs there and I thought some of it was pretty good. One day Fred said if your name ain't Hank Williams or Patty Page you don't have any business being on MGM records. So, I'm gonna try and get you another deal. So he got us a deal at Capitol Records. He actually produced the first session—*The Family Who Prays*—I forgot what the other three were—that one deal lasted for the rest of the Louvin Brothers career, and way beyond that...

How did your stints in the military affect your career?

CL: Well, in 1945 I joined, because I couldn't get a job, and the music wasn't feeding us. Everybody kept saying the draft will get you before you learned anything musically. I got mad and joined the Army Air Force, but I got out 14 months later I got out and in 1947 that's when we went to work with Eddie. Then we were doing quite well, and then I got my greetings from the draft board in Memphis. I marched down there to tell them how stupid they were that I'd been there and done that. They said we know all about that—but you didn't have 24 months active duty so you're subject to the draft. So they drafted me. I was three weeks away from being 27, which was the cut off. My wife was four months pregnant. They said she could do that without me here; she'd do just as good if I was there or not. They shipped my butt to Korea. I stayed over there pretty close to 14 months all together.

While I was there Ira worked at the post office, and did a DJ show on WMPS in Memphis. Then when I got out of the Army that time I was a civil service regular employee at the post office, but I wasn't a substitute clerk like when I left. Ira said, "I know where we can make a killing." I said, where's that?" And he said Birmingham. On WBOK there. They're gonna pay us $100 a week sponsor money and we'll hire a couple of pickers for 50 bucks a week and everything we make on the road is ours. Well, that was a bad mistake because there was a duet that had been in Birmingham for years—Rebe and Ray. They had sung Louvin Brothers songs so much that when we went to Birmingham all the people thought we were impersonating them. So, we didn't do well at all, almost lost our shirt.

We were truly gonna quit the business. I said to Ira—because we auditioned a half a dozen times at the Opry, but we auditioned for Jim Denney—he was a stage manager. We thought he was the boss, and nobody corrected us. I called Ken Nelson from a payphone—we're already lost our phone. I ask him if he knew anybody. He said I know Jack Stapp—that was a new name to me. I said, well Ira and I are gonna quit the business if we can't get on the Opry. We won all the awards gospel music had to offer, but in those days the gospel people didn't like us because we played stringed instruments. They thought of us as a carnival act. The country folks didn't dig us that much because we would quiet an audience, actually make them feel guilty that they were out instead of in church. Anyway, Ken said, give me your number, I'll call you back. I said we don't have a number Ken, but I'll stick right here by this pay phone until you call back. It wasn't any more than an hour when he called back. He had talked with Mr. Stapp and told him I got this duet that I'd like to have on the Opry. I don't know what Jack Stapp said, but he must a stuttered cause Mr. Nelson said, 'If you don't want em, then the Ozark Jubilee does'—that was a television show out in Springfield, Missouri, that the Opry was afraid of because they were the first country show on television. So, through a bluff Jack Stapp said okay, tell em they're on. They'll start this Friday night. And that was on a Tuesday. It took six months to talk Ken Nelson into allowing us to mix our music—part secular, part gospel and we recorded "When I Start Dreaming Late," in late 55 and that did more for us than 20 years of trying we'd put into it.

That song is on your new CD...

CL: Yes sir. It did well. It put us in a place we didn't even know existed. We did extremely well there for four or five years I'd guess.

Y'all had a nice run there in 57, 58, 59...how did the rock and roll scene affect the Louvin Brothers?

CL: Well, it was late 55. We worked 100 days with Elvis Presley. Actually, when we first started the tour Elvis was opening for us. Hank Snow was on that tour and so were some of the Carter Family. See, Hank put up fifty-percent of the money to buy Elvis' recording contract and his manager's contract. Mr. Parker played dirty, very simple. For example, he'd give away 30 or 40 tickets to the little Woolworth workers and say 'you don't have to pay nothing to get in. all you have to do is yell 'We want Elvis.' They did that to Hank Snow for three or four days and Parker's dream came true and Hank said, 'I don't want anything to do with the punk. Just give me my $25,000 back and I'm out of here.' Of course, that's exactly what Mr. Parker wanted to hear. So he got him out and that gave him fifty-percent ownership of Elvis for the rest of Elvis' life. Even after he died until Elvis' ex-wife sued him. You can't keep getting fifty percent of something when the star is dead.

Talk a little about the classic record the Louvin Brothers recorded in 1960, *Satan Is Real*. What do you remember about that record?

••••••

CL: Well, my wife and I were living up on a little farm in Good-lettsville, Tennessee, and about a half a mile from us was a rock quarry—it wasn't active anymore and Ira and I had written this song. We wanted it to be the name of an album. So, my wife Betty, and I—our oldest son had a Lionel train and it was on a sheet of plywood. We were so close with money, so close to going under that we didn't have the money to go buy another sheet of plywood. So we took the train off that one and ripped it in two which made it 16 feet tall and together we built what we were told what the bogeyman would look like. He'd have a pitchfork and he'd have horns—very scary looking.

We painted it up and Capitol Records sent a photographer Ken Veeder from Hollywood to take the pictures. So we took car tires and filled them full of kerosene—had it all ready, and it started sprinkling' rain. Well, this Ken Veeder got very nervous and didn't want his camera to get any water on it. We'll do this later, he said. We've got two weeks work in this already. If we can stand out here and play like we're enjoying it you can go ahead and shoot that camera. So, he did. The rest of it is history. A couple years back somebody asked this rock and roll artist to choose the top 50 album covers of all time, and *Satan Is Real* came in fifth. I thought that was phenomenal. We just looked at that book today.

Well, I discovered your music through Gram Parsons...

CL: I never met Gram. I credit him with introducing the Louvin Brothers to (you) and to Emmylou. He told Emmylou I want to play you something. He got her to sit down and listen, and she asked who's that girl singing the high part? And he said that's not a girl, that's Ira Louvin. So, that's how she met the Louvin Brothers music. She was very kind to us she cut four or five (songs). We're still friends today, Emmylou and I. Her first number one song, the first release she had "If I Could Only Win Your Love" was a Louvin Brothers song. Gram introduced the Louvin sound to a lot of people because they tell me—it's an Emmylou story—that Gram would pay people in California to go around to all these old record stores and pawnshops to see if they could find any Louvin Brothers music. He'd pay them for their trouble. I wish I could have met him.

•• • • ••

Your music, as I've gotten older, carries an even heavier weight once you experience some adverse turns in life. You could say those songs serve as medicine to troubled souls...

CL: My brother—he didn't live it—I'm not saying that, but he was pretty close to a biblical scholar. He knew the book. You could listen to the songs. You knew he knew the book. That's basically what Louvin Brothers music was about. The way you're living today might not be the way you want to die. I've gotten thousands of letters stating the fact that Louvin Brothers music turned them around, and put them on the right track. That makes you feel pretty good. I don't know if they'll be a reward for that or not, I doubt it, but down here it makes you feel good.

Losing your brother must've altered your life...you played music together a long time. How did you carry on?

CL: James, it was all I knew how to do. I'd already been doing 20-25 years—since '41 as a duet. I didn't know how to do anything else. I didn't want to go back to the farm, I knew that (laughs). I couldn't go back to the post office because I asked for a leave of absence, and the postmaster said, 'You have to make up your mind if you want to be a hillbilly or a postal employee, and your request is denied. I told him where he could put his job and it wasn't where the sun would shine. I'm sure he would've had thrown me out if I went back.

What's been the hardest thing for you to learn after all these years?

CL: Some of the business hasn't been that hard to learn James, it's a few of the things I was supposed to unlearn. I today—and we're talking 41 or 42 years later—when I'm singing a Louvin Brothers song and I have some people who help me with harmony and today everybody has their own microphone. We always worked one microphone. When it comes time for the harmony I step to the left to give the harmony a chance to get in the other side. It's a habit that I haven't been able to break. Old habits are extremely hard to break. It's not too hard to learn something, but life changes and you would like to forget that, and it's harder to do than it was to learn it.

•••••••

Let's talk about your new CD. When did you start planning to cut these songs?

CL: I was sitting right where I'm sitting now and the telephone rang and it was Josh Rosenthal from New York. He introduced himself and said two years ago I seen your show in Albany, New York, and I checked you out. You haven't had an international release in ten years, and I said that's exactly right. You've done your homework. Now what? Well, how would you like to record on my label? I needed it, so I said I'd like to. He said, if you'll record the songs I send down I guarantee you I can get this played on college radio. If they play it on college radio you can work the universities. That sounded very interesting because that's how Lester, Earl, and Willie got well was playing the colleges. So, he sent the songs down and there were two or three Carter Family songs, "On A Green Hillside," "Worried Man Blues," and "Kneeling Drunkard's Plea." I heard those songs when I was very young on a battery radio with what they called Carter family transcriptions. Now, Ira and I recorded "Kneeling Drunkard's Plea." I never recorded "Grave On a Green Hillside' or "The Worried Man Blues." He sent those, he sent a Jimmie Rodgers song. He chose "Must You Throw Dirt In My Face," that was a 1958 release of ours. "When I Stop Dreaming." "The Christian Life," There's one more...

"Knoxville Girl"...

CL: "The Knoxville Girl," of course we certainly didn't write that. That's a three-hundred-year-old English folk song. We sang it first after everyone else had forgotten it. My brother and I were working in Knoxville and we started singing that song. People imagined that was written about Knoxville, Tennessee, because they got a river that runs right through there. It sounded logical and turned out to be the most requested song Ira and I ever sang. We didn't go anywhere and not get a request for that song. We might have a number one record like: "I Don't Believe You Met My Baby," but they might not request that song, but somebody would always demand "Knoxville Girl." I just thought it would be sensible if we put that on there and Mr. Rosenthal did also. So we recorded three, two hour sessions; it was supposed to be three hour sessions, but by the time the guys got there, got in tune, and had coffee and all this, and hour would have gone. So we would record two hours and it was time for the guys to eat and the session was over. We did this three times, and recorded 20 songs. Out of the 20 songs I had to go back and re-record two of them. The first one's they call scratch versions, but I never just slouched through a song with the attitude that 'hey, I can come back later and do it again.' So 18 of them were acceptable but they only chose 12 for the CD. We still got 8 more laying there—a Johnny Cash number.

Any plans for the song you wrote last night?

CL: Well, it was a gospel song, "Awake With A Smile." Someday I hope you'll hear it.

I hope so. You've got some musical guests on this album. Talk about them, starting with George Jones.

CL: Well, "Possum" is a good friend of mine. I asked him. Josh wanted George on that record. But I went over to his house and set it up. On the CD that I had just had brand new out at the time, called *If Only In A Song,* but I had cut an old Tom T. Hall song called "Back When We Were Young," a great new version of it. I wanted Tom T on it, so he did that talking (on the new CD), "Blues Stay Away." He sung one little old line at the end of it. Bobby Bare came with Tom T that day—I think they were going fishing later. Mark Never got him to record some also on that one and I think he recorded some on "Worried Man Blues." I was there when Elvis Costello came. I never met Jeff Tweedy. He brought them in without calling me because I would have drove down—I'm 75 miles out—but I would've been glad to drive down and met the people. Josh tells me he's going to do something I've never been a part of—on my 80th birthday—this coming July he said he was going to rent the Ryman. That's the way we're going to celebrate the 80th birthday.

You'll have to make sure they roll the cameras and tapes for that one.

CL: (laughs) We might even get a little video out of that…

•••••••

Why not? It's good to hear someone who's been around as long as you still out on the stage playing your music. The new CD is amazing.

CL: You made a statement earlier in our conversation that you felt like a character in a Louvin Brothers song…I'll remember that…that's very good…

I mean that in the highest sense of a compliment. When I was 20 I loved your music because of my romantic view of the pure country harmonies. But now, I hear it on a whole other level. The stakes have been raised…under the right circumstances those songs will send you to your knees.

CL: Did you ever hear—I can tell almost from your conversation what you're going through. Did you ever hear the song in the Louvin Brothers catalogue called "What Can Any Man Do For A Woman That I Haven't Done For You." It's a mean song if you're not in the right mood. Ira was killed with his fourth wife. He just couldn't seem to say or do the right things. He had two or three wives most anybody could've lived with, but he had very little patience for the human race. He could take a piece of wood and make something you wouldn't believe, and he'd work on it for three months to finish it—had all the patience in the world—but when it come to people he didn't have much patience. I think that's what happened to his marriages.

Well, you've got some live shows coming up, right?

CL: Before we hit the shows…are you aware of the 24th of February?

No sir.

CL: Well, you have a personal invitation. It's on a Saturday in Nashville at Grimey's Record Store. We're going to have a CD party. The record's released on the 20th—so the CD party's on the 24th; starts about 5 o'clock. We'd love to have you up.

I'd be honored…

CL: I'll be disappointed if I didn't get to meet you. There's no charge, and believe me, we'd love to have you there.

You said earlier you didn't think there'd be a reward for making people feel good down here, but I think there will. The messages in your songs are eternal, and surely there's a reward for the message they send.

CL: You wouldn't believe how many times I've been asked, 'did you and your brother think 50 years ago—now 56 years ago—50 years later that the songs would still be around—still be available to buy?' I'd say no, we never thought about anything like that. We were trying very hard to make a living. You live in the right now world. The business I'm in is feast or famine. You think you've got it made. You think you've got the world by the tail, and next week the world's got you by the tail. Back then we were just trying to stay closer to the feast. We were never thinking 55 years down the road. I don't believe anybody could tell the truth and say, yeah, I knew when I cut that people will love it after 55 years. It's nice.'

The Louvin Brothers were no act; everything was a message in the musicianship. A serious message...

CL: Yes, it is. I've worked a lot solo with a preacher—his name was Freddie Clarke—and he was a charismatic preacher. I found out for sure where the Louvin Brothers gospel music songs live. The people know them as well as the old hymnbooks. The foot-stomping' songs like "I Can't Say No", "There's A Higher Power"—stuff like that, I've seen people run from the back of the church—across the tops of the pews, and never kick nobody in the head, or step on hands—I thought they were coming for me, but they come up make a big circle and go back down the other side. That's where the music really lives. Ira and I, we didn't work a lot of churches. He thought that—and I'm sure I felt the same—that that's begging. We definitely weren't beggars. Sometimes it might've been good to have some sense enough to have done that, but we didn't. We'd sing in a few churches, knowing, when we went there, the preacher knew not to take an offering for us because that's where the begging comes in. We'll come sing, but that's all. These days I go to church and within ten or fifteen minutes after church starts, somebody will get the word to the preacher that I'm in the house. Then they'll want you to get up and sing.

Then if you don't...

CL: Oh, they'll embarrass you to death. They'll say well I know why he's not getting up...we'll have to give him a nice round of applause. That will put me out the door. But I've had it happen. It's hard to go to church and be a listener. They want you to be a participant, and I do that once in awhile, of course I got the long finger and the ringer finger shortened—half an inch or three quarters of an inch on my left hand and I can't play the guitar anymore. But I have a lady who sings with us that plays guitar like I used to or probably better—I know better. So, anywhere I go, I have to impose on somebody to come along and play the guitar. I don't like to do that because that's the way they make a living. I don't want to ask them on this only day off to get dressed up and come up and play guitar for me and sing a few songs.

Will she go out on the road with you for those shows? Do you know what band you'll use? I'm sure you do...

CL: I know everyone except the drummer. We'll have Dianne Berry as a singer, she does all out boy-girl duets—we do a lot of Louvin Brothers music in trio form—the third part of the harmony will be Mitchell Brown. The acoustic or electric, whatever we use, this great picker named Bill Kelly. We haven't chosen on the drums yet, if we use drums it'll probably just be a snare because I like things quiet.

Make sure you get them to record all that stuff.

CL: We'll be singing some of those things with this group at the CD party. People ask what the funniest thing is, at the time it was funny, and then later on you don't appreciate it as much. My brother and I were working in Aurora, Colorado, in a club, and we had to work until 2 or 3 in the morning. Aurora has the largest veteran's hospital in the world. A nice looking little Red Cross girl came over to the show and asked Ira if we would get up like 9 in the morning, come to the hospital, and do some songs. She was exceptionally cute, and there was no telling what Ira thought he'd get out of it—he agreed to do it the next morning. We get up the next morning, come to the hospital, and do some songs. We get up the next morning, and we had a boy who worked with us—Jimmy Capps—great guitarist—he's in the house band at the Opry now, but he played my guitar because we were strolling and he couldn't play his electric…Ira played the mandolin…

We went in the rooms in the hospital where you had to wear a mask over your face—just one patient—but you'd go in there and sing them a song. Every place we'd go, the little Red Cross girl would say we have a wonderful surprise for you this morning—from the Grand Ole Opry, the Louvin Brothers. They're going to sing you some songs. So, we'd sing a song and go room to room. We did maybe eight rooms. Then we went to where they all congregate—like the auditorium, a pretty big room. We went in and there was a lady lying on one of those beds with wheels and she's laying there and she's got a wet washcloth over her face. So we walked in and the little Red Cross girl made her speech and this lady laying in the bed said 'O my God,' that's all I need…'

Ira went up to her head, Jimmy went towards one side and I got on the other side and we sang about ten songs right down on top of her. I don't know if it killed her or what. After getting up with very little sleep, and you go to do something that you hope will be appreciated and this gal comes off with that statement. We thought it was cruel of her, and we made more noise right by her. She didn't talk anymore. We sang her some potent tunes.

Well, I appreciate you talking to me. I look forward to seeing you on the 24th.

CL: If you need anything else call me. Just remember James, time changes everything. If you be patient, it'll happen.

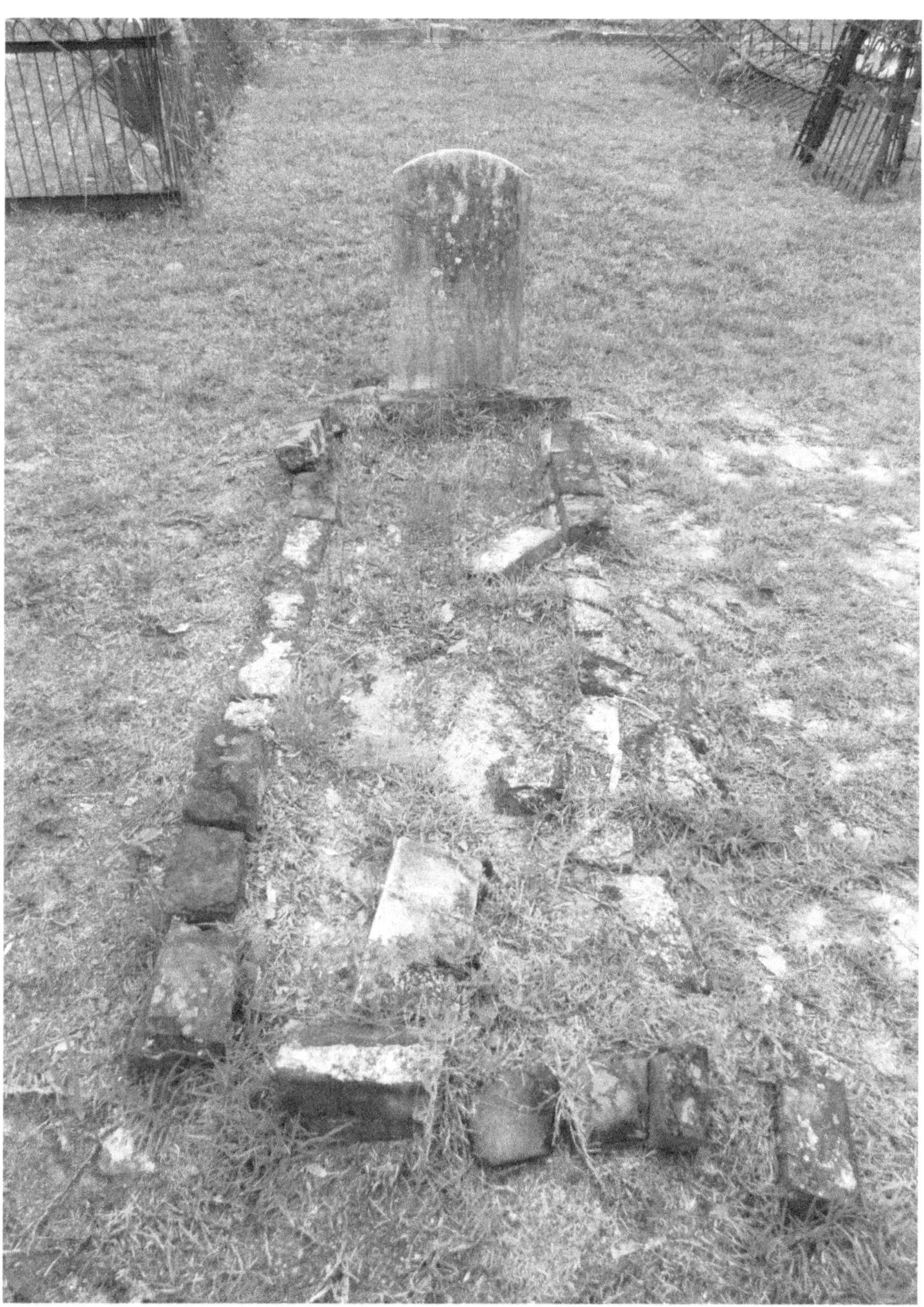

"Insured Beyond The Grave"
Brunswick, Georgia

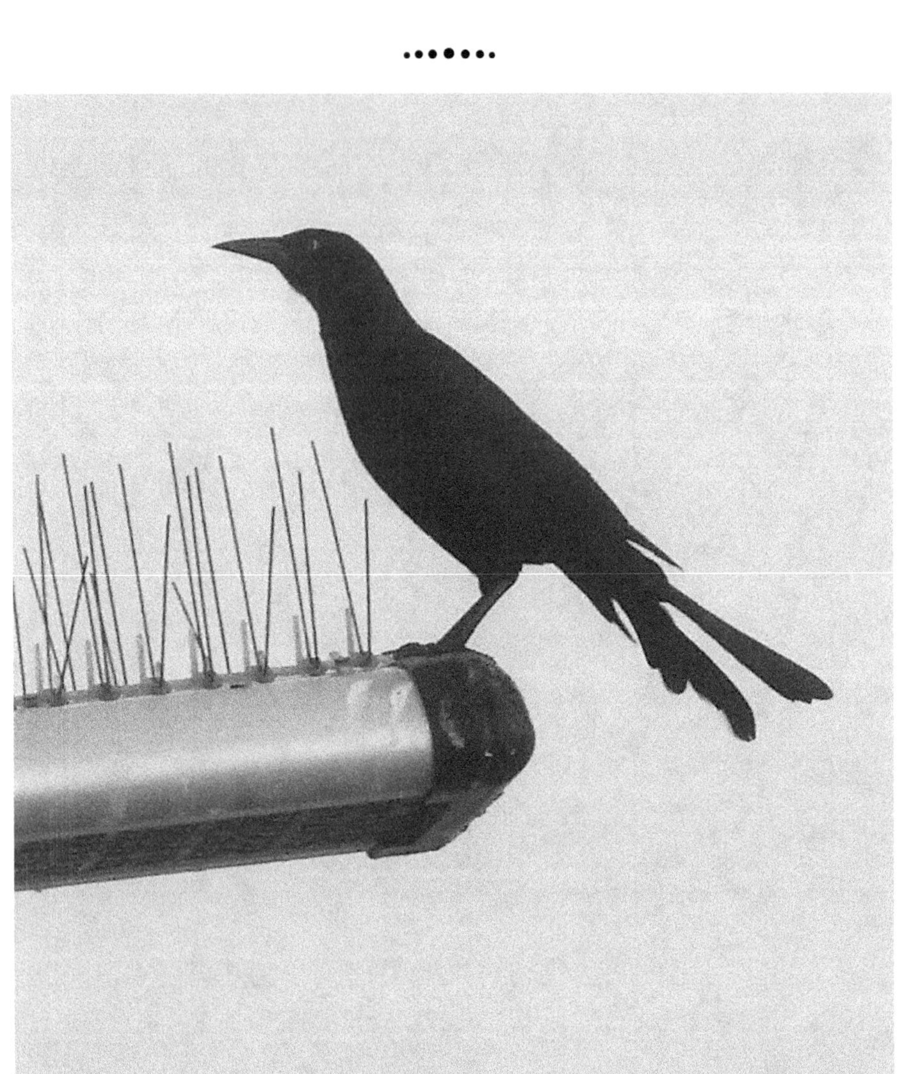

"Black Crow"
Saint Simons Island, Georgia

www.ingramcontent.com/pod-product-compliance
Lightning Source LLC
Chambersburg PA
CBHW071602030726
47593CB00001BA/274